LIBRARY
OF
ADVENTIST THEOLOGY

# SIN
AND
# SALVATION

*Series Editors:*

George R. Knight
Woodrow W. Whidden II


Other books by George R. Knight include:

*A Search for Identity*
*A Brief History of Seventh-day Adventists*
*Ellen White's World*
*Exploring Ecclesiastes and the Song of Solomon*
*Exploring 1, 2, 3 John and Jude*
*Exploring Galatians and Ephesians*
*Exploring Hebrews*
*Exploring Mark*
*If I Were the Devil*
*Joseph Bates*
*Lest We Forget*
*Meeting Ellen White*
*Organizing for Mission*
*Reading Ellen White*
*The Apocalyptic Vision and the Neutering of Adventism*
*The Cross of Christ*
*Walking With Ellen White*
*Walking With Paul in the Book of Romans*

To order, call **1-800-765-6955**.


Visit us at
**www.reviewandherald.com**
for information on other Review and Herald® products.

# SIN
## AND
# SALVATION

*God's Work for
and in Us*

GEORGE R. KNIGHT

REVIEW AND HERALD® PUBLISHING ASSOCIATION
Since 1861 | www.reviewandherald.com

The Review and Herald® Publishing Association publishes biblically based materials for spiritual, physical, and mental growth and Christian discipleship.

The author assumes full responsibility for the accuracy of all facts and quotations as cited in this book.

An earlier edition of *Sin and Salvation: God's Work for and in Us* was published in 1992 as *The Pharisee's
Guide to Perfect Holiness: A Study of Sin and Salvation,* by Pacific Press Publishing Association.

Unless otherwise noted, Bible texts in this book are from the Revised Standard Version of the Bible,
copyright © 1946, 1952, 1971, 1973 by the Division of Christian Education of the National Council of
the Churches of Christ in the U.S.A. Used by permission.

Texts credited to NIV are from the *Holy Bible, New International Version.* Copyright © 1973, 1978,
1984, International Bible Society. Used by permission of Zondervan Bible Publishers.

Bible texts credited to Phillips are from J. B. Phillips: *The New Testament in Modern English,* Revised
Edition. © J. B. Phillips 1958, 1960, 1972. Used by permission of Macmillan Publishing Co.

This book was
Edited by Gerald Wheeler
Designed by Trent Truman
Cover photo: © ernestking/istockphoto.com
Interior designed by Heather Rogers
Typeset: Bembo 11/13

PRINTED IN U.S.A.

12  11  10  09  08                    5  4  3  2  1

**Library of Congress Cataloging-in-Publication Data**
Knight, George R.
  Sin and salvation : God's work for us and in us / George R. Knight. — [Rev. ed.].
     p. cm. — (Library of Adventist theology ; bk. 2)
  Rev. ed. of: The Pharisee's guide to perfect holiness. 1992.
  Includes bibliographical references and indexes.
  1. Perfection--Religious aspects—Seventh-day Adventists. 2. Holiness—Seventh-day Adventists.
3. Justification (Christian theology) 4. Sanctification—Seventh-day Adventists. 5. Seventh-day
Adventists—Doctrines. I. Knight, George R. Pharisee's guide to perfect holiness. II. Title.
  BT766.K55 2008
  234--dc22

                                   2007049618


ISBN 978-0-8280-2068-8

# Dedicated to

**Roger and Peggy Dudley**
who have exemplified caring love in my life.

# Contents

# A Word to the Reader

There is no more important topic than God's plan of salvation for a lost world. *Sin and Salvation* is the second volume in my series on God's redemptive plan. The first, *The Cross of Christ*, specifically focused on God's work *for* us and the meaning of Christ's sacrifice on the cross. The present book continues the treatment of God's work *for* people but extends it into the realm of His work *in* them in such areas as sanctification and perfection. The two volumes together survey the broad scope and the overall theme of the redemptive plan.

Beyond that, *Sin and Salvation* seeks to show the interrelatedness of the components of salvation. The book's undergirding thesis is that different concepts of sin lead to varying approaches to "achieving" righteousness. It argues that the greatest mistake of the dominant Pharisaic view at Christ's time was its definition of sin. A false definition led the Pharisees to unfruitful (and even destructive) views of righteousness and perfection. The problem and confusion, unfortunately, never died with the first century Pharisees. It is alive and well today.

Seventh-day Adventists have also wrestled with the ongoing struggle to understand how people get saved. Some have emphasized human effort, sanctification, and some sort of sinless perfection; others have argued that salvation is basically legal (forensic) justification, and that human sanctification is vicariously achieved through Christ's perfect life; yet others, downplaying human effort, have implied that "Jesus does it all"—our part is to sit back and enjoy the ride once we have accepted Jesus.

Like many of my books, this one has evolved from my personal experience. During the past 45 years, I have at various times taught two of the above approaches and flirted with the third, only to discover that all are less than adequate. Thus, the present attempt at understanding a complex subject.

Ever since my conversion from agnosticism in 1961, I have wrestled with what it means to be saved—with what God can do *for* us and *in* us. This book, therefore, is in one sense a result of my personal experience. But even beyond that, it is the fruit of countless encounters with people in the midst of living the Christian life, scholarly studies, and biographical reminiscences on the topic. There is nothing more important in my life than how to be right with God and how to be prepared to enjoy His kingdom of love in both the present age and the age to come.

As a result, *Sin and Salvation* is more than a book on abstract theology. Theology at its best not only informs the mind, but also guides daily life. A theology that cannot stand up to the crises and challenges of daily living is less than adequate. It is my hope that the suggestions made in this study will not only enlighten the minds of my readers, but also provide them with insight into the intensity and dynamics of the daily struggle faced by people living in a world of sin.

Besides *The Cross of Christ,* the present book is closely related to the subject matter of several of my other books. First and foremost is *I Used to Be Perfect: A Study of Sin and Salvation* (1994, 2001), which both summarizes and extends the thesis set forth in *Sin and Salvation*. I have also treated many of its themes in *Exploring Galatians and Ephesians* (2005), *Walking With Paul Through the Book of Romans* (2002), and, from a historical perspective, in my three books related to the discussions of righteousness by faith at the 1888 General Conference session—*From 1888 to Apostasy: The Case of A. T. Jones* (1987), *Angry Saints: Tensions and Possibilities in the Adventist Struggle Over Righteousness by Faith* (1989), and *A User-friendly Guide to the 1888 Message* (1998).

In many ways, *Sin and Salvation* has been the most difficult of my books to write. Despite the temptation to skirt the difficult topics involved in its scope, I have sought to face each of them responsibly. No book, of course, can do justice to the depth and complexity of the plan of salvation. While it is our privilege to begin such study in our earthly existence, an understanding of the richness of God's work will continue to develop throughout eternity.

One thing especially surprised me during my study for this book, and that was the amount of agreement between Christians of various backgrounds and denominations on the essential elements of what God does *for* and *in* people in His great salvific work. Even Adventists of apparently opposite postures generally found common ground when *pushed* to be specific by the "hard questions" of theory and life. Most of the warfare in the Christian community is not so much over the central concerns but with where to draw lines and how to define stages and words.

While I have found that problem discouraging, it is also hopeful in the sense that there is a great deal more shared understanding on the subject among Christians than I first perceived. As my study progressed, I more and more fully saw the wisdom of the words of Anglican bishop J. C. Ryle, who wrote: "The last day will show who is right and who is wrong" in our understanding of holiness. "In the meantime, I am quite certain that to exhibit bitterness and coldness towards those who cannot conscientiously work with us is to prove ourselves very ignorant of real holiness."*

I should add a word about style. In this book I have attempted the difficult marriage between a popular style and scholarly precision. The result is something of a compromise, which I hope will edify the reader while also being responsible to the deeper concerns of the subject.

Overall, I have sought to write in clear, broad strokes that set forth the gospel themes in bold relief and as part of a unified package. I should also note that chapters 8 and 9 address more specifically Adventist concerns than the rest of the book. I gave extra space to them because they have been central features in Adventist discussion and eschatology.

The present book first apeared in 1992 under the title of *The Pharisee's Guide to Perfect Holiness: A Study of Sin and Salvation*. Outside of editorial changes, the content has remained mostly the same. The two exceptions are that I have expanded and enriched the sections on "the issue of universal justification" and the Greek philosophic definition of perfection as sinlessness.

My debts in writing this book have been many. Special thanks goes to Raoul Dederen, Atilio Dupertuis, and Robert Olson for reading the entire manuscript of the initial publication, and to Robert Johnston for reading the first chapter. Their critiques and suggestions aimed at making the manuscript more accurate. The book is better because of their input and might have been even stronger had I followed all of their counsel. Joyce Werner is also to be thanked for entering my handwritten manuscript into the computer.

Special appreciation for the present version of the book goes to Mika Devoux for providing a cleaned up computerized version of the scanned copy; to my wife, Bonnie, for entering the seemingly endless rounds of corrections into the computer; and to Gerald Wheeler and Jeannette Johnson, for guiding the book through the publication process.

I trust that *Sin and Salvation: God's Work for and in Us* will be a blessing to its readers as they seek to live their lives "in Christ."

**George R. Knight**
*Rogue River, Oregon*

---

* J. C. Ryle, *Holiness: Its Nature, Hindrances, Difficulties, and Roots* (Welwyn, Eng.: Evangelical Press, 1979), pp. xiv, xv.

# Chapter 1

# Pharisees Are Good People

I still get upset when I read the Bible.[1] Take, for example, the New Testament portrayal of the Pharisees. In spite of the impression left by the biblical picture of them, the Pharisees were the best of people. *The Jewish Encyclopedia* is undoubtedly right when it claims that no complete "estimate of the character of the Pharisees can be obtained from the New Testament writings, which take a polemical attitude toward them."[2]

In a similar vein, we find a great deal of truth in the accusation by *Encyclopaedia Judaica* that it is "mistakenly held that New Testament references to them as 'hypocrites' or 'offspring of vipers' (Matt. 3:7; Luke 18:9 ff., etc.) are applicable to the entire group." The leaders of the Pharisees were themselves well aware of the insincere among their numbers and frequently describe them as "sore spots" and "plagues of the Pharisaic party."[3]

Most Christians need to revise their picture of the Pharisees. They were not merely good people—they were the best of people. Not only were they morally upright, but they were desperately earnest in their search for God and in their protection of His holy name, law, and Word.

Certainly the church and the world would be infinitely better if more of us daily came to God with the central Pharisaic question: "What shall I do to inherit eternal life?" (Luke 10:25; cf. Matt. 19:16). Here was a people totally dedicated to serving God from the time they arose in the morning to when they retired at night.

Not only were the Pharisees intellectually dedicated to doing right, but they realized the highest level of morality in their daily lives. Jesus never contradicted the Pharisee in Luke 18 who thanked God in prayer that he was "not like other men, extortioners, unjust, adulterers" (verse 11). Nor did Christ take issue with the young man who claimed to have "observed" the Ten Commandments from his youth (see Matt. 19:18-20). It stretches the imagination even to attempt to conceive of a people more intent on obedience and ethical living than the Pharisees. A brief look at some of their praiseworthy characteristics should help us put them in perspective.

First and foremost, they loved and protected the Bible as the Word of God. They were intent on preserving the relevant meaning of Scripture. That goal, however, ran into trouble when it encountered divergences of opinion on the exact meaning of a biblical passage. As a result, they developed the theory that along with the written text there was, and always had been from Moses' time, an unwritten tradition that supplemented the written text and pointed to its true meaning.[4] Thus the oral tradition of the Pharisees was really a product of their reverence for the holy Word of God.

A second high point for the Pharisees was their love of and dedication to God's law. R. Travers Herford sums up that aspect of Pharisaism concisely when he states that "the primary concern of the Pharisees was to make the Torah [law] the supreme guide of life, in thought, word and deed, by study of its contents, obedience to its precepts, and, as the root of all, conscious service of God Who had given the Torah."[5]

The Pharisees were deeply committed to not breaking the law of God. Consequently, they devised a system to avoid violating it. With their oral traditions they built a "fence for the Law" to "protect it by surrounding it with cautionary rules to halt a man like a danger signal before he gets within breaking distance of the divine statute itself."[6]

Thus, for example, they developed 1,521 oral rules for the Sabbath alone.[7] By the time of Christ, the Pharisees had countless of these fences or rules that affected every aspect of their daily lives. The Jews of Christ's day could tell you how large a rock people could carry on the Sabbath day, how far they could take it, and how many cubits they could throw it. Their oral tradition covered every aspect of life, and an individual had to be zealously sincere about religion to live the pharisaic life.

Beyond strict Sabbath observance, the Pharisees were energetic and sacrificial tithers, even going so far as to separate every tenth leaf of their mint plants and other garden herbs as being the Lord's (see Matt. 23:23). And, of course, they would never eat or even touch any food or item regarded as unclean.

People can say what they like about the Pharisees, but one thing all must admit is that they led lives totally dedicated to serving God and obeying His law. Jesus commended them for such a life (see Matt. 23:23). And Paul, looking back to his Pharisaic years, could say that "as to righteousness under the law" he was "blameless" (Phil. 3:6).

14

A third commendable aspect of Pharisaism was its missionary and evangelistic zeal. They would "scour sea and land to make a single convert" (Matt. 23:15, Phillips). The Pharisees not only sought to convert non-Jews to their religious views and practices, but also other Jews. Thus, writes Joachim Jeremias, the Pharisaic group set forth the rules of purity laid down for the everyday life of the priests as the ideal for every Jew. "In this way they meant to build up the holy community of Israel" into the "true Israel" of God (God's remnant). As a result, while the average Jew did not like the superior airs of the Pharisees, the common people "looked to the Pharisees . . . as models of piety, and as embodiments of the ideal life."[8]

A fourth positive aspect of the Pharisees is that they were "adventists." They looked forward with intense desire to the coming of the Messianic kingdom. But they tied it to the faithful keeping of the law. Some of them believed that Messiah (Christ) would come if God's people kept Torah (the law) perfectly for one day. As a result, they fully dedicated their lives to bringing about that day through perfect holiness.[9]

The Pharisees were an elite corps of highly dedicated men, being about 6,000 strong in the time of Christ. The New Testament refers to the religious scholars among them as the "scribes." One interpretation of the name *Pharisee* is "the separate ones." By extension, it would represent "the holy ones, the true community of Israel."[10]

The sect of the Pharisees developed after the Babylonian captivity. God had allowed the Jews to be taken into captivity because (1) they had not been faithful to His law, and (2) they had adopted the ways of their pagan neighbors. After the 70-year captivity, Ezra early became a central figure in steering the Israelites toward God's commands and away from the compromising culture of their day.

The Pharisees first appear as an organized group in the second century B.C. during the Maccabean crisis. The "separated ones" adopted a lifestyle and a theological outlook that would preserve faithfulness to God so that Israel need not repeat its captivity. Thus, in their search for holiness, they separated themselves from the surrounding cultures and their customs, from the this-worldly and compromising practices of the priestly Sadducees, and from the careless ways of the common people. Because the Pharisees sought to pave the way for the coming of the Christ through godly living, their motivations were praiseworthy in every way.[11]

Given this positive view of the Pharisees, one of the most shocking and revolutionary teachings of Christ is that "unless your righteousness ex-

15

ceeds that of the scribes and Pharisees, you will never enter the kingdom of heaven" (Matt. 5:20). How could anyone strive harder or live for God more earnestly than these elite moralists, these storm troopers for the kingdom of God?

### The Fly in Pharisaism's Theological Ointment

The central problem in the dominant tradition of Pharisaic Judaism's approach to God and salvation was an inadequate view of sin and its effect on human ability. The rabbinic[12] perspective came to view sin generally as a specific act rather than as a condition of the heart and mind. Likewise, the dominant Pharisaic tradition saw neither Adam or his descendants as morally different because of the Genesis fall. In other words, human beings since the Fall have had the same ability to live the righteous life as Adam did before it. Thus G. F. Moore writes, "There is no notion that the original constitution of Adam underwent any change in consequence of the fall, so that he transmitted to his descendants a vitiated nature in which the appetites and passions necessarily prevail over reason and virtue." Nor was "the will to good . . . enfeebled."[13]

While it is true that the rabbis taught that people have a *yeser ha-ra'* (an evil impulse), they also assumed that God had created Adam with it in the first place. The impulse to evil can be subdued and brought into service to God and humanly controlled through studying and meditating upon the Torah (law) and by applying the law to daily living. "The mind [and life] thus preoccupied with religion," Moore writes, "excludes temptations from without and evil devisings within."[14]

E. P. Sanders penned, in summing up the rabbinic position, that "the possibility exists that one might not sin. Despite the tendency to disobey, man is free to obey or disobey."[15] Thus persons could technically live sinless lives under their own steam.

The Jews, however, realistically recognized that strict obedience was rare, so they also taught repentance and forgiveness. But even repentance they defined as a kind of salvation by human works in which a person abandons evil deeds and does good. Thus one's sins become "white as snow" (Isa. 1:18) through moral reformation. While God's forgiveness is genuine, the high point in rabbinic teachings on grace as God's unmerited favor is that God gave Israel the law and a covenant relationship with Himself in which obedience to the law as a response to God's gracious election is central. "The 'righteous' man" in actual practice, therefore, "is not he who obeys the Law flawlessly, but he alone who *strives* to regulate his life by the

Law" and "is repentant when he fails." George Eldon Ladd points out that the sincerity and primacy of one's purpose to keep the law and "the strenuous endeavor to accomplish it are the marks of a righteous man."[16]

Thus Jewish teaching, while recognizing the reality of and need for grace, forgiveness, and repentance, put obedience to the law at the center of humanity's relationship to God. That led in daily practice to legalistic approaches, even though Judaism at its best recognized and taught that the matter of greatest importance was the spirit of the law as exemplified in love for God (see Deut. 6:5; 10:12) and for one's neighbor (see Lev. 19:18).

During the centuries that Pharisaism developed, the role of the law went through a significant change in Jewish thinking. Ladd indicates that the importance of the law came to overshadow the concept of God's gracious covenant and became "the condition of membership in God's people." Even more important, observance of the law became "the basis of God's verdict upon the individual. Resurrection will be the reward of those who have been devoted to the Law." The law became the hope of the faithful and central to justification, salvation, righteousness, and life.[17]

That emphasis, not surprisingly, led eventually to a kind of legalistic bookkeeping among the Jews. We can think of their approach in terms of a moral balance scale in which the godly are those whose merits outweigh their transgressions, while the ungodly are those whose transgressions are heavier. The Jewish *Mishnah* puts it nicely when it says, "The world is judged by grace, yet all is according to the excess of works [that be good or evil]."[18]

The *Talmud* later presented the same thought: "One who performs mostly good deeds inherits the Garden of Eden, and one who performs mostly transgressions inherits *Gehenna* [hell]." The real problem for the judgment, of course, would be the "intermediates"—those whose merits and faults balance each other. That problem proved to be a point of exciting debate between the Pharisaic schools of Hillel and Shammai in the New Testament period. According to one tradition, God's grace comes in to tip the balance in favor of righteousness.[19]

*The important point to note is that the Pharisaic merit system of righteousness atomized sin. That is, it defined sin primarily as a series of actions*, even though Judaism at its clear-thinking best recognized sin as a rebellious state of mind and as an offense against God.[20] Walther Eichrodt notes that the atomization of sin into specific actions was undoubtedly aided by the fact that when the "Old Testament speaks of sin *the chief emphasis* unquestionably *falls on its current concrete expression."* Beyond that, the Pharisaic concept of law thrust the deeper meaning of sin as rebellion against God into the background. Given their balance-scale approach, the transgression of each individual command of the law was sin.[21]

As we noted earlier, the Pharisees' approach to law and sin led them to develop an ever-increasing number of rules in an attempt to safeguard themselves against unwittingly breaking the letter of the law. The Jews applied their oral tradition to every possible life situation, resulting in a massive body of written and oral law that they had to observe. "To violate one of them was equivalent to rejecting the whole Law and refusing God's yoke."[22]

With this information in hand, we should not be surprised to find the rich young ruler asking Jesus "what good deed" he needed *to do* "to have eternal life" (Matt. 19:16). Nor should it puzzle us to find Jesus answering the young man according to his own perspective by giving him an itemized list of commandments (verses 18, 19). Jesus met him on his own ground, but Christ's final suggestion regarding the road to righteousness and becoming "perfect" shifted the issue from the atomized letter of the law to its spiritual intent in relation to both loving God and one's neighbor. Calling for an end to selfish and self-centered living, Jesus emphasized total dedication to God. Such a concept was too much for the young man, who beat a hasty retreat from a Teacher who had such high ideals (verses 20-22). It is infinitely easier to keep the letter of the law than its spirit.

One of the greatest tragedies of Pharisaism is that in its sincere attempt to live up to the letter of the individual biblical and oral commandments, it missed the intent of the whole. *The essence of the Pharisaic problem was viewing the nature of sin as being a series of acts rather than being primarily a condition of the heart and a rebellious attitude toward God.*

Unfortunately, *a mistaken concept of sin led them into a fatal misunderstanding regarding righteousness. If one defines sin as a series of actions, the next logical step is to see righteousness as a series of behaviors or actions.*

With that mentality, they could develop their balance scale approach to righteousness and God's final judgment. From that perspective, the rich young ruler could ask what deeds he still needed to perform. Christ's answer to him ("If you would be perfect") reflects the fact that the Pharisees of His day were seeking to bring about the kingdom of God by living "perfect" lives. While their intent was praiseworthy, their faulty view of sin led them to a faulty approach to righteousness.

Unfortunately, in spite of the New Testament, the effort to bring about the kingdom of God through an atomized view of sin and righteousness is still alive and well in the twenty-first century—even in Adventism. In fact, Adventism's most prominent theologian of the 1930s and 1940s took exactly the same position as the Pharisees on sin and righteousness.

In speaking of sanctification as the work of a lifetime, M. L. Andreasen noted that it begins at conversion and continues throughout life. "Every victory," he wrote, "hastens the process. There are few Christians who have not gained the victory over some *sin* that formerly . . . overcame them." Many a man enslaved to the tobacco habit has triumphed over tobacco, and it ceases to be a temptation for him. "*On that point he is sanctified. As he has been victorious over one besetment so he is to become victorious over every sin.* When the work is completed, when he has gained the victory over pride, ambition, love of the world—over all evil—he is *ready for translation.* He has been tried in all *points.* The evil one has come to him and found nothing. Satan has no more temptations for him. *He has overcome them all.* He stands *without fault* before the throne of God. Christ places His seal upon him. . . .

"Thus it shall be with the last generation of men living on the earth. Through them God's final demonstration of what He can do with humanity will be given. . . . [The final generation] will be subjected to every temptation, but they will not yield. They will demonstrate that it is possible to live without sin—the very demonstration for which the world has been looking. . . . It will become evident to all that the gospel really can save to the uttermost."[23]

The above quotation is extremely important in Adventist theology. Whole schools of Adventist thought base themselves upon its approach to sin, righteousness, and perfection. While not denying God's ability to save to the uttermost and the need for a "spotless" final generation of earthlings (Rev. 14:5), the present book will argue that Adventist theology has two distinctly different approaches to sin that lead to several (more than two) distinctively different approaches to righteousness and perfection within the denomination.

The present volume also argues, in connection with the above point, that the greatest mistake of the Pharisees of old was in their definition of sin. Chapter 2 will take up the topic of sin. The rest of the book, chapters 4 through 10, will develop an approach to righteousness, perfection, and "translation faith" that grows out of a well-rounded view of the biblical teaching on sin. Meanwhile, we need to spend a bit more time with our friends the Pharisees.

19

## The Problem With Being Good

The parable of the Pharisee and the publican (Luke 18:9-14) is probably the best New Testament illustration of the problem of human goodness. "Two men," related Jesus, "went up into the temple to pray, one a Pharisee and the other a tax collector. The Pharisee stood and prayed thus with himself, 'God, *I* thank thee that *I* am not like other men, extortioners, unjust, adulterers, or even like this tax collector. *I* fast twice a week, *I* give tithes of all that *I* get.' But the tax collector, standing afar off, would not even lift up his eyes to heaven, but beat his breast, saying, 'God, be merciful to me a ["the" in the Greek text] sinner!' I tell you, this man went down to his house justified rather than the other; for every one who exalts himself will be humbled, but he who humbles himself will be exalted."

We should note several things about the Pharisee's prayer. First, it is a catalog of his own virtues, the negative first, then the positive. Not only is he not like others, but he can list his merits. Five times he uses the personal pronoun *I* in relation to his virtue. Thus William Barclay points out that "the Pharisee was really giving himself a testimonial before God."[24] Such a catalog is obviously based on an atomization of sin. The Pharisee could quantify his righteousness—he could count his merits.

Second, not only could he quantify his righteousness, but he could compare himself with the tax collector and come out feeling good about himself. More important, he used his neighbor's failures to build his self-image. Luke therefore adds that our Pharisee friend not only trusted in himself, but he "despised others" who were not as good as himself. That problem, unfortunately, has continued to plague Pharisaic personalities down through history.

Third, the parable indicates that the Pharisee, in spite of his goodness, was totally lost spiritually. Not only was his prayer "with" or "to" himself (verse 11), but he had no sense of his lostness. In his confidence and zeal to be good, he concluded that he had succeeded. We could compare him to Rabbi Simeon ben Jochai, who once said: "If there are only two righteous men in the world, I and my son are these two; if there is only one, I am he!"[25]

In the parable the Pharisee demonstrates that he does not understand either the nature or the depth of sin. Sin, his actions imply, could be rooted out by trying harder and doing more. One outcome was a form of "degenerate sanctification" that drove a wedge between faith in God and daily living. The result was "destructive of true religion."[26]

Thus the parable of Luke 18 represents the way in which the pursuit

20

of righteousness can go wrong.[27] The foundation of the problem was that the Pharisee viewed both sin and righteousness as a series of actions rather than as a condition of the mind and a relationship to God. Beyond that, he failed to see that human beings are sinners by nature, whose very goodness—given the bent of the human mind—merely leads people deeper into the core of sin—that is, pride and self-sufficiency.

In speaking to that problem, P. T. Forsyth noted that *there is no sin more subtle than the sin of goodness*—the sin of "the good people who do not know that they are not good." In another connection, Forsyth identifies Pharisaism as "Antichrist" because it is a human-centered religion. Ellen White agreed with that assessment when she wrote that "the principles cherished by the Pharisees are such as are characteristic of humanity in all ages. *The spirit of Pharisaism is the spirit of human nature.*"[28]

*Without a knowledge of the depth of sin, people lack a "fundamental ingredient" in their self-understanding.* Such a knowledge helps us understand "why humans do certain things, from the milder trespasses to the actions of a very ruthless criminal." An adequate concept of sin enables us to realize, Bernard Ramm notes, that "we are sinners in our 'mission control center.'" Out of that center come the orders for action. A realization of the depth and nature of sin also helps us understand *the sin of goodness* and the human need for total reliance on salvation through God's mercy.[29]

The Pharisee of Luke 18, unfortunately, had none of those insights. As a result, Christ tells us that this man, who had sought to justify himself in his prayer, went away unjustified. "Of all sins," we read in *Christ's Object Lessons*, that of "pride and self-sufficiency" "is the most hopeless, the most incurable." That is so because goodness feels no need. Thus Puritan writer William Perkins could think of the merely good person as "a beautiful abomination."[30]

Not only do the world's Pharisees feel no need of anything, but those who pride themselves on their moral goodness and religious achievements generally set themselves up as judges of other people. Ellen White put it nicely when she wrote that all who trust in their own goodness "will despise others. As the Pharisee judges himself by other men, so he judges other men by himself. His righteousness is estimated by theirs, and the worse they are" the better he feels about himself. "His self-righteousness leads to accusing. 'Other men' he condemns as transgressors of God's law." In that attitude he becomes one with Satan as an accuser of God's people (Rev. 12:10).[31]

Such are the fruits of the sin of goodness. One of the first outward symptoms of this most serious of all spiritual diseases is the development of a critical spirit.

Still, another symptom of Pharisaism is the tendency to multiply rules and regulations. While, as subsequent chapters will emphasize, high Christian standards are important, certain ways of relating to them are unhealthy. Sickness in the realm of rules and regulations comes about when they get viewed as ends in themselves rather than as means to enable a person to love one's Lord and neighbor in a fuller way.

In all sincerity, the Pharisees multiplied rules to protect God's law. After all, so the "logic of the slippery slope" runs, if a person commits the slightest indiscretion on the Sabbath, it could lead to Sabbath breaking. So they developed, as pointed out earlier, 1,521 laws to fence the Sabbath in and protect it. Likewise, they expanded their dietary regulations. In a similar vein, their zeal for ceremonial cleanliness in ritual worship led them into fanatical application of cleanliness in every area of life. Not only did this multitude of regulations fence in the law and protect it, but it also provided more items that one could count for righteousness as individuals daily weighed in on the balance scale of salvation. Such an approach, however, left less zealous people with merely more and more "sins."

Unfortunately, such a way of viewing laws, sin, and righteousness, while seeking to honor God and protect His law, tended to lead to the opposite effect. Thus Jesus reminded the Pharisees that their laws were not all important when He noted that "the Sabbath was made for man, [and] not man for the Sabbath" (Mark 2:27). *In their zeal for their rules they had forgotten the law of love that makes the rules meaningful.* In fact, their focus on rules led them to persecute those who violated them, as we see in the cases of the healed cripple found carrying his bed on the Sabbath (John 5:9-15) and the man born blind whom Jesus also healed on the Sabbath (John 9:1-34).

To the Pharisees, the letter of the law (in this case, that no work should be done on the Sabbath) was more important than its spirit. Jesus stood against their emphasis. Unfortunately, their attitude led to blind Pharisaic hatred and death on the cross.

The Pharisees' role in the crucifixion represented the apex of spiritual confusion. In their desire to protect the law, they crucified the Messiah who gave the law. While they had a rigid orthodoxy, they lacked love. They confused moral goodness and orthodoxy with religion. Saul of Tarsus exemplified that mindset. William Coleman vividly describes Saul as one who "had entered that severe circle of those who would murder because they loved."[32]

That love, however, focused on the wrong ideal. Just because people are sincere in their motives does not mean they are correct in their actions. The old wineskins of Saul's concepts of sin and righteousness would not burst until his experience on the Damascus road (Acts 9:1-9). Thenceforth he would preach a different gospel.

A closely related problem to Pharisaic hardness of heart was the tendency to make an outward show of their religion. After all, Coleman points out, "What is the point of living a righteous life if no one knows about it?" Thus "the only thing more important than being humble is to look humble."[33] Two of the most obvious outward signs of Pharisaic piety were their ostentatious use of phylacteries (little cases containing written portions of the law, fastened to the forehead and left forearm) and tassels (extensions of the corners of Jewish garments that served as reminders of the law). With the pretentious use of such symbols by the Pharisees in mind, Jesus said: "They do all their deeds to be seen by men; for they make their phylacteries broad and their fringes long, and they love the place of honor at feasts and the best seats in the synagogues, and salutations in the market places, and being called rabbi by men" (Matt. 23:5-7).

"How do we look?" became the key question for many Pharisees. Many of their daily religious practices were calculated to have the maximum effect at public display. Thus if prayer time caught them in the middle of a road, they would bow, while traffic waited "until the solemn occasion ran its course" (cf. Matt. 6:5, 6). Jesus locked horns with the Pharisees repeatedly because they too often placed the emphasis on the external rather than the internal.[34]

It was to the hypocritical aspects of Pharisaism that Christ directed some of His most scathing rebukes. "Well did Isaiah prophesy of you hypocrites, as it is written, 'This people honors me with their lips, but their heart is far from me'" (Mark 7:6; cf. Isa. 29:13). On another occasion the "gentle Jesus" accused them of being "blind guides," who strained out a gnat while "swallowing a camel!" (Matt. 23:24).

The ancient Jews were well aware of the problem of Pharisaic hypocrisy. The Talmud enumerates seven classes of Pharisees, of which five were either hypocrites or eccentric fools: "(1)'the shoulder Pharisee,' who wears, as it were, his good actions ostentatiously upon his shoulder; (2)'the wait-a-little Pharisee,' who ever says, 'Wait-a-little until I have performed the good act awaiting me'; (3)'the bruised Pharisee,' who in order to avoid looking at a woman runs against the wall so as to bruise himself and bleed; (4)'the pestle Pharisee,' who walks with head down like the pes-

23

tle in the mortar; (5)'the ever reckoning Pharisee,' who says, 'Let me know what good I may do to counteract my neglect'; (6)'the God-fearing Pharisee,' after the manner of Job; (7)'the God loving Pharisee,' after the manner of Abraham."[35]

We can surmise that many Pharisees in the last two groups responded to Jesus in a positive manner. They too were fed up with pharisaic abuses. Thus some of the Pharisees warned Jesus against one of Herod's plots (Luke 13:31), and Nicodemus courageously risked his career and life to play a central part in the Lord's burial (John 3:1; 19:38-40). Apparently after Pentecost a fair number of Pharisees converted to the risen Christ (Acts 15:5). But even as Christians they had to struggle mightily to shed the trappings of their old religion with its multiplication of rules, focus on externals, emphasis on human merit, and tendency to criticize and even persecute those who did not live up to what they chose to impose on themselves and the church (see, for example, Acts 15 and the book of Galatians).

It was one of the unfortunate experiences of the early church that the spirit of the Pharisees crept into Christianity. Like the Trojan horse of Homeric times, that mentality was a deadly threat to true Christianity. Paul spent a great deal of his ministry combating "baptized Pharisaism," but he failed to destroy it.

### Pharisaism Is Alive and Well

The sad truth is that Pharisaism continues to exist in the church, and even within Adventism. The reason that it is still alive and well is that *it is a state of mind rather than a historic group.* In essence, the Pharisee is what the Bible calls "the natural man"—the person who can feel good about himself or herself in part because of a confusion between upright living and true righteousness.

In many ways, a central problem with the Pharisees is their genuine goodness. Such people feel no need for Christ. From a human perspective, they are proud of their moral accomplishments. "You can do something with a hardened sinner," writes P. T. Forsyth. "He can be broken to pieces. But I do not know what you can do with a viscous [sic] saint, with those who are wrapped in the wool, soaked in the comfort of their religion, and tanned to leather, soft and tough as a glove, by its bitterest baptisms. . . . Is there anything more comfortable, and selfish, and hopeless . . . ? When religion becomes perverted to be a means of mere comfort and dense satisfaction, it becomes an integument [outer covering] so tough that even the grace of God cannot get through it."[36]

One of the great problems of morally respectable people is that they cease to realize how lost they are in their natural state and how totally dependent they are upon God's grace. That problem is especially acute when such individuals are blessed with an abundance of material goods. Street people recognize their lack, but those the Bible characterizes as Laodicea know not that they "are wretched, pitiable, poor, blind, and naked." They feel no need of refinement "by fire," of "white garments," and of "salve" to anoint their eyes (Rev. 3:15-18).

With that problem in mind, it is not difficult to agree with Coleman, who writes that "the Pharisees are our not-too-distant cousins. They have done very little that we have not worked hard to match in action or in spirit. We have used them as whipping posts when in fact they make better mirrors."[37]

If the first temptation of the modern Pharisee is to take pride in his or her spiritual accomplishments, the second is to be critical of others. As Emil Brunner put it, "Where is the man who would not be a Pharisee? Which of us does not desire a little throne where he can sit in judgment on others?"[38]

There may be nothing more destructive than a critical spirit. Yet, interestingly enough, many so-called Christians are filled with criticism of their pastor, their church, and those who do not agree with them. Just listen to them for a while. The modern Pharisees are just as "good" at criticism as their ancient counterparts. *Whenever anyone is more critical than positive, they provide evidence of Pharisaism.* Such a spirit ripped apart the Adventist General Conference session held at Minneapolis in 1888.[39] And the same spirit continues to ravage Adventism as its "superior types" multiply regulations and criticize everything from the way people worship God to what others may be eating (or not eating) for breakfast.

*A problem with Pharisees is that while they may know all the rules about caring, they have never learned to really care about people.* Back in 1888, Ellen White referred to such people as "moral icebergs, cold, sunless, dark, and forbidding."[40]

All of us have known such individuals, and some of us (including myself) even have partaken of their spirit in our zeal for the fine points of Adventist lifestyle and doctrine. We have had our study groups and endless discussions on the minutiae of the law, but from time to time the frightening reality hits home that it is easier to spend a dozen hours discussing the letter of religion than it is to spend a few minutes obeying its spirit.

## Sin and Salvation

To be honest, I personally find it easier to multiply regulations than to truly care for other people. The shocking truth is that *a Pharisee lurks within the skin of each of us, seeking to impose its spirit on an unsuspecting world and an undeserving church.* We not only are tempted to follow the Jews of old in recreating a "Mishnah" of oral interpretations to impose upon our neighbors, but—worse yet—some of us seek to put our own theological straitjacket on God. The Pharisees of every generation are busy creating the God of heaven in their own religious image.

---

[1] See George R. Knight, *The Cross of Christ: God's Work for Us* (Hagerstown, Md.: Review and Herald, 2008), pp. 13-17.

[2] *The Jewish Encyclopedia*, s.v. "Pharisees."

[3] *Encyclopaedia Judaica*, s.v. "Pharisees."

[4] George Foot Moore, *Judaism in the First Centuries of the Christian Era: The Age of the Tannaim* (Cambridge, Mass.: Harvard University Press, 1946), vol. 1, pp. 235-262; *The Universal Jewish Encyclopedia*, s.v. "Pharisees."

[5] *The Universal Jewish Encyclopedia*, s.v. "Pharisees."

[6] Moore, *Judaism*, vol. 1, p. 259.

[7] *Ibid.*, vol. 2, p. 28. See examples in *Seventh day Adventist Bible Students' Sourcebook*, s.v. "Sabbath."

[8] Joachim Jeremias, *Jerusalem in the Time of Jesus* (Philadelphia: Fortress, 1969), pp. 265-267.

[9] *Babylonian Talmud*, Sanhedrin 97b; Shabbath 118b; *Jerusalem Talmud*, Taanith 64a.

[10] Josephus, *The Antiquities of the Jews*, XVII.2.4; Jeremias, *Jerusalem*, pp. 246, 252.

[11] On the rise of the Pharisees, see Moore, *Judaism*, vol. 1, pp. 3-124. Louis Finkelstein, *The Pharisees: The Sociological Background of Their Faith* (Philadelphia: Jewish Publication Society of America, 1938), vol. 1, pp. 73-81; Jeremias, *Jerusalem*, pp. 246-267; *The International Standard Bible Encyclopedia*, 1977-1988 ed., s.v. "Pharisees."

[12] Rabbinism was a postbiblical development in Judaism, but scholars generally consider its viewpoints to be the dominant ones among the Pharisees during the New Testament period.

The past three decades have witnessed a vigorous debate about the place of the law in Judaism and about the nature of rabbinc Judaism itself. For a helpful overview, see Stephen Westerholm, "The 'New Perspective' at Twenty-Five," in *Justification and Variegated Nomism,* D. A. Carson, Peter T. O'Brien, and Mark A. Seifrid, eds. (Grand Rapids: Baker Academic, 2004), vol. 2, pp. 1-38.

[13] *Encyclopaedia Judaica*, s.v. "Sin"; Moore, *Judaism*, vol. 1, p. 479.

[14] Moore, *Judaism*, vol. 1, pp. 479, 489-492.

[15] E. P. Sanders, *Paul and Palestinian Judaism* (Philadelphia: Fortress, 1977), pp. 114, 115.

[16] Moore, *Judaism*, vol. 1, pp. 509, 510, 521; George Eldon Ladd, *A Theology of the New Testament* (Grand Rapids: Eerdmans, 1974), pp. 496, 498, 499.

[17] Ladd, *A Theology of the New Testament*, p. 497.

[18] *Theological Dictionary of the New Testament*, s.v. "*dikaios*"; *Mishnah*, Aboth 3:16 (brackets in original).

[19] Yerushalmi Peah 1:1, quoted in Roger Brooks, *The Spirit of the Ten Commandments* (San Francisco: Harper & Row, 1990), p. 10; Werner Foerster, *From the Exile to Christ*

(Philadelphia: Fortress, 1964), pp. 218, 219; J. A. Ziesler, *The Meaning of Righteousness in Paul* (Cambridge, Eng.: Cambridge University Press, 1972), p. 122.

[20] For discussions of sin as rebellion, see e.g., Solomon Schechter, *Aspects of Rabbinic Theology: Major Concepts of the Talmud* (Peabody, Mass.: Hendrickson, 1998), p. 219; Bruce D. Chilton and Jacob Neusner, *Classical Christianity and Rabbinic Judaism: Comparing Theologies* (Grand Rapids: Baker Academic, 2004), pp. 185-192.

[21] Moore, *Judaism*, vol. 1, pp. 461, 465, 466; Walther Eichrodt, *Theology of the Old Testament*, trans. J. A. Baker (London: SCM, 1967), vol. 2, p. 401; *Theological Dictionary of the New Testament*, s.v. *"hamartano."*

[22] J. Bonsirven, *Palestinian Judaism in the Time of Jesus Christ*, trans. W. Wolf (New York: Holt, Rinehart and Winston, 1964), p. 95; see also Matt. 11:29; Acts 15:10.

[23] M. L. Andreasen, *The Sanctuary Service*, 2d ed., rev. (Washington, D.C.: Review and Herald, 1947), p. 302. (Italics supplied.)

[24] William Barclay, *The Gospel of Luke*, 3d ed., Daily Study Bible (Edinburgh: The Saint Andrew Press, 1956), p. 232.

[25] Rabbi Simeon ben Jochai, quoted in *ibid.*, p. 233.

[26] G. C. Berkouwer, *Faith and Sanctification* (Grand Rapids: Eerdmans, 1952), p. 120.

[27] Peter Toon, *Justification and Sanctification* (London: Marshall Morgan and Scott, 1983), p. 18.

[28] P. T. Forsyth, quoted in A. M. Hunter, *P. T Forsyth* (Philadelphia: Westminster, 1974), p. 58; P. T. Forsyth, *The Justification of God* (London: Latimer House, 1948), p. 116; Ellen G. White, *Thoughts From the Mount of Blessing* (Mountain View, Calif.: Pacific Press, 1956), p. 79. (Italics supplied.)

[29] Bernard Ramm, *Offense to Reason: A Theology of Sin* (San Francisco: Harper & Row, 1985), pp. 146, 147. (Italics supplied.)

[30] Ellen G. White, *Christ's Object Lessons* (Washington, D.C.: Review and Herald, 1900), p. 154; Alan Simpson, *Puritanism in Old and New England* (Chicago: University of Chicago Press, 1955), p. 8.

[31] White, *Christ's Object Lessons,* p. 151.

[32] William L. Coleman, *The Pharisees' Guide to Total Holiness* (Minneapolis, Minn.: Bethany House, 1977), p. 113.

[33] *Ibid.*, p. 116.

[34] *Ibid.*, p. 29.

[35] *The Jewish Encyclopedia*, s.v. "Pharisees."

[36] P. T. Forsyth, *The Work of Christ* (London: Hodder and Stoughton, n.d.), pp. 161, 162.

[37] Coleman, *Pharisees' Guide*, p. 123.

[38] Emil Brunner, *The Mediator*, trans. Olive Wyon (New York: Macmillan, 1934), p. 494.

[39] George R. Knight, *From 1888 to Apostasy: The Case of A. T Jones* (Washington, D.C.: Review and Herald, 1987), pp. 44, 45; George R. Knight, *Angry Saints: Tensions and Possibilities in the Adventist Struggle Over Righteousness by Faith* (Washington, D.C.: Review and Herald, 1989), pp. 80-99.

[40] E. G. White to G. I. Butler, Oct. 14, 1888.

Chapter 2

# Sin: Original and Not So Original

Modern secular culture, in spite of all its wealth and knowledge, is caught in a paradoxical vacuum when it comes to an understanding of the problem it faces. On the one hand, writes psychiatrist Karl Menninger, "try as we may, it is difficult to conceive of our universe in terms of concord; instead, we are faced everywhere with the evidences of conflict. Love and hate, . . . creation and destruction—the constant war of opposing tendencies would appear to be the dynamic heart of the world."[1]

On the other hand, modern culture generally stands helpless in the face of evil because it has thrown away the explanatory key. Thirty-five years after penning the above statement, Menninger still wrestled with the issue—this time in a pathbreaking volume entitled *Whatever Became of Sin?* In discussing the foundations of modern culture, he points out that "sins had become crimes and now crimes were becoming illnesses." The upshot is that too often the concept of illness has become a device for escaping moral responsibility. Society, he argues, cannot find health until it comes to grips with the lost concept of sin.[2]

Another psychiatrist, O. Hobart Mowrer, put the issue succinctly when he wrote: *"Just so long as we deny the reality of sin, we cut ourselves off, it seems, from the possibility of radical redemption [recovery]."*[3]

These psychiatrists, coming from a professional group traditionally unfavorable to both Christianity and "sin," have put their finger on the core problem of the Bible and human existence. Christian theologians have recognized the centrality of sin from the time of the New Testament. G. C. Berkouwer writes that "any attempt to minimize our sin is radically opposed by the whole of the scriptural message." James Stalker adds that "all heresies spring out of an inadequate sense of sin."[4]

The apostle Paul helps us see that a correct understanding of sin is not only all important for grasping the human problem, but that it is also the crucial element in understanding salvation. The book of Romans, for ex-

28

ample, bases its argument on both the depth and the universality of sin. Chapter 1 demonstrates that the Gentiles are sinners, while the second chapter drives home the point that the Jews are no better, since they "are doing the very same things" (Rom. 2:1). The foundation stone for Paul's doctrine of redemption is the declaration that "both Jews and Greeks, are under the power of sin." "All have sinned and fall short of the glory of God" (Rom. 3:9, 23).

Only after bringing his readers to that conclusion can Paul start to develop an adequate doctrine of salvation. In fact, he begins that task in the very next verse. Because all are sinners (verse 23), all who are saved must be "justified by his grace as a gift, through the redemption which is in Christ Jesus" (verse 24).

The next few chapters then go on to expand upon how God overcomes the problem of sin in human lives through justification and sanctification—theological terms we will spend a great deal of time discussing in chapters 4 and 5. Meanwhile, the rest of the present chapter will, in the tradition initiated in the book of Romans, flesh out the nature of sin.

*It is important to recognize that an inadequate doctrine of sin will of necessity lead to an inadequate doctrine of salvation.* Edward Vick correctly states that "the first element in Christian perfection [or any other aspect of salvation] is recognizing that we are sinners." That, he points out, does not merely mean that we recognize that we have committed sinful acts *a, b,* and, *c.* "It means acknowledging that we are the kind of people who do such things. . . . To recognize that we are sinners means that we recognize there is a power that lords it over us and prevents us from being what God intends us to be. That power is the power of *sin.*"[5]

*Consequently, it is impossible to overestimate the importance of the depth of the sin problem.* When Paul wrote that both Jews and Gentiles "are under the power of sin" (Rom. 3:9), he meant it.

Because the Pharisees underestimated the power of sin, they thought that they could overcome sin through overcoming sins *a, b,* and *c.* The problem central to that procedure is that even after we have stopped committing sins *a, b,* and *c,* the power of sin itself still remains, and we are still sinners. Our external tinkering, in spite of all the effort we may have expended, has solved nothing.

In short, the adequacy of our view of sin will determine the adequacy of our understanding of salvation. Millard J. Erickson perceptively notes that "if man is basically good and his intellectual and moral capabilities are essentially intact, then whatever problems he encounters with respect to his standing before God will be relatively minor." For such people, the essential problem of life may be ignorance or socioeconomic deprivation. In that event, a tuning of the economic system or "education will solve the problem; a good model or example" of the way of righteousness may be all that is required. "On the other hand, if man is corrupt or rebellious, and thus either unable or unwilling to do what he sees is right, a more radical cure will be needed." Thus the more radical our understanding of sin, "the more supernatural the salvation we will deem needed."[6]

Pharisees down through the ages have consistently underplayed what Paul calls the "power" of sin in human lives. As a result, they have overestimated humanity's ability to deal with the sin problem. Ellen White speaks to that point when she pens that "education, culture, the exercise of the will, human effort, all have their proper sphere, but here they are powerless. They may produce an outward correctness of behavior, but they cannot change the heart; they cannot purify the springs of life. There must be a power working from within, a new life from above, before men can be changed from sin to holiness. That power is Christ."[7]

## Original Sin

### The Universality of Sin

One of the great facts of life is the problem of sin. On every hand we find ourselves faced with it. One commentary on its power and prevalence is that every state must have its army, police, judges, courts, and penal systems. Theologian John Macquarrie highlights the problem when he writes that as we "look at actual human existing, we perceive a massive disorder in existence, a pathology that seems to extend all through existence, whether we consider the community or the individual." Reinhold Niebuhr was just as succinct when he wrote that "where there is history . . . there is sin."[8]

Thus even if the Bible did not exist, there would still be a doctrine of sin. It is written into the very fabric of existence. The pagan writers of antiquity as well as the philosophical, literary, sociological, psychological, political, and other theorists of the present day attest to its universality. Secular novelist John Steinbeck put it accurately when he penned: "I believe that there is one story in the world, and only one. . . . Humans are caught—in their lives, in their thoughts, in their hungers and ambitions, in their avarice and cruelty, and in their kindness and generosity too—in a net of good and evil."[9]

30

Because of such insights, James Orr could write that "the Christian doctrine of Redemption [and the Fall] certainly does not rest on the narrative in Gen. iii, but it rests on the reality of the sin and guilt of the world, which would remain facts though the third chapter of Genesis never had been written."[10]

Christians, of course, do have Genesis 3 as the account of *the* original human sin. Not only do we have Genesis 3, but we have Romans 5:12, which declares that "sin came into the world through one man and death through sin, and so death spread to all men because all men sinned."

Romans 5 is not alone in the biblical declaration of the universality of sin. Romans 3:9-23 repeatedly sets forth the fact that "all have sinned," while Jeremiah 17:9 declares that the human heart "is deceitful above all things, and desperately corrupt." Beyond that, Ephesians indicates that people are "by nature children of wrath" (Eph. 2:3), and Romans flatly states that "God has consigned all men to disobedience" (Rom. 11:32). According to David, this *state* of sinfulness exists from birth. "Behold," he wrote, "I was brought forth in iniquity, and in sin did my mother conceive me" (Ps. 51:5).

While Romans 5:12 establishes the facts that (1) Adam sinned and (2) all people sinned as a result of Adam's sin, the apostle "did not undertake to define the exact manner in which this result was accomplished." In actual fact, suggests Bernard Ramm, "Paul is not primarily dealing with the indictment of humanity as sinful. He is instead describing the glorious redemption in Christ." The formal indictment had already appeared in Romans 1:17-3:23.[11]

Even though Romans 5 does not explain the process for the transmission of the consequences of Adam's sin to his posterity, other texts in both testaments indicate that it does take place. Genesis 5:3, for example, declares that "Adam . . . became the father of a son in his own likeness, after his image." Here a distinction is implied between the unfallen Adam having been created in the image of God and his son being born after Adam's post-fall likeness. That theme surfaces again in Genesis 8:21, in which God claimed at the conclusion of the Flood story that "the imagination of man's heart is evil from his youth."

In a similar vein, Jesus told Nicodemus that "that which is born of the flesh is flesh, and that which is born of the Spirit is spirit" (John 3:6). Here, as in Paul's writings (see Rom. 7:17, 18; 8:5, 8, 9, 13; Gal. 5:24), flesh refers to humanity's moral condition rather than to its physical nature.

Viewed from another perspective, the problem of sin arising in Genesis

3 does not end there. It continues on into Genesis 4 with the Cain and Abel story, into Genesis 6 with Noah's generation, and into every corner of the rest of both Scripture and world history.

The concept of original or initial sin helps us understand both ourselves and the world around us, even though we cannot fully grasp the mechanics of its transmission. Without some idea of original sin, wrote Blaise Pascal, "we remain incomprehensible to ourselves."[12]

### The Nature of "Original Sin"

Given the fact that both the Bible and our daily world demonstrate the universality of sin, our next question must relate to its nature. What is it that Adam's children somehow receive as the heritage of the fall? The two most popular answers are guilt and a fallen nature.

Many have rejected the concept of inherited guilt. One was the prophet Ezekiel, who wrote: "The soul that sins shall die. The son shall not suffer for the iniquity of the father, nor the father suffer for the iniquity of the son" (Eze. 18:20). Moses used the same argument when he declared that "the fathers shall not be put to death for the children, nor shall the children be put to death for the fathers; every man shall be put to death for his own sin" (Deut. 24:16).

The reason for these injunctions is that sin is personal. In the book of James we read that "whoever knows what is right to do and fails to do it, for him it is sin" (James 4:17). Sin is not only personal it is also moral. As we shall see later in this chapter, sin is a willful choice against God. Because sin is both moral and personal, Ramm can rightly conclude that "the guilt of one person cannot be imputed to another," and nineteenth-century theologian Washington Gladden can refer to the idea of God's punishing individuals for Adam's sin as "immoral theology."[13]

Ellen White, on the other hand, in at least one place seems to be saying that we inherit guilt. "The inheritance of children," she penned, "is that of sin. Sin has separated them from God. Jesus gave His life that He might unite the broken links to God. As related to the first Adam, men receive from him nothing but guilt and the sentence of death."[14] Along that same line is God's comment in the Ten Commandments that He will visit "the iniquity of the fathers upon the children to the third and the fourth generation of those who hate me" (Ex. 20:5; cf. ch. 34:7; Num. 14:18; Deut. 5:9).

But we need to read both of the above statements within the full context of God's revelation. While there is no doubt about God visiting the father's iniquity upon the children of future generations, it is the reason for such a visitation that we must understand if we are to make sense of the Bible's apparently contradictory statements.

Ellen White helps us see through the problem when she writes in regard to Exodus 20:5: "It is inevitable that children should suffer from the consequences of parental wrongdoing, but they are not punished for the parents' guilt, except as they participate in their sins. It is usually the case, however, that children walk in the steps of their parents. By inheritance and example the sons become partakers of the father's sin. Wrong tendencies, perverted appetites, and debased morals, as well as physical disease and degeneracy, are transmitted as a legacy from father to son, to the third and fourth generation."[15]

James Denney also helps us understand the relationship between inheritance and guilt. "Heredity," he writes, "is *not* fate—what we have received from our parents does not weave around us a net of guilt and misery through which we can never break" if we belong to God. It is immoral and cowardly unbelief to claim that the actions of our forebears have determined out fate. "The sins of fathers are only ruinous when sons make them their own. The inherited bias may be strong, but it is not everything that is in any man's nature, and it is only when he ignores or renounces the relation to God, and freely makes the evil inheritance his own, that he makes it into a condemnation."[16]

If that is so, it forces us to ask, "Why is it that everyone sins? Why is sin a universal human experience? Why has no one escaped its clutches?"

Albert Knudson points us to the answer. He suggests that we are faced with the universality of both sin and guilt. But between the two there is an inconsistency. Guilt implies freedom, yet the universality of sin seems to indicate a cause prior to people's deciding or willing to sin. "*If sin is due to free choice, there would seem to be no reason why it should be universal. Its universality suggests an element of necessity, an inborn tendency or bias toward evil, that precedes the exercise of freedom.*"[17]

Ellen White grasped the same point when she noted that we have not only "cultivated tendencies to evil," but also inherited tendencies. Because of these inherited tendencies to sin, a child need not be taught to sin.[18]

No matter how ignorant a people may have been, J. C. Ryle points out, "they have always known how to sin!" That is because we are "by nature children of wrath" (Eph. 2:3). "Out of the heart of man, come evil thoughts, fornication," and so on (Mark 7:21). "The fairest babe," writes Ryle, "is not, as its mother . . . fondly calls it, a little 'angel,'. . . but a little 'sinner.' "[19] Not that it consciously sins as a baby, but it is a sinner in the sense that it is born with a tendency to choose sin as soon as it is old enough to do so.

John Faulkner summarizes the biblical viewpoint of original sin nicely when he writes that "original sin means that the parents of our race by voluntary transgression received a wrong bent which by natural laws they transmitted to their offspring." Thus Ellen White can speak of the "corrupt channels of humanity."[20]

While guilt and sin cannot be transmitted from one generation to the next, the inbuilt tendency or propensity to sin can. That inborn inclination to sin (the carnal or fleshly mind [Rom. 8:7]) remains the primary tendency in an individual until reversed by the conversion or born-from-above experience.

Having said all these things about little children being potential sinners tilted by their nature toward evil, perhaps it is time to note that they are born with more than a tendency to sin. That fact became evident in the great battles over the sinfulness of human nature fought in nineteenth-century theology.

Leonard Woods took the position that young children must be born evil because moral depravity (1) is as universal as reason and memory, (2) demonstrates itself as soon as children are old enough to reveal their feelings, (3) cannot be ascribed to any change in the nature of children after their birth, (4) manifests itself spontaneously and is difficult to eradicate, and (5) enables one to predict that every child will be a sinner.[21]

Henry Ware replied to Woods, arguing that his five arguments could as readily establish natural holiness as natural depravity. After all, Ware pointed out, if it is true that children exhibit sinful affections, it is also the case that they manifest good affections. Second, if depraved affections appear early, so do good affections. Third, if we cannot trace sinful tendencies to changes subsequent to birth, neither can we virtuous tendencies. Fourth, both sinful and virtuous reactions are spontaneous and difficult to eradicate. Fifth, if it is predictable that all children will sin, it is equally so that they will also manifest some good traits.[22]

Some theologians recognized the fact that humans have both good and evil tendencies at birth. William Newton Clarke, for example, claimed that every individual received a double inheritance of good and evil. On the other hand, he argued against persons being morally neutral. To the contrary, "God has certainly endowed humanity with a tendency to rise; . . . nature is favorable to goodness." Goodness, in fact,

34

could be brought about by improving "the common stock." In other words, humanity can be made better through environmental and social engineering.[23]

Ellen White agreed with Clarke to a certain extent. Thus she wrote that "a perception of right, a desire for goodness, exists in every heart. But against these principles there is struggling an antagonistic power." For her, however, nature was favorable to evil rather than goodness. In every person, she penned, there is "a bent to evil, a force which, unaided, he cannot resist." Individuals can overcome their evil propensity only through the "power" of Christ.[24]

Unlike some of her interpreters, Ellen White did not hold that individuals are born morally neutral. Rather, "every" person inherits "a bent to evil." That "bent" is so fixed, as we will see in chapter 4, that only the converting power of Christ can correct its downward pull. Social engineering and genetic tinkering are not sufficient to correct the deep seated sin problem.

Outside of Christ, the Bible knows of no child who lived a life completely free of sin and who was "born again" or "born from above" at the time of its natural birth. Having God-fearing parents is not enough to tilt the scales of inborn depravity.[25] Even children born to the best of Christian families need to overcome spiritual pride, self-sufficiency, and self-centeredness. And it is those items, rather than the more obviously wicked acts, that stand at the center of sin. We will return to that topic in the next section of this chapter.

The fact that some people do not know the time of their conversion does not mean that they have not been converted. The most difficult cases of sin in the New Testament are the older sons and shiny coins of Luke 15. Such "moral heroes" are often the most hopeless of all sinners, because they are outwardly such upright people. Feeling no need, they too often never come to themselves (Luke 15:17). Their moral rectitude, unfortunately, makes them critical of others (verses 25-30). That attitude is an indication that their heart is not right, despite the fact that their outward actions are exemplary. As we discovered in the experience of the Pharisees, nothing is more deceptive than the sin of goodness.

The most difficult group to convert in Christ's ministry were those who felt no need of conversion. Such is the peril of Pharisees, both ancient and modern. *Whether we like it or not, recognize it or not, or confess it or not, every person has a "bent" to evil that needs correcting—even if that inclination is thoroughly camouflaged by Christian pedigree and outward goodness.*

35

### The Results of "the" Original Sin

Before leaving the topic of original sin, we need to examine the results of "the" original sin. Genesis 3 presents a vivid picture of what it led to. First and foremost were the religious consequences of sin—Adam and Eve became alienated from God. The Bible says they "hid themselves from the presence of the Lord God" and that they were "afraid" of Him (Gen. 3:8-10). Having dethroned God and "love to God from its place of supremacy in the soul," they became separated from Him.[26]

Such alienation is quite understandable on the human plane. For example, children who have violated their mothers' will do not wish to meet them or to look them in the face. There is something in their heart that they wish to hide. Likewise, guilt renders God's presence unbearable. Sin ruptured the oneness between people and God.

The sin-caused alienation between God and humanity would have been bad enough if it had been only a passive hiding from God's presence, but sin by its very nature is active against God. Thus James claims that the natural world is at "enmity [hostility] with God" (James 4:4). And Paul tells us that God reached out to save us while we were His enemies (Rom. 5:10; Col. 1:21, 22).

"Now an enemy," penned Leon Morris, "is not simply someone who falls a little short of being a good and faithful friend. He belongs to the opposite camp." Sinners, by definition, "are putting their effort into the opposite direction to that of God."[27]

A second result of sin was its social implications. They immediately emerged during the universe's first family argument. When God asked Adam if he had eaten the forbidden fruit, Adam quickly blamed Eve. "The woman whom thou gavest to be with me, she gave me fruit of the tree, and I ate" (Gen. 3:12). So much for the world's only perfect marriage.

The great tragedy of the social effects of the original sin was that they did not stop with Genesis 3. The message of Genesis 4-11 is one of the ever-widening social effects of sin. They move from the tragic brotherhood of Cain and Abel in Genesis 4 to become an underlying motif of all Scripture.

A third set of results of the original sin were the personal implications. Sin affects each person's relationship with his or her "self." After God finished questioning Adam, He turned to Eve. "What," He asked her, "is this that you have done?" "The devil made me do it," she replied (Gen. 3:13, paraphrased). Here we come face to face with the problem of people being unwilling and, in most cases, unable to face up to themselves and to evaluate correctly their actions and underlying motives. "The heart is deceitful above all things" (Jer. 17:9).

The religious, social, and personal effects of sin grow out of a shift that took place in human nature at the Fall. Whereas God had originally created Adam and Eve in His image (Gen. 1:26, 27), their children bore their parents' fallen image (Gen. 5:3). Their fallen condition, as we have already seen, had a "bent" toward evil.

The Bible is rich in imagery picturing fallen humans. Their "minds and consciences are corrupted" (Titus 1:15). Beyond that, through all history they have been "lovers of self, lovers of money, proud, arrogant, abusive, disobedient to their parents, ungrateful, unholy," and so on (2 Tim. 3:1-5; cf. Gen. 6:5, 6; Rom. 1:18-32). The Bible's description of the "natural person" is never pleasant, even though some individuals may have sins that are more socially acceptable than others. The central focus of the scriptural accusation is that the unconverted heart and mind are unspiritual (Rom. 8:4-8).

The Fall affected every individual's spiritual orientation. Thus Ellen White can write that "the heart of man is by nature cold and dark and unloving." "By nature the heart is evil." Even though Adam originally had a well-balanced mind and pure thoughts, "through disobedience, his powers were perverted, and selfishness took the place of love."[28]

Those problems, as we noted above, have continued to affect his posterity. Some individuals may claim not to be infected by the sin virus, but that in itself goes against both God's revelation and human observation. Puritan divine Thomas Gataker aptly described the natural heart when he suggested that it "is like a book that is spoiled by mistakes and misprints" and "like a wasteland 'wherein weeds of all sorts come up of themselves naturally,' and which yields nothing good without careful attention." Bernard Ramm claims that the problem with the sinner "is not this or that failing," but that "the whole psyche is like a ship whose rudder is fixed at a wrong angle."[29]

The "rudder" of human life, of course, is the will—that "power of decision, or of choice" that "is the governing power in the nature of man." It was the all-important will that the Fall "bent" toward evil. The essence of the effects of the original sin that has affected all generations since Adam is a misdirected will evidenced in daily life by the human tendency to choose the evil over the good. Thus, while there was a Fall, there is also a continuous falling. "Every sin committed," Ellen White wrote, "awakens the echoes of the original sin." One result is that every human being down

37

through history except Christ has sinned and fallen short of the glory of God (Rom. 3:23).[30]

The plan of salvation, as expounded by the New Testament, presupposes the universality of human sinfulness. Immediately after Paul makes his point concerning the all inclusiveness of sin in Romans 3:23, he begins his exposition of salvation through Christ in verse 24.

## SIN Is Love: The Core of SIN

That sin is love should come as no surprise to the Christian. The Bible has several words for love, but the most significant is *agapē*. *Agapē* reflects the kind of love that God has for human beings. He cares for them supremely for their own best good, even though they do not deserve it. *Agapaō* is the verb used often by the New Testament writers to speak of God's relationship with human beings. *Agapē* in the New Testament also refers to a way of life patterned on God's love for people.[31]

His hope for people is that they will love (*agapaō*) Him and one another even as He has loved them (see Matt. 22:36-40). The problem comes in when love focuses on the wrong thing. Thus Jesus condemned the Pharisees because they had "love" (*agapaō*) for "the best seat in the synagogues" (Luke 11:43). Likewise, Demas left the Christian way when he fell "in love [*agapē*] with this present world" (2 Tim. 4:10). Similarly, John admonishes his readers not to "love [*agapaō*] the world or the things of the world." Such individuals do not have the love of the Father in them (1 John 2:15).

These passages do not say that there is anything wrong with the world. But they do teach that to put anything in God's place is wrong. *Sin is love focused on the wrong object.* It is to love the object more than its Creator. And it makes no difference whether that thing is an external object or one's own person. To love anything or anyone more than God is sin. Sin is love aimed at the wrong target, accompanied by a way of life based on the direction of that aim.

That definition stands at the very foundation of Eve's sin in Genesis 3. Sin, of course, had existed prior to Genesis 3. It originated in heaven, when Lucifer sought to become equal with God—that is, when he loved himself more than his Maker (Isa. 14:12-14).[32] Lucifer's rebellion eventuated in "war . . . in heaven." The result was that "the great dragon was thrown down, that ancient serpent, who is called the Devil and Satan, the deceiver of the whole world—he was thrown down to the earth" (Rev. 12:7-9).

We find the deceptive serpent again facing Eve in Genesis 3. There this most "subtle" creature began to undermine God's authority. He first sought to get Eve to doubt God's word (Did He really say not to eat of the tree? [verse 1]). Next, Satan implanted doubt as to whether God really meant what He said (Certainly God doesn't kill people for touching fruit! [verses 2-4]). Third, the tempter threw doubt on God's goodness, implying that He was selfishly hoarding the best things for Himself (verses 5, 6). "Be like God" was the suggestion. Since God can't be trusted, you might as well do your own thing. Put your confidence in your own self. Become the master of your own destiny.

Following that line of reasoning, "she took of its fruit and ate" (verse 6). The questions we must now ask are: "When did Eve sin? What was her sin?"

I would like to point out that *Eve's sin was not in taking the fruit and eating.* Those actions were a *result* of sin rather than the primary sin itself.

*Eve sinned when she threw out God's word to her and accepted Satan's suggestion. She sinned when she told God to get lost so that she could do her own thing. And she sinned when she rebelled against God and put her will at the center of her life, loving her own opinion more than His.*

*Out of her rebellious sin flowed sinful acts. The act was not the sin but the result of sin ruling her heart.* She fell before she took the fruit. Eve fell when she placed love for something (the fruit) and/or someone (herself) before her love for God. As a result, James Orr can claim rightly that the essence of sin is making my will rather than God's will "the ultimate law of my life."[33]

### Most Sincere Christians Are Not Concerned With SIN

At this point I would like to suggest that most Christians, including Seventh-day Adventists, are not really interested in SIN. They are concerned with such acts as murder, theft, and dishonesty, but not SIN. Warts or blemishes on the surface, they are symptomatic of SIN, but are not the basic SIN itself.

Now don't go away angry. I know the Bible says that "sin is the transgression of the law" (1 John 3:4, KJV) and that Ellen White said that "the only definition of sin is that it is the transgression of the law."[34] But let us look at the total biblical perspective on both sin and law. The present chapter will treat the first of those tasks, while the second will be the topic of chapter 3. For the moment, we can say sin is at least three things: (1) a state of rebellion, (2) a broken relationship, and (3) an action.

Sin at its most basic level is not some impersonal evil or "residual animal behavior" or bad trait built into human character. Rather, it is *rebellion* against the God of the universe (Isa. 1:2, 4; Hos. 7:13).[35] Thus sin is personal rather than impersonal. "Against thee, thee only," says the psalmist, "have I sinned" (Ps. 51:4). Sin is a personal attack against God's authority. The "flesh" (unconverted human nature), writes Paul, "is hostile to God" (Rom. 8:7). The sinner is in the relationship of "enemy" to God (Rom. 5:10). Beyond being personal, sin is moral. It is a deliberate act of the will to rebel against God. Fundamentally, sin is a choice against God.

Herbert Douglass correctly observes that "sin is a created being's clenched fist in the face of his Creator; sin is the creature distrusting God, deposing Him as the Lord of his life." In like manner, Emil Brunner claims that sin "is like the son who strikes his father's face in anger, . . . it is the bold self-assertion of the son's will above that of the father."[36]

The story of Eve depicts sin as the desire to be "like God" (Gen. 3:5). It is the choice of Cain to "do it his way" rather than God's (Gen. 4:1-7). "Sin, in the Biblical view," Orr wrote, "consists in the revolt of the creature will from its rightful allegiance to the sovereign will of God, and the setting up of a false independence, the substitution of a life-for-self for life-for-God."[37] The dynamic that fueled the rebellion of the prodigal son (Luke 15:11-32), sin has driven all too much human activity down through the corridors of history.

From this perspective, it is easy to see that all sin follows the disregarding of the first great commandment and the first of the Ten Commandments: "You shall love the Lord your God with all your heart, and with all your soul, and with all your mind"; "You shall have no other gods before me" (Matt. 22:37; Ex. 20:3).

We should recognize that sin as rebellion is not merely a set of discrete acts, but, as we saw in our discussion of original sin, a state of fallenness. Human beings have a sinful nature that leads them to do sinful acts. For that reason, James Denney points out, "every sincere man is sorry not only for what he has done, but for what he is. The sin which weighs on us, . . . which defeats us, which makes us cry, 'O wretched man that I am! Who shall deliver me?' is more than isolated acts. . . . It is our very nature which needs to be redeemed and renewed."[38]

Sin as a state of rebellion and exaltation of one's will over that of God is closely tied to self-centeredness. It was no accident Ellen White wrote that "under the general heading of selfishness came every other sin." Again, she penned: "There is nothing more offensive to God than this narrow, self-caring spirit."[39]

Intricately linked to selfishness, self-centeredness, and an unhealthy self-love is the problem of pride. It was through rebellious pride and self-sufficiency that Lucifer became the devil, that Eve became the mother of a sinful race, and that Christ's 12 disciples failed to receive His blessing as they continually bickered over who was the greatest (see Isa. 14:12-15; Eze. 28:13-17; Gen. 3; Matt. 18:1). C. S. Lewis has remarked that "pride leads to every other vice: it is the complete anti-God state of mind."[40] Out of such a rebellious nature will flow sinful acts.

Sin as rebellion is intimately tied to sin as a broken relationship. The most obvious thing about Genesis 3 is that the Fall fractured all of humanity's relationships. Central to those broken relationships was human alienation from God. Isaiah writes to Israel of old that their "iniquities" had "made a separation" between themselves and their God. Their "sins" had "hid his face" from them (Isa. 59:2). Paul wrote that the unconverted person is "estranged" from God (Col. 1:21).

Because the Bible defines sin in reference to God, *sin is a relational concept.* There are only two ways of relating to God. We can say yes to His will or no to that will. We have no other options. Saying yes to God we call the faith relationship. But saying no to Him is rebellious sin. No moral creature can ignore God. *Either we respond to Him in faith or in sin.*[41]

If sin is a broken relationship to God, then righteousness and faith will of necessity center on a reconciliation of that relationship.[42] And if sin is rebellious distrust of God, then faith must center in trust. Sin, therefore, is not ethical, but religious. *Thus sin is not a broken relationship to a code of law, but a rebellious and broken relationship to the Lord of the law.*

By this time, someone will be saying that my presentation sounds dangerously like what some have pejoratively termed the "new theology." If so, I hope to demonstrate that it is the "new theology of the Sermon on the Mount."

Sin as a state of rebellion and sin as broken relationship are directly related to sin as act. Jesus made that plain when He said that "what comes out of the mouth proceeds from the heart, and this defiles a man. For out of the heart come evil thoughts, murder, adultery, fornication, theft, false witness, slander" (Matt. 15:18, 19; cf. Mark 7:20-23). "Out of the abundance of the heart the mouth speaks. The good man out of his good treasure brings forth good, and the evil man out of his evil treasure brings forth evil" (Matt. 12:34, 35). The same concept underlies Jesus' saying that an evil tree brings forth evil fruit and James's thought that a brackish spring pours forth brackish water (Matt. 7:17, 18; James 3:11).

Brunner catches that biblical insight when he points out that the Bible views the heart as "the organ of the whole personality." Sin has its seat in humanity's twisted heart. The heart "is the Headquarters of the General Staff, . . . it is the summit of the personality, the Self, which rebels against the Lord."[43] For that reason the Bible equates conversion with receiving a "new heart" (Eze. 11:19; 18:31; Eph. 3:17).

Being a sinner is not committing a series of unrelated acts, but having an evil heart that gives birth to a lifetime of evil actions. John Macquarrie says it nicely when he writes that "the sinful attitude expresses itself in sinful acts, and of course in popular usage 'sin' usually means some actual sin or deed of wrongdoing. Theologically, however, the interest lies rather in the attitude than in the particular deeds which flow from it, for it is the attitude that is the fundamental evil."[44]

This discussion does not mean that individual acts of sin are not important. After all, doesn't the Bible say that "sin is the transgression of the law" (1 John 3:4, KJV)? Again, Ellen White was certainly correct when she wrote that "there is no definition given in our world but that transgression is the transgression of the law."[45]

Individual acts of transgression are sins. Beyond that, they are the outward symptoms of SIN—the visible manifestations of a sinful heart and nature. We can portray the biblical idea graphically as follows:

## SIN ⟶ sins

That is, the sinful heart, the heart in willful rebellion against God, produces acts of sin in the daily life.

Ramm meaningfully comments that "sin may be defined as transgressing the law, but that does not measure its seriousness."[46] That very problem, as we saw in chapter 1, led to the shortcomings of the Pharisees. Because they viewed sin as a series of discrete actions, they naturally tended to view righteousness also as a series of discrete actions. Thus their inadequate view of sin set them up for an inadequate view of salvation.

Paul Althaus notes that the scholastic theologians of Martin Luther's day made the same mistake. They only thought "of the transgressions of the law in [terms of] thoughts, words, and deeds."[47] The medieval church had pictured salvation as an overcoming of those acts. That, of course, was the point that forced Luther to begin the Protestant Reformation.

Christian salvation is much deeper than merely cleaning up one's outward life, as important as that is. It calls for a total transformation of the heart and life and a renewed relationship to God. Out of that transformed heart, as we shall see in chapters 4 and 5, will flow changed actions.

The problem with the "atomic theory" that views sin as separate acts of transgression is that it does not account for or even permit a moral nature. A human being is not a series of good and evil actions, but a person with a "bent" toward God or against Him. Overcoming sin is not merely trying hard to be better. G. C. Berkouwer observes that the Bible views "man in terms of his total life direction: man the sinner, the guilty one, the rebel against his God. In the biblical perspective there is no possibility of escape and no way out of man's guilty lostness." Scripture, therefore, describes human beings in terms of bondage, slavery, servitude, and a process of degeneracy that cannot be reversed without God's intervention. Humanity is "dead in sin" and "lost" (Rom. 6:6; Eph. 2:1, 5; 4:18; Col. 2:13; Luke 19:10). Only in the cross can we see the depth of sin and the magnitude of the action needed to cure it.[48] God is in the business of saving people, not in merely polishing up their exteriors.

### Some Further Aspects of Sin

Before moving away from a definition of sin as a state of rebellion, a broken relationship, and a series of acts, we should briefly examine a few more aspects of sin. First, temptation is not sin. Jesus was tempted, but He did not sin. Neither have I sinned when I am tempted. Sin takes place when I recognize the temptation for what it is, decide to continue to dwell and/or act on it, and in effect tell God to "scram" for the time being.

Second, an act of sin may be either one of commission or omission. Unfortunately, most Christians think of sins only in terms of performing an evil act, while failing to see that sin is infinitely broader than doing wrong things. It also includes one's failure to do the loving thing for one's neighbor. "The condemning power of the law of God," Ellen White writes, "extends, not only to the things we do, but to the things we do not do. . . . We must not only cease to do evil, but we must learn to do well."[49] In the word picture of Jesus in the last judgment, the "good" Pharisees are caught totally off guard because they focused merely on sins of commission while overlooking sins of omission (Matt. 25:31-46).

My point is that we can leave off doing "bad" things while still being essentially selfish and mean. The real test of total transformation and the internalization of God's principles is a life that constantly reaches out in love to serve others. Thus the bulk of Pharisaic righteous activity fell far short of God's infinite ideal. With that in mind, we can agree with H. Wheeler

Robinson's evaluation that both our sinfulness and the activity of God's grace are much more profound than most people have ever imagined.[50]

Because of the distorted focus on sin as acts of commission, most schemes of perfection emphasize the negative. One can generally not do things through sheer willpower, whereas "genuinely" caring for your enemy takes the total transforming power of the Holy Spirit. Thus even the "good" person still needs the conversion experience. The real question is not whether we hate God, but whether we love Him and His created children more than we love our "selves."

A third aspect of sin to note is that not all sins have the same seriousness. Ellen White writes that "the sin that is most nearly hopeless and incurable is pride of opinion, self-conceit." In *Steps to Christ* we read that "God does not regard all sins as of equal magnitude; there are degrees of guilt in His estimation." While "no sin is small" in His sight, God, unlike humans, estimates their proper weightiness. Human beings might emphasize such outward sins as drunkenness, "while pride, selfishness, and covetousness too often go unrebuked. But these are sins that are especially offensive to God; for they are contrary to the benevolence of His character, to that unselfish love which is the very atmosphere of the unfallen universe." Those who fall into the grosser sins, White adds, feel a sense of shame and the need of grace, but not those who are prideful.[51]

That is why the "vegetarian" sins of the Pharisee are more dangerous and harder to cure than those of the publicans. Pharisees and perfectionists of all eras have too often fallen before the weightier, but "invisible," sins.

A fourth aspect of sin that we need to recognize is the tendency to trivialize sin. Some people get nervous when they hear sin defined in terms of broken relationships and "unmeasurables" such as pride and self-centeredness. They envision heresy and antinomianism (lawlessness) behind such statements. Such believers see sin as a "quantity" that we can weigh and count, rather than as a quality of life.

The quantitative view of sin nearly always leads to a focus on the smallest units of sin as one moves from sin to righteousness. Thus, the Pharisees spent endless hours debating the fine points of sin and righteousness, such as how far one could walk on the Sabbath day. The quantitative approach to sin was aptly expressed by the "saint," who, in the midst of a discussion of possible lessons from the sins of David, remarked that "we don't all have the same problem. For some of us it is eating granola between meals."

One supposes that when our friend gets the victory over granola between meals, she will move on to "greater" conquests as she finds smaller and smaller bits of sin still resident in her being.

The nice thing about the quantitative approach, from the human perspective, is that it breaks sin (and thus righteousness) into manageable chunks, and one can get the feeling of progress and victory. Meanwhile, once one defines sin in terms of such things as wearing costume jewelry or certain dietary habits, one has essentially "contained" it in that definition, and thus one can go about his or her life without worrying about it. In other words, by restricting "sin" to such concepts as wearing jewelry, I can then feel good about driving any type of car I like or wearing the finest suits. I don't think I will ever get over the physician who was death on wedding bands (because he had a "proof text") but drove a gold-colored Cadillac. Truly he had made sin manageable. Certainly he had a type of righteousness. But he had trivialized both sin and righteousness. It reminds one of those Pharisees who strained out the gnats while swallowing the camels.

The qualitative approach to sin and righteousness is not less demanding than the quantitative. To the contrary, it is infinitely more so, because from its perspective neither sin nor righteousness can be compartmentalized or contained. It does not have a lower view of law, but rather a higher one. Instead of being concerned with merely tinkering with external actions and "Christian improvement" in lifestyle, it seeks total transformation of heart, mind, and life. Refusing to break sin into smaller and smaller units, it focuses on the largest units of sin—those that contain the smaller. But beyond "sin-units," which are relatively meaningless in terms of God's basic law, it looks toward sin and righteousness in the light of the quality of the relationship between people and their God and their neighbors.

Unfortunately, the qualitative approach is beyond mere human effort. It depends on God's grace in ways not needed in the smaller-and-smaller-units approach. For example, I can stop eating granola between meals on my own steam. I can possibly, even, with a great deal more effort, stop meditating on the delights of Bathsheba on a moment-by-moment basis through mental discipline. But I am beyond the limits of human ability if I am commanded to continually love those who abuse me. That takes the dynamic, transforming power of God's grace. While I might feel some pride in getting the "victory" over "granola between meals" or lustful meditations of romping through the daisies with my personal Bathsheba, all pride is humbled in the dust when it comes to overcoming the real problems in my life.

By the way, lest some should mistake my meaning here, when people love God and neighbor, that love *will* transform how they eat and how they think about and treat their neighbors. The qualitative approach to sin and righteousness always includes quantitative aspects, but the opposite is not true. I know people who have gotten "the victory" over granola between meals yet who are very ugly about those who do not agree with their theological viewpoints and who have not achieved similar "heights" of religious progress. The Pharisees live on. Trivialized views of sin, unfortunately, lead to trivialized views of "righteousness."

## Sins That Are Not Sins

While there are sins that are sins, there are also sins that are not sins. A good place to start on a discussion of this topic is in the book of James. James wrote that "whoever knows what is right to do and fails to do it, for him it is sin" (James 4:17). Paul also tied sin to human knowledge when he penned that "through the law comes knowledge of sin" (Rom. 3:20; cf. 4:15; 7:7).

But what if a person doesn't know the law, yet goes against its precepts? Has that person "sinned"? Or what about the individual who commits wrongs but is not aware of it? Has he or she "sinned"? In other words, are there sins of ignorance or unintentional sins?

Paul apparently thought there were such sins. He wrote to Timothy that he had "formerly blasphemed and persecuted and insulted" Christ. Legally he had sinned, even though it had not been conscious ethical action. The apostle went on to point out that he had "received mercy" because be had "acted ignorantly in unbelief" (1 Tim. 1:13).

Did that sin need to be forgiven as sin? Paul's answer is yes. God's grace "overflowed" him. "Christ Jesus," Paul penned, "came into the world to save sinners. And I am the foremost of sinners." The apostle had received "mercy" (verses 14-16).

The difference between conscious sins and unconscious ones is explicit in the Old Testament. Thus David could ask God both to "clear" him from his "hidden faults" and to keep him back from "presumptuous sins" (Ps. 19:12, 13). H. C. Leupold characterizes David's hidden faults as "sins of weakness inadvertently committed. They are the sins that we ordinarily do not even discern as being committed by us." On the other hand, the psalmist's "presumptuous sins" are those committed "in defiance of the Lord."[52]

Moses had also talked of several varieties of sins. We could equate sinning with a "high hand" (Num. 15:30) with David's sins of presumption,

46

but the oft repeated concept of one who "sins unwittingly" (Lev. 4:2, 13, 22, 27; Num. 15:27) undoubtedly, if one reads the context, includes a degree of conscious disobedience. Thus "unwitting sin" included "both conscious acts of disobedience and offenses committed as the result of human weakness and frailty."[53] But even sinful actions that were purely accidental and included no intent to do wrong to another person came under the Mosaic legislation (e.g., Ex. 21:12-14).

Specific known sins had specific personal sacrifices in the Levitical legislation. But, in addition, the people had the daily evening and morning burnt offerings to take care of their inadvertent sins. The yearly Day of Atonement also made provision for "sins the people had committed in ignorance" (Heb. 9:7, NIV). The only sins that people could not atone for in the Old Testament sacrificial system were openly presumptuous sins that they refused to repent of and/or stop committing. Such persons had no hope in either the Old Testament (see Num. 15:30, 31) or in the New (Heb. 10:26).

At this juncture, it is important to recognize that the most comprehensive definition of sin is not sin as transgression of the law. Arnold Wallenkampf set forth the broader aspects nicely when he wrote that "the apostle Paul gives the definitive definition of sin when he says that 'whatever does not proceed from faith is sin' (Rom. 14:23)." Thus Wallenkampf can speak of "moral" (deliberate) and "amoral" (acts of ignorance) sins. He is careful to note that sins of ignorance or sins connected with immaturity or human weakness (amoral sins) "will cause our eternal death unless we accept Jesus as our Saviour."[54]

Wesleyan theology makes a helpful distinction between the ethical and legal concepts of sin. The ethical concept involves intention to sin, while the legal concept "includes any infraction of the perfect will of God."[55]

The division between ethical and legal concepts of sin is based upon John Wesley's teaching that there are sins "properly so called" and sins "improperly so called." The first consists of voluntary transgression of a known law, while the second represents "involuntary transgression of a Divine law, known or unknown." Both proper and improper sins, he writes, need "atoning blood."[56]

Wesley equates improper sin with "mistakes" rather than willful "rebellion." Improper sins flow from ignorance, bodily weakness, reflexive actions, and so on. We should note, however, that the line between proper and improper sin in daily life is not always clear. For example, when I become angry, is my attitude voluntary or involuntary? "Perhaps," writes

J. R. McQuilkin, "it was involuntary to begin with, but if one continues in a state of anger, it surely becomes voluntary." It is also important to recognize that an improper sin becomes a proper one if a person's attention gets called to it, and that individual refuses to change (see James 4:17).[57]

While Ellen White did not use Wesley's terminology, she had the same concepts. "If one who daily communes with God errs from the path," she penned, ". . . it is not because he sins willfully; for when he sees his mistake, he turns again, and fastens his eyes upon Jesus, and the fact that he has erred, does not make him less dear to the heart of God." Again, Ellen White wrote, "To be led into sin unawares—not intending to sin . . . is very different from the one who plans and deliberately enters into temptation and plans out a course of sin."[58]

Thus willful sin for Ellen White is the same as Wesley's proper sin, while unwillful sin (error or sins of ignorance) can be equated with sin improperly so called. Both Wesley and Ellen White also refer to improper sins as "mistakes."[59]

The point to note in this section is that the Bible writers, Ellen White, and theologians such as Wesley refer to improper sins as sins rather than merely as evil.[60] Beyond that, it is important to remember that both the atoning death of Christ and the Old Testament system cover both willful sins and sins of ignorance. This teaching will be of importance as we seek to unlock the meaning of perfection in the Bible and Ellen White's writings in chapters 7 through 9.

**Concluding Perspective**

We have spent a great deal of time on the problem of sin, because an incorrect understanding of it will of necessity lead to an inadequate view of salvation. J. C. Ryle points out that "if a man does not realize the dangerous nature of his soul's disease, you cannot wonder if he is content with false or imperfect remedies."[61]

An understanding of sin is also a prerequisite for an adequate concept of perfection. "Whenever the concept of sin is deformed, or naturalized or rationalized," claims Hans LaRondelle, "the idea of perfection consequently suffers under the same verdict."[62]

The problem is that sin is deceptive. Ellen White writes that "many are deceived concerning the condition of their hearts. They do not realize that the natural heart is deceitful above all things, and desperately wicked" (Jer. 17:9). That problem is especially difficult for those suffering from the sin of goodness (e.g., Luke 15:25-29). Those who think of themselves as "reasonably good" feel no need to become partakers of God's grace.[63]

Anselm, a medieval scholar, held that only "the one who has truly pondered the weight of the cross" "has truly pondered the weight of sin."[64]

To cure the illness of sin takes death and resurrection, first in Christ and then in each of His children. Just as Christ had His cross, so must we have ours. But beyond the cross, and intimately connected to it, is the resurrection life. Most of the remainder of this book will cover these topics. But first we must look at the law and its function in God's universe and in our individual lives.

---

[1] Karl Menninger, *Man Against Himself* (New York: Harcourt, Brace & World, A Harvest Book, 1938), p. 3.

[2] Karl Menninger, *Whatever Became of Sin?* (New York: Hawthorn, 1975), pp. 45, 48, *passim*.

[3] 0. Hobart Mowrer, *The Crisis in Psychiatry and Religion* (Princeton, N.J.: D. Van Nostrand, 1961), p. 40.

[4] G. C. Berkouwer, *Sin* (Grand Rapids: Eerdmans, 1971), p. 287; James Stalker, *The Atonement* (New York: American Tract Society, 1909), p. 88.

[5] Edward W. H. Vick, *Is Salvation Really Free?* (Washington, D.C.: Review and Herald, 1983), p. 86.

[6] Millard J. Erickson, *Christian Theology* (Grand Rapids: Baker, 1986), p. 562.

[7] Ellen G. White, *Steps to Christ* (Mountain View, Calif.: Pacific Press, n.d.), p. 18.

[8] Ramm, *Offense to Reason*, p. 157; John Macquarrie, *Principles of Christian Theology*, 2d ed. (New York: Charles Scribner's Sons, 1977), p. 69; Reinhold Niebuhr, *The Nature and Destiny of Man: A Christian Interpretation* (New York: Charles Scribner's Sons, 1964), vol. 2, p. 80.

[9] Emil Brunner, *The Christian Doctrine of Creation and Redemption*, trans. Olive Wyon (Philadelphia: Westminster, 1952), p. 90; Ramm, *Offense to Reason*, pp. 10-37; John Steinbeck, *East of Eden* (New York: Bantam, 1967), p. 366.

[10] James Orr, *The Christian View of God and the World* (New York: Charles Scribner's Sons, [1897]), p. 182.

[11] Albert Barnes, quoted in H. Shelton Smith, *Changing Conceptions of Original Sin* (New York: Charles Scribner's Sons, 1955), p. 129; Ramm, *Offense to Reason*, p. 50.

[12] Blaise Pascal, quoted in Ramm, *Offense to Reason*, p. 1. Cf. Blaise Pascal, *Pensées* 7.445.

[13] Ramm, *Offense to Reason*, p. 76; Washington Gladden, quoted in Smith, *Changing Conceptions of Original Sin*, p. 176.

[14] Ellen G. White, *Child Guidance* (Nashville: Southern Pub. Assn., 1954), p. 475.

[15] Ellen G. White, *Patriarchs and Prophets* (Mountain View, Calif.: Pacific Press, 1958), p. 306.

[16] James Denney, *Studies in Theology* (London: Hodder and Stoughton, 1895), pp. 90, 91.

[17] Albert C. Knudson, *The Doctrine of Redemption* (New York: Abingdon-Cokesbury, 1933), p. 263. (Italics supplied.)

[18] Ellen G. White, *The Desire of Ages* (Mountain View, Calif.: Pacific Press, 1898), p. 671. Cf. White, *Patriarchs and Prophets*, p. 306.

[19] Ryle, *Holiness*, pp. 5, 3.

[20] John Alfred Faulkner, *Modernism and the Christian Faith* (New York: Methodist Book Concern, 1921), p. 280; Ellen G. White, *Selected Messages* (Washington, D.C.: Review and Herald, 1958), book 1, p. 334.

[21] Leonard Woods, quoted in Smith, *Changing Conceptions of Original Sin*, pp. 79, 80.

[22] Henry Ware, quoted in *ibid*, pp. 82, 83.

[23] William Newton Clarke, *An Outline of Christian Theology* (New York: Charles Scribner's Sons, 1898), pp. 244, 245.

[24] Ellen G. White, *Education* (Mountain View, Calif.: Pacific Press, 1903), p. 29. Cf. H. R. Mackintosh, *The Christian Experience of Forgiveness* (London: Nisbet, 1927), p. 63.

[25] For an opposite position to this, see Marvin Moore, *The Refiner's Fire* (Boise, Idaho: Pacific Press, 1990), p. 132, n. 6. The idea that a person can be born "born again" is quite pervasive in certain sectors of Adventism.

[26] James Orr, *God's Image in Man*, 2d ed. (New York: A. C. Armstrong and Son, [1906]), p. 223.

[27] Leon Morris, *The Atonement* (Downers Grove, Ill.: InterVarsity, 1983), pp. 136, 137.

[28] White, *Mount of Blessing*, p. 21; White, *The Desire of Ages*, p. 172; White, *Steps to Christ*, p. 17.

[29] Thomas Gataker, quoted in B. W. Ball, *The English Connection: The Puritan Roots of Seventh-day Adventist Belief* (Cambridge, Eng.: James Clarke, 1981), p. 68; Ramm, *Offense to Reason*, p. 149.

[30] White, *Steps to Christ*, p. 47; E. G. White, *Review and Herald*, Apr. 16, 1901, p. 241.

[31] See *The New International Dictionary of New Testament Theology*, s.v. "Love." Cf. Daniel Day Williams, *The Spirit and the Forms of Love* (New York: Harper & Row, 1968), pp. 16-51; C. S. Lewis, *The Four Loves* (New York: Harcourt Brace Jovanovich, 1960).

[32] For the use of Isa. 14:12-14 as applying to Lucifer, see Knight, *The Cross of Christ*, p. 20.

[33] Orr, *God's Image*, p. 216.

[34] E. G. White, MS 8, 1888, in *The Ellen G. White 1888 Materials*, (Washington, D.C.: Ellen G. White Estate, 1987), p. 128.

[35] Herman Ridderbos, *Paul: An Outline of His Theology*, trans. J. R. De Witt (Grand Rapids: Eerdmans, 1975), p. 105; Ramm, *Offense to Reason*, pp. 81, 95; Edmond Jacob, *Theology of the Old Testament*, trans. A. W. Heathcote and P. J. Allcock (New York: Harper & Row, 1958), p. 283; Eichrodt, *Theology of the Old Testament*, vol. 2, p. 400.

[36] Herbert E. Douglass, *Why Jesus Waits*, rev. ed. ([Riverside, Calif.]: Upward Way Publishers, 1987), p. 53; Brunner, *The Mediator*, p. 462. Cf. Brunner, *Christian Doctrine of Creation and Redemption*, p. 92.

[37] Orr, *Christian View of God*, p. 172.

[38] James Denney, *The Christian Doctrine of Reconciliation* (London: James Clarke, 1959), p. 196.

[39] Ellen G. White, *Testimonies for the Church* (Mountain View, Calif.: Pacific Press, 1948), vol. 4, p. 384; White, *Christ's Object Lessons*, p. 400.

[40] C. S. Lewis, *Mere Christianity* (New York: Macmillan Paperbacks, 1960), p. 109. Cf. George R. Knight, *Philosophy and Education: An Introduction in Christian Perspective*, 4th ed. (Berrien Springs, Mich.: Andrews University Press, 2006), pp. 184-192.

[41] For more on this topic, see Gustaf Aulén, *The Faith of the Christian Church*, trans. E. H. Wahlstrom (Philadelphia: Muhlenberg, 1960), pp. 231-236; Emil Brunner, *The Letter to the Romans* (Philadelphia: Westminster, 1959), p. 161.

[42] See Knight, *The Cross of Christ*, pp. 73-75.

[43] Brunner, *Christian Doctrine of Creation and Redemption*, p. 94.

[44] Macquarrie, *Principles of Christian Theology*, p. 261. Cf. Martin Luther, in Paul Althaus,

*The Theology of Martin Luther*, trans. R. C. Schultz (Philadelphia: Fortress, 1966), pp. 144, 145.

[45] E. G. White, MS 9, 1890, in *1888 Materials*, p. 537.

[46] Ramm, *Offense to Reason*, p. 40.

[47] Althaus, *Theology of Martin Luther*, p. 153.

[48] Berkouwer, *Sin*, p. 241. See also, Denney, *Studies in Theology*, pp. 80-85; Knudson, *Doctrine of Redemption*, pp. 240, 241; Ramm, *Offense to Reason*, p. 40.

[49] White, *Selected Messages*, book 1, p. 220.

[50] H. Wheeler Robinson, *Redemption and Revelation* (London: Nisbet, 1942), p. 241.

[51] White, *Testimonies for the Church*, vol. 7, pp. 199, 200; White, *Steps to Christ*, p. 30.

[52] H. C. Leupold, *Exposition of the Psalms* (Grand Rapids: Baker, 1969), p. 183.

[53] R. K. Harrison, *Leviticus*, Tyndale Old Testament Commentaries (Downers Grove, Ill.: InterVarsity, 1980), pp. 60, 61.

[54] Arnold Valentin Wallenkampf, *What Every Christian Should Know About Being Justified* (Washington, D.C.: Review and Herald, 1988), p. 25.

[55] Laurence W. Wood, "A Wesleyan Response" and "The Wesleyan View," in *Christian Spirituality: Five Views of Sanctification*, ed. Donald L. Alexander (Downers Grove, Ill.: InterVarsity, 1988), pp. 39, 113.

[56] John Wesley, *A Plain Account of Christian Perfection* (Kansas City, Mo.: Beacon Hill Press of Kansas City, 1966), p. 54.

[57] *Ibid.*, p. 55; J. Robertson McQuilkin, "The Keswick Perspective," in *Five Views on Sanctification* (Grand Rapids: Zondervan, 1987), p. 172. See also, Leo George Cox, *John Wesley's Concept of Perfection* (Kansas City, Mo.: Beacon Hill Press of Kansas City, 1964), p. 180; Leon and Mildred Chambers, *Holiness and Human Nature* (Kansas City, Mo.: Beacon Hill Press of Kansas City, 1975), *passim*.

[58] Ellen G. White, *Review and Herald*, 12 May 1896, p. 290; Ellen G. White, *Our High Calling* (Washington, D.C.: Review and Herald, 1961), p. 177.

[59] Ellen G. White, *Gospel Workers* (Washington, D.C.: Review and Herald, 1948), p. 162; Wesley, *A Plain Account of Christian Perfection*, 55; White, *Selected Messages*, book 1, p. 360.

[60] For a treatment of the opposite position to the one presented in this passage, see Dennis E. Priebe, *Face-to-Face With the Real Gospel* (Boise, Idaho: Pacific Press, 1985), pp. 28-30.

[61] Ryle, *Holiness*, p. 1.

[62] H. K. LaRondelle, *Perfection and Perfectionism* (Berrien Springs, Mich.: Andrews University Press, 1971), p. 3.

[63] White, *Selected Messages*, book 1, p. 320; White, *Mount of Blessing*, p. 7.

[64] Anselm, quoted in Ramm, *Offense to Reason*, p. 38.

51

Chapter 3

# Unlawful Uses of the Law

W e know," the apostle Paul writes in an insightful passage, "that the law is good, if . . . one uses it lawfully" (1 Tim. 1:8). The astounding truth is that we can misuse the law. Paul implies that we can abuse it, and that God's perfect law is bad when employed for ends for which it was never made. One of the great temptations of human nature is to misapply God's law.

Paul was well aware of the problem, because he had been a Pharisee who had had "reason for confidence in the flesh"; one who was "blameless" "as to righteousness under the law" (Phil. 3:4, 6). In his pre-Christian experience, the apostle had prided himself in his moral accomplishments for God. In the best Pharisaic sense of the word, he had been a moral athlete who strained every nerve to please God through obeying His commandments.

In other words, Paul had held the Pharisaic position that "a man can attain to a right relationship with God by keeping meticulously all that the law lays down. If he fulfills all the works of the law, he will be right with God."[1] The way to being counted as right or just before God was through observing God's law. Obedience led to justification. The law had been for him a means of achieving righteousness.

It was that very concept that the converted Paul came to see as an "unlawful" use of God's law. In another connection he wrote that the moral law (including the Ten Commandments) was "holy and just and good" (Rom. 7:12). "Good for what?" is the question that we must ask. Even that which is good, holy, and just can be put to bad, unholy, and unjust uses if employed for a purpose for which it was not created. The law of God must be used lawfully (for its intended purpose) if it is to have a beneficial effect in the Christian life. But when mispplied, it becomes an agent of death.

Neither Christ nor the New Testament writers downplayed the importance of the law. But they did seek to put it in its proper place. That is nowhere more clear than in Paul's theological masterpiece—the epistle to the Romans. We noted in the previous chapter that before he could effectively deal with salvation (beginning in Romans 3:24), he first had to demonstrate the depth and universality of human sin. That topic was his main burden in Romans 1, 2, and 3:1-23. In Romans 3:23 the apostle sums up his argument by forcefully concluding that the Jews were no better than the Gentiles, "since all have sinned and fall short of the glory of God." Therefore all must be "justified by his grace," which is made available through Christ's sacrifice and "received by faith" (Rom. 3:24, 25).

The point we want to stress at this time is that not only did Paul use the first three chapters of Romans to prove the universality of sin, but he also began to develop in them the weakness and helplessness of the law in dealing with the sin problem. In Romans 3:20, therefore, he makes a frontal assault on the Pharisaic approach to righteousness by claiming that "no human being will be justified [made right or righteous] in his [God's] sight by works of the law, since through the law comes knowledge of sin." That issue had to be made and added to the apostle's conclusions regarding sin before he could begin to deal adequately with God's solution to the sin problem.

The weakness of the law for salvation became a theme in Paul's epistles. "The law," he penned, "brings wrath" (Rom. 4:15; cf. 6:23). "A man is not justified by works of the law" (Gal. 2:16). "All who rely on works of the law are under a curse; for it is written, 'Cursed be every one who does not abide by all things written in the book of the law, and do them.' Now it is evident that no man is justified before God by the law" (Gal. 3:10, 11).

In short, the law reveals that we have a serious problem in our lives, but it offers no solutions. It simply leaves people with a death sentence hanging over their heads. Thus Paul got upset when people sought to use law to gain salvation (Gal. 3:1-3). Martin Luther, who once claimed that "if ever a man could be saved by monkery that man was I," came to the same conclusion as his Pharisaic forerunner—Paul. Both Paul's and Luther's "opposition to every method of obtaining salvation by means of a legal formula," G. C. Berkouwer suggests, "is obstinately intense," because such techniques became "competitors to Christ."[2]

Paul's rebuff, Berkouwer continues, "is not directed against the law, but against the sinful man who thinks himself good enough to obtain righteousness before God and who uses the law as a ladder."[3]

The importance of the law for Paul is indicated by the fact that immediately after stating that it could not be used to become right with God (Rom. 3:20), that all people were under condemnation because of the universality of sin (3:23; cf. 4:15; 6:23), and that salvation came through God's grace accepted by faith (3:24, 25, 28), he was quick to add that the way of faith does not "make void the law." To the contrary, the way of faith is to "establish the law" (3:31, KJV). Paul would spend much of Romans 7 through 15 expounding the meaning of Romans 3:31 for Christian living, but first he needed to continue his discussion of how a person becomes "saved" from God's "wrath."

The discussion of how a person becomes right with God (becomes justified) is the focal point of Romans 4 and 5. Only after getting a person saved does Paul move on to discuss the role of the law in the saved person's life (chapters 7-15). The present book will follow the same progressive argument that Paul set forth in Romans. First, however, we need to examine the purpose of the law and its true nature. After all, "the law is good, if any one uses it lawfully" (1 Tim. 1:8). What does it mean to use the law lawfully?

**The Purpose of the Law**

The first purpose of the law is to reveal God to us. "The moral law which God gave to man in the beginning," Loraine Boettner observed, "was no arbitrary or whimsical pronouncement, but an expression of His being. It showed man what the nature of God was."[4]

We should see the law of God as an expression of God's character and will. It is not arbitrary. God does not command love and forbid murder because of some passing idea, but because "his very nature issues in his enjoining certain actions and prohibiting others. God pronounces love good because he himself is love. Lying is wrong because God himself cannot lie." The revealed law is a reflection of His character.[5] It was not an accident when Paul claimed that the law is "holy and just and good" and "spiritual" (Rom. 7:12, 14).

The law as a reflection of God's character points to its second purpose. It serves as a standard of judgment of what the ideal human character is like. God created human beings after His own "image" and "likeness" (Gen. 1:26, 27). His ideal for every person was that he or she should perfectly reflect His character. Thus Ellen White can write, "The conditions of eternal life, under grace, are just what they were in Eden—perfect righteousness, harmony with God, perfect conformity to the principles of His law."[6]

Not only was the law of God a standard in Eden, but it will perform the same function in the final judgment at the end of time (Rom. 2:12-16; Rev. 14:6, 7, 9, 12; Eccl. 12:13, 14).[7]

The law as a standard of judgment is closely related to a third function of the law—that of pointing out and condemning sin in the human heart and life. "Through the law," Paul wrote, "comes knowledge of sin." "If it had not been for the law, I should not have known sin" (Rom. 3:20; 7:7). Wrath and death are the fruit of the broken law (Rom. 4:15; 5:12, 17; 6:23). John Wesley picturesquely summarized the condemning function of the law when he wrote that one purpose of the law is to awaken "those who are still asleep on the brink of hell."[8]

One of the great realities of life is that people often have no awareness of many of their most serious shortcomings and sins. I, for example, am much more conscious of my children's sins than of my own. Their sins are a constant irritation if I choose to focus on them. They, likewise, are quite aware of where I am missing the mark.

While our judgments of others may be somewhat accurate, God desires that we come to grips with our personal faults. Thus, James claims, He gave us His law to function as "a mirror" (James 1:23-25). Before I leave for work in the morning, I go to the mirror to discover what is right and what is wrong with my face and hair. The mirror tells me that not all is ready for public exposure, that there is egg on my face and my hair is only half-combed.

Now the function of the mirror is to point out things that need improvement. With that knowledge I can go to the soap, washcloth, and comb. It will not do to rub my face on the mirror to get the egg off or to run the mirror through my hair in an endeavor to comb it. The purpose of the mirror is to point out needed improvements—it is not the instrument that can make those changes.

So it is with God's law. When I compare myself with the law, I find that I have problems in my life. But the law cannot of itself correct those problems. It has another function—to tell me that I am a sinner. The law points out my problems and needs, but it does not solve them.

A fourth purpose of the law is to point beyond itself and human sinfulness. The problem with the law is that, once broken, it offers me no hope. In the light of the broken law, I am a sinner who deserves condemnation and eternal death (Rom. 6:23). I am hopeless before a law that I have broken even one time in thought, word, or action. God's law offers no mercy or pardon. It sets standards of righteousness, but provides no remedies once broken.

55

In the light of the broken law, the sinner is both helpless and hopeless. God uses the law, therefore, to lead us beyond human hopelessness to Jesus Christ as the answer to humanity's lostness. Paul likens the law in Israel's national experience to a sort of school bus driver, who transports children to and from school. The law is not the teacher, but the one who brings individuals to the teacher. Thus the law led or drove Israel to Christ in a historical sense (Gal. 3:23-25).

On a personal level, the law still performs the same function in human lives. The condemnation of the broken law drives us to Christ, to whom we can confess our sins and receive both forgiveness and cleansing (1 John 1:9; 2:1, 2). Once the law has performed its function of bringing us to our Teacher (Christ), it ceases to serve that purpose. It no longer has the driving-leading role, until we depart from the Teacher again. Then it springs into action once more and leads us back to our only source of hope and pardon.

The sixteenth- and seventeenth-century Puritans were expressing the driving-to-Christ function of the law when they characterized it as "a fiery serpent." It "'smites, stings, and torments the conscience'" and thereby "'drives us to the Lord Jesus lifted up in the gospel, like the brazen serpent in the wilderness, to heal us.'" Again, "'in Puritan thinking, the sharp needle of the law, as it pricks the conscience, was found to be attached to the scarlet thread of the Gospel.'"[9]

Thus, Hans LaRondelle writes, "The law of God does not destroy the gospel of Christ, but rather reveals the need and indispensability of the gospel of grace." It is with that concept in mind that Paul could write that "I through the law died to the law" as a way of salvation (Gal. 2:19). The law had, points out Herman Ridderbos, "beaten" Paul "to death" and condemned him in its judgment. But he became right with God (justified) through faith in Christ's death on the cross (see Gal. 2:16-21).[10]

A fifth function of the law is to act as a moral guide and a standard of righteousness for Christian living. While the law cannot save a person from sin, it does have a valid role in the converted Christian's life. Puritan John Flavel couldn't have phrased it better when he wrote that "*the law sends us to Christ to be justified, and Christ sends us to the law to be regulated.*"[11]

Wesley said essentially the same thing when he claimed that "on the one hand, the law continually makes way for, and points us to, the gospel; on the other, the gospel continually leads us to a more exact fulfilling of the law."[12]

Paul's statement in Romans 3:31 that faith upholds or establishes the law rather than overthrowing it is foundational to the arguments set forth by Flavel and Wesley. The rest of the book of Romans provides excellent evidence for their conclusions. And we can say the same for the New Testament in general.

The New Testament is clear that while the law is *not* a method of salvation, it does serve in the converted Christian life as a normative definition of sin and a guide to Christian living.

While Paul, as a Christian, is no longer under the condemnation of the law (Rom. 8:1), he is still "under the law of Christ" (1 Cor. 9:21). Dutch Calvinist Berkouwer can therefore write that "now the commandments are to the believer the gracious gift of the Savior-God," and Wesleyan Melvin Dieter can suggest that for the converted person the law "becomes a gospel" as it lures us "to the life of love, which is the end of the law." In a similar vein, Anthony Hoekema can equate Christian law keeping with living by the Spirit, when he writes that "Spirit-led believers are precisely the ones doing their best to keep God's law. . . . The Christian life . . . must be a law-formed life."[13]

John Calvin, the great reformer of Geneva, defined the role of the law in the Christian's life as well as anyone. The "principal use" of the law, he claimed, "finds its place among believers in whose hearts the Spirit of God already lives and reigns. . . . Here is the best instrument for them to learn more thoroughly each day the nature of the Lord's will to which they aspire."[14] We will return to the "principal use" of the law in chapter 5.

Meanwhile, we should emphasize again that one of the greatest and most serious confusions of religious history is the failure to make a clear distinction between what one must do to be moral and what one must do to be saved. That was the deadly mistake of the Pharisees. Not realizing the depth of the sin problem, they believed that they could become righteous by keeping the law. Because they did not understand the purpose of the law or the power of sin in their lives (Rom. 3:9), Berkouwer claims, "the law of God held no terror for them."[15]

Not taking into account the effects of the Fall (original sin and its results), they still thought that they could overcome sin as the unfallen Adam (and later Christ, the second Adam) overcame sin. To combat that popular error, Ellen White wrote that "it was possible for Adam, before the fall, to form a righteous character by obedience to God's law. But he failed to do this, and because of his sin our natures are fallen and we cannot make ourselves righteous. Since we are sinful, unholy, we cannot perfectly obey the holy law."[16]

J. H. Gerstner expands on the above insights. "The Pharisees' erroneous interpretation of the law [and law keeping]," he explained, "rested on an erroneous view of mankind. They regarded the fall of Adam as simply the first example of a person deciding wrongly; people can still live correctly after the fall if guided by the law."[17]

Paul, Martin Luther, John Calvin, John Wesley, Ellen White, and a host of others down through history would consistently argue against that theology. Unfortunately, however, Pharisaism raises its head in every generation, often with a contemporary, up-to-date theological explanation. Such views are not dead among Seventh-day Adventists even in the twenty-first century.

## Will the "Real LAW" Please Stand Up

The Ten Commandments are not the "real law." In fact, in the context of universal history throughout eternity, they might be termed a late development.

One doesn't have to think too long or too hard to reach the conclusion that the law as expressed in the Ten Commandments is neither eternal nor universal. Take the fourth commandment, for example. It plainly states that God gave the Sabbath as a memorial of the creation of the planet Earth (see Ex. 20:8-11; Gen. 2:1-3). Even the seven-day cycle (of twenty-four hours each) points to our planet and solar system as the determinants of the Sabbath law found in the Decalogue. The Sabbath law of the Decalogue, however, does represent a universal and eternal *principle* that undergirds it. We could do a similar analysis for some of the other specific commands of Exodus 20.

Ellen White is in agreement with that line of thought. "The law of God," she penned, "existed before man was created. The angels were governed by it. Satan fell because he transgressed the *principles* of God's government. . . .

"After Adam's sin and fall nothing was taken from the law of God. *The principles of the ten commandments existed before the fall*, and were of a character suited to the condition of a holy order of beings. *After the fall, the principles of those precepts were not changed, but additional precepts were given to meet man in his fallen state.*"[18]

Again she wrote: "The law of God existed before man was created. It was adapted to the condition of holy beings; even angels were governed by it. After the Fall, the principles of righteousness were unchanged." But, Ellen White penned in another connection, after Adam's transgression the

58

principles of the law "were definitely arranged and *expressed* to meet man in his fallen condition."[19]

While the new "expression" and "arrangement" of the law after the Fall undoubtedly included ceremonial aspects, it also involved the negativization of the law. After all, no one had to remind the holy angels of heaven not to steal, commit adultery, or murder.

The angels kept the law without knowing it because it was written in their hearts. "Love," we read, "is the *great principle* that actuates the unfallen beings."[20] They did not have to be told "You shall not kill" or "You shall not steal" because they were positively motivated from the heart to care for one another. Only after the entrance of sin did the law have to be reformulated in negative terms for beings driven by selfishness and negative motivations.

*The correct identification of what Charles Colson refers to as "the Law behind the law"[21] is of utmost importance, because any accurate discussion of righteousness and/or perfection depends upon a correct understanding of God's law.*

The Old Testament has at least three laws: the moral, the civil, and the ceremonial. Beyond that, Scripture refers to the books of Moses and even the entire Old Testament as "the law." Thus the word *law* in the Bible has many meanings.

In the New Testament, however, Jesus makes the nature of the LAW behind the laws crystal clear. When asked concerning the great commandment, He replied: "You shall love the Lord your God with all your heart, and with all your soul, and with all your mind. This is the great and first commandment. And a second is like it, You shall love your neighbor as yourself. On these two commandments depend all the law and the prophets"(Matt. 22:37-40; cf. Deut. 6:5; Lev. 19:18).

Paul and James agree with Jesus, but point toward a further reduction of the law to one basic precept. Thus Paul can say that "love is the fulfilling of the law" (Rom. 13:10) and "the whole law is fulfilled in one word, 'You shall love your neighbor as yourself'" (Gal. 5:14). Meanwhile, James not only is in harmony with Paul, but expresses the ultimate unity of the law. James noted that "whoever keeps the whole law but fails in one point has become guilty of all of it" (James 2:11).

The concept underlying these New Testament discussions of law has several facets. First, the law is unified. Instead of many principles undergirding the law, it has but one. At its most basic level, we can sum up the law in one word—*love*.[22] That is the same word that John used to encapsulate the character of God. In 1 John 4:8 we read that "God is love." That makes good sense if the law is a reflection of His character.

But the Bible begins to spell out the meaning of love so that humans and other created beings can see its significance in concrete situations. For unfallen beings, one can think of the necessary law as having two parts— love to God and love to one another. After the Fall, however, the law needed further explication because of the degeneracy of the human race. While there is substantial evidence of the existence of the ideas contained in the Ten Commandments before Sinai, God chose to formally expound the two great principles of the law as 10 precepts when He founded the nation of Israel as His special people (Ex. 19, 20).

The first four commandments illustrate concrete aspects of the principle of loving God, while the last six particularize specific ways of loving one's neighbor.

Thus we might depict the progression of law from one to two to 10 in the following way:

**LAW ⟶ laws**

The idea is that the laws of God flow out of the LAW of God.

That concept reminds us of what we discovered about sin in chapter 2. There we noted that sins (as acts of rebellion) flow out of SIN (as fallen nature). Thus

**SIN ⟶ sins**

In later chapters we will see that the unity of SIN and the unity of LAW are directly related to the unity of righteousness. We will find that RIGHTEOUSNESS as converted nature will lead to righteousness as acts. Thus

**RIGHTEOUSNESS ⟶ righteousness**

We noted earlier that one of the foundational problems of Pharisaism was the atomization of sin into a series of acts. The atomization of sin is directly related to the atomization of law and righteousness. While Christians ought to understand the nature of sins, laws, and righteous acts, they must also comprehend SIN, LAW, and RIGHTEOUSNESS if they are to come to a biblical understanding of perfection. Because the Pharisees of old did not understand SIN and LAW, they could not understand RIGHTEOUSNESS. The entire New Testament stands against their misunderstandings.

Beyond unity, a second aspect of biblical law is that it is essentially positive rather than negative. Jesus plainly indicated that negative religion is not sufficient when He told the story of the person who swept his life clean and put it in order, but failed to fill it with vital, outgoing Christianity. The final condition of that person, He claimed, was worse than in the beginning (Matt. 12:43-45). "A religion which consists in *thou shalt nots*," writes William Barclay, "is bound to end in failure."[23]

The same truth appears in Jesus' dealing with the rich young ruler. The young man was excellent at the "thou shalt nots," but he balked when Jesus suggested the endless possibilities entailed in really caring for other people. Jesus pointed him beyond the negative 10 to the positive law of love. That, of course, was more than he was ready to commit himself to. He felt relatively comfortable with the negative law but was not ready for the unlimited reach of the law into every area of his life (Matt. 19:16-22).

Peter's question about how often he should forgive his brother brings out the same lesson. He doubled the rabbinic rule of three forgivenesses and added one for good measure. After all, seven forgivenesses is quite a few when you think about it. Christ's answer of 490 implied endless forgiveness. That answer, of course, was more than the disciple had bargained for. In actuality, Peter (along with other "natural" humans) really wanted to know when he could *stop* loving his neighbor. When can I be pensioned off from all this "niceness" and give people what they deserve? is the real question. Christ's answer in the parable of the two debtors is, Never (see Matt. 18:21-35).

Like Peter, we are more comfortable with the negative than the positive. We want to know when we have fulfilled our quota of goodness so that we can relax and be our normal selves. The negative limits the scope of righteousness and makes it humanly manageable and achievable. Thus legalists of all stripes must of necessity focus on the thou shalt nots. The Christian alternative is the endless righteousness expressed in caring to God and humanity that one finds summarized in the two great commandments to love.

Strangely, many think that an emphasis on the two great commandments is a watering down of the demands laid upon the Christian in daily living. Christ repeatedly demonstrated the opposite to be true. In those two commands, wrote Ellen White, "the length and breadth, the depth and height, of the law of God is comprehended." In the Sermon on the Mount Christ expounded on the principles of the law and began to demonstrate their far-reaching inner meaning. It is the "principles,"

Ellen White suggested, that "remain forever the great standard of righteousness."[24]

The negative approach to religion stems from a negative approach to law. The world has seen too much negative religion. Pastor Kirk Brown once told me that "the major qualification in some people's minds to being a Christian is the ability to say don't." Unfortunately, that caricature is all too true for many people who need to come to grips with a higher standard. It is a relatively simple thing for me to avoid committing adultery compared with the unending challenge of loving all my neighbors as myself (Matt. 7:12; 22:39).

The negative precepts of the Ten Commandments inform me about certain aspects of love to God and my fellow beings, but, important as they are, they are only the tip of the LAW itself. One can never be saved or become perfect by not working on Sabbath or avoiding theft.

Whether we like it or not (and the Pharisees of old certainly didn't), Jesus put the standard of righteousness higher than "normal" people care to reach. Barclay summed up the issue when he wrote: "The priest would have said that religion consists of sacrifice; the Scribe would have said that religion consists of Law; but Jesus Christ said that religion consists of love."[25]

"By this," said Jesus, "all men will know that you are my disciples, if you have love for one another" (John 13:35). It is significant that He never stated that His disciples would be recognized because they kept the Sabbath, paid tithe, or took care of their health. Those items of conduct are important in Christian living, but they are not its core. One of the great tragedies of life is when Christians treat each other unjustly because of a disagreement over lifestyle or doctrinal issues. While they may be technically correct in their theology and need to get their point across, their approach demonstrates that they are better at swallowing camels than they are at following Christ's example. Their doctrinal and lifestyle "purity" needs to be baptized in Christianity. Then it will have some meaning.

### The Christian and the Law

When Paul comments that he "through the law died to the law, that" he "might live to God," he was not saying that the law died (Gal. 2:19). The law still functions for Christians as a standard of righteousness and as a condemner of sin, but it can never be seen as a way of salvation. "Paul," points out Emil Brunner, "never fights against the Law," but only against its improper uses.[26]

Bishop Ryle spoke correctly of the Christian's relationship to the law when he wrote that "genuine sanctification will show itself in habitual respect to God's law, and habitual effort to live in obedience to it as the rule of life. There is no greater mistake than to suppose that a Christian has nothing to do with the law and the Ten Commandments, because he cannot be justified by keeping them." The New Testament ties Christian liberty to keeping the "law of liberty" (James 2:12) in opposition to being under bondage to sin (see Rom. 6:18, 19).[27]

A Christian can relate to the law in two basic ways. The first is legalism. Legalism, suggests James Stewart, has three characteristics: (1) "It is a religion of *redemption by human effort*"; (2) it represents a "*tendency to import a mercenary spirit into religion*" (e.g., This "is what I have done: now give me my reward!"); and (3) it has a "*fondness for negatives.*"[28]

Richard Rice notes that "legalism is incredibly naive" because it "drastically underestimates the effects of sin on human beings." Sin not only destroys our ability to keep the law (see Rom. 3:9), but it places every person under condemnation (see ch. 5:12). "But legalism," Rice adds, "is more than naive; it is downright sinful. It arises from the proud assumption that fallen human beings can do something on their own to merit divine favor, when nothing could be farther from the truth."[29]

The key to understanding Paul's statements against the law is that a legalistic approach to the law makes one independent of God. Thus the person who earns the salvific reward through obedience to the law has room to boast of his or her accomplishment (Rom. 3:27; 1 Cor. 1:29). That leads to pride, the very antithesis of faith (Phil. 3:4, 7; Rom. 4:2).[30]

W. L. Walker points out the obvious when he says that "legalism . . . is 'natural,' and readily finds favour with men."[31] It is nice to think that we can do something to earn our salvation (or at least part of it), but the truth is just the opposite (Eph. 2:8-10). Paul went to the heart of the matter when he claimed that "if justification [or righteousness] were through the law, then Christ died to no purpose" (Gal. 2:21).

Salvation does not change the law, but it transforms our relation to it. Beyond delivering us from the condemnation of the law (Rom. 8:1), salvation supplies us with a powerful incentive to keep it.[32]

If Christ's clearest teaching on the relation between law and grace in salvation is in the parable of the Pharisee and the tax collector (Luke 18:9-14), the story of Zacchaeus (19:1-10) may be His best illustration of a saved person's spiritual law keeping as a response to God's grace. As soon as Zacchaeus was saved, he was out sharing half his goods with the poor and

restoring fourfold to those people he had defrauded. His new life in its relationship to the law was an evidence of his salvation. Zacchaeus reversed
the style of his life from selfishness to serving others. That is transformation
and evidence of a new birth.

We could not find a greater contrast than the one between the converted tax collector and that of the rich young ruler (Matt. 19:16-22).
When a person is converted, there begins a natural outflow of God's love
from the heart, rather than a mere meticulous keeping of the letter of the
law.

The Christian's relation to the law is included in what the Bible calls
the new covenant experience. Jeremiah and the book of Hebrews tell us
that the ideal spiritual experience takes place when God puts His laws into
our minds and writes them on our hearts (Jer. 31:31-34; Heb. 8:10).

It is normal for a Christian to keep the law, because its very principle
of love to God and neighbor is written in the "fleshy tables of the heart"
(2 Cor. 3:3, KJV). Thus the Christian is closer to God's law than the le-
galist. Because true Christians have been "born from above" (John 3:3, 7,
margin) and have transformed hearts and minds (Rom. 8:4-7), a desire to
be in harmony with God's law is an integral part of their lives. The new
attitude to God's law is a sign that His grace has redeemed them. We will
return to that topic in chapter 5, but first we want to examine a bit more
the initial process of being saved by grace.

---

[1] William Barclay, *The Letter to the Romans*, 2d ed., Daily Study Bible (Edinburgh: The
Saint Andrew Press, 1957), p. 53.

[2] Richard Rice, *The Reign of God: An Introduction to Christian Theology From a Seventh-
day Adventist Perspective* (Berrien Springs, Mich.: Andrews University Press, 1985), pp. 245,
246; Luther, quoted in William Barclay, *The Letter to the Galatians*, 2d ed., Daily Study Bible
(Edinburgh: The Saint Andrew Press, 1958), p. 23; G. C. Berkouwer, *Faith and Justification*
(Grand Rapids: Eerdmans, 1954), pp. 77, 72, 73, 76.

[3] Berkouwer, *Faith and Justification*, p. 77.

[4] Loraine Boettner, *Studies in Theology*, 5th ed. (Grand Rapids: Eerdmans, 1960),
p. 286.

[5] Erickson, *Christian Theology*, pp. 802, 803.

[6] White, *Mount of Blessing*, p. 76.

[7] Ellen G. White, *The Great Controversy Between Christ and Satan* (Mountain View,
Calif.: Pacific Press, 1950), p. 436.

[8] John Wesley, *The Works of John Wesley*, 3d ed. (Peabody, Mass.: Hendrickson, 1984
[reprinted from 1872 edition]), vol. 5, p. 449.

[9] Ball, *English Connection*, 131-133.

[10] Hans LaRondelle, *Christ Our Salvation: What God Does for Us and in Us* (Mountain
View, Calif.: Pacific Press, 1980), p. 40; Herman N. Ridderbos, *The Epistle of Paul to the*

Churches of Galatia, The New International Commentary on the New Testament (Grand Rapids: Eerdmans, 1953), p. 104; *The International Standard Bible Encyclopedia*, 1977-1988 ed., s.v. "Law in the NT."

[11] John Flavel, quoted in Ball, *English Connection*, p. 133. (Italics supplied.)

[12] Wesley, *Works*, vol. 5, pp. 313, 314.

[13] Berkouwer, *Faith and Sanctification*, p. 175; Melvin E. Dieter, "The Wesleyan Perspective," in *Five Views on Sanctification*, p. 26; Anthony A. Hoekema, "The Reformed Perspective," in *ibid.*, pp. 87, 88.

[14] John Calvin, *Institutes of the Christian Religion*, 2.7.12.

[15] Berkouwer, *Faith and Sanctification*, p. 119.

[16] White, *Steps to Christ*, p. 62.

[17] *The International Standard Bible Encyclopedia*, 1977-1988 ed., s.v. "Law in the NT."

[18] Ellen G. White, *Spiritual Gifts* (Battle Creek, Mich.: SDA Pub. Assn., 1864), vol. 3, p. 295. (Italics supplied.)

[19] White, *Selected Messages*, book 1, pp. 220, 230. (Italics supplied.)

[20] White, *Mount of Blessing,* p. 109; E. G. White to Brethren and Sisters of the Iowa Conference, Nov. 6, 1901, in *1888 Materials*, p. 1764. (Italics supplied.)

[21] Charles Colson, *Kingdoms in Conflict* (Grand Rapids: Zondervan, 1987), p. 237. (Italics supplied.)

[22] See John McIntyre, *On the Love of God* (New York: Harper & Brothers, 1962), p. 240, for the necessary link between the love of God and love to fellow humans. For another treatment of the unity of God's law, see Alden Thompson, *Inspiration: Hard Questions, Honest Answers* (Washington, D.C.: Review and Herald, 1991), pp. 110-136.

[23] William Barclay, *The Gospel of Matthew*, 2d ed., Daily Study Bible (Edinburgh: The Saint Andrew Press, 1958), vol. 2, p. 57.

[24] White, *Selected Messages*, book 1, pp. 320, 211.

[25] Barclay, *Matthew*, vol. 1, p. 363.

[26] Brunner, *Romans*, p. 140.

[27] Ryle, *Holiness*, p. 26. See also, Berkouwer, *Faith and Sanctification*, pp. 179-181.

[28] James S. Stewart, *A Man in Christ: The Vital Elements of St. Paul's Religion* (New York: Harper & Row, n.d.), pp. 84-87.

[29] Rice, *Reign of God*, p. 243.

[30] See Ladd, *New Testament Theology*, p. 500; Brunner, *Romans*, p. 140.

[31] W. L. Walker, *The Gospel of Reconciliation or At-one-ment* (Edinburgh: T. & T. Clark, 1909), p. 182.

[32] See Rice, *Reign of God*, p. 246.

Chapter 4

# Justification the Work of a Lifetime
# Sanctification the Work of a Moment

The monks and hermits who lived in the desert early in the church's history provide the supreme example of how not to deal with sin. Those men desperately desired to free themselves from all earthly things, particularly bodily desires.

To accomplish their task, they went alone into the Egyptian desert with the idea of living in solitude and thinking of nothing but God. The most famous of the solitary monks was Saint Anthony (251?-356).

In his zeal, Anthony lived the hermit's life, fasted, went without sleep, and tortured his body. For 35 years he lived in the desert in nonstop battle with the devil.

Anthony's biographer tells his story: "First of all the devil tried to lead him away from discipline, whispering to him the remembrance of his wealth, cares for his sister, claims of kindred, love of money, love of glory, the various pleasures of the table, and the other relaxations of life, and, at last, the difficulty of virtue and the labour of it."

Writing of the great conflict that constantly took place between the forces of good and evil in Anthony's imaginings, his biographer penned: "The one would suggest foul thoughts, and the other counter them with prayers; the one fire him with lust, the other, as one who seemed to blush, fortify his body with prayers, faith and fasting. The devil one night even took upon him the shape of a woman, and imitated all her acts simply to beguile Anthony."

For 35 years Anthony struggled with temptation, and at the end he was no closer to victory than at the beginning.[1]

Anthony, of course, was only one of many ascetics in the early church. Another believer desperate for salvation was Saint Simeon Stylites (ca. 390-459). Simeon, after having been buried up to his neck for several months, next decided that his way to holiness was to sit on top of a 60-foot pillar, where he would be removed from all temptation. For 36 years (until his death) Saint Simeon remained atop his pole. Not only did his body "drip" with vermin, but he performed excruciating exercises far above the desert floor. Once, for example, he is said to have touched his feet with his forehead more than 1,244 times in succession.

Other ascetic athletes of God incarcerated themselves in cells so small that they could neither lie at full length nor stand at full height. Many of them gave up bathing and wore skin garments with the hair next to the flesh. And still others reportedly subsisted on grass, which they cut with sickles.[2]

Such men were obviously desperately sincere in their desire to get right with God. They were following a path that Paul the Pharisee had earlier traveled and that Martin Luther and John Wesley and the writer of this book (after his verbal declaration, soon after his "conversion," to be the first perfect Christian since Christ) would later stumble down.

To the present day, many still live lives of austerity in a frantic attempt to achieve a life acceptable to God. The exact nature of what they do may change across time and from person to person, but the underlying principle remains the same—that there is something that humans can do to make it easier for God to save them; that there is something we can do to improve our standing before Him.

Sincerity and desperate earnestness, however, are not enough. In the initial chapters of this book we learned first that human beings since Adam have been born with a bent toward evil and "are under the *power* of sin" (Rom. 3:9). Of themselves they are unable to do anything to get right with God or stay right with Him, no matter how sincere they are or how hard or long they try.

Second, we learned in the previous chapter that the law does not provide the Christian with any help, in spite of the fact that the natural person desires to use it as a ladder to heaven and as "an occasion of pride . . . and self-righteousness." To the contrary, law, Carl Braaten writes, "drives the self-reliant person into despair. It pulls the props out from under a person; it casts one into the slough of despondency, self-accusation, anxiety, and suicide."[3]

More important, however, "the law prepares the way for the hearing of the good news of divine grace freely offered."[4] Given the personal and legal facts of the human situation, it is little wonder that Paul, Augustine, Luther, Wesley, and countless other Christians have rejoiced when they finally realized what God has done for a fallen race through Christ Jesus. The welcome news, Paul exclaimed in the foundation text to the book of Romans, is that the gospel (good news) "is the power of God for salvation to every one who has faith" (Rom. 1:16). Again, the apostle wrote, "By grace you have been saved through faith; and this is not your own doing, it is the gift of God" (Eph.2:8).

Those inspired thoughts bring us to the place where we can begin to understand the solution to the problems we have examined in the first three chapters. We will begin by "unpacking" some of the great words of salvation.

### Getting What We Don't Deserve

One thing ought to be clear up to this point: that human beings deserve nothing from God but eternal death (Rom. 6:23). They have rebelled against Him, put their selfishness at the center of their lives, are under the condemnation of the law, and are even betrayed into boastful spiritual pride by those of their characteristics that might be defined as "good." No wonder the Bible refers to humans as not only being confused, but as lost in sin (see Luke 19:10; 15:6, 9, 24; Matt. 1:21).

Now if people merit severe punishment and instead receive a beautiful, priceless gift, they are getting something they do not deserve. That is the everyday definition of what the Bible calls *grace*.

"The free grace of God," pens Braaten, "is a 'spontaneous' and 'unmotivated' love. God loves human beings because of his own inclination to do so. There are no love-worthy qualities within us that drive God to love us. God loves the unlovable. God even loves the ungodly, the enemies of religion and morality, the publicans and sinners of every age."[5]

At the base of His grace is *agapē* love. God loves us in spite of ourselves. That theme runs from Genesis through Revelation. Thus, while the "*wages* [something we have earned] of sin is death," "the *free gift* [grace] of God is eternal life in Christ Jesus our Lord" (Rom. 6:23). "God shows his love for us in that while we were yet sinners [rebels against God's rulership in our lives] Christ died for us" (Rom. 5:8). Christ did not die for good people, but "for the ungodly" (Rom. 5:6).

God's grace shines through Scripture even where the Bible never uses the word, as evidenced by the following texts: "You did not choose me, but I chose you" (John 15:16). "We have seen and testify that the Father has sent his Son as the Savior of the world" (1 John 4:14). "The Son of man came not to be served but to serve, and to give his life as a ransom for many" (Matt. 20:28). These passages, and countless others, make it clear that the concept of grace does not arise out of an abstract theory about the nature of God, but out of the revelation of His very character as seen in both testaments.

Grace always starts with God's caring initiative. Thus we find Him, immediately after the entrance of sin, seeking the undeserving Adam and Eve in Eden (see Gen. 3:8-11); God choosing Israel in Egypt, not because of its righteousness, but because of its destitution (see Eze. 16:1-14; Deut. 7:6-11); God as the shepherd searching in the wilderness for the lost sheep, as the woman crawling through the rubble on a dirty floor in search of the lost coin, and as the father pulling up his skirts to *run* out to meet a son who had figuratively "spit in his face" (see Luke 15). Christ came not only to die for prostitutes and dishonest, treacherous tax collectors such as Zacchaeus, but "to seek and to save" all "the lost" (Luke 19:10). "God so loved the world that he gave his only Son, that whoever believes in him should not perish but have eternal life" (John 3:16).

Salvation in the Bible is always God's initiative. "We do not first repent of our sins and then come to Jesus," wrote James Denney; "it is the visitation of our life by Jesus to which we owe our first repentance and then all other spiritual blessings."[6] The human part in the drama of salvation is one of responding to the divine initiative.

The revelation of God's grace revolutionized the life of Paul. As a Pharisee he held that God justified only those who obeyed the law. Justification was a certification of human goodness. But as a Christian, he recognized that Christ had reached out and touched him while he was in the process of killing Christians (Acts 7:58; 8:3; 9:1-9).

With those ideas in mind, it is easier to see why ex-slave trader John Newton could write and sing about:

> "Amazing grace! how sweet the sound
>   That saved a wretch like me!
>  I once was lost, but now am found,
>   Was blind, but now I see."

Luther, in a similar spirit, could write of Jesus, who "has snatched us poor lost men from the jaws of hell, won us, made us free, and brought us back to the Father's goodness and grace."[7]

Like all the other words related to sin and salvation, *grace* is primarily a term denoting a personal relationship between God and humanity. It represents a love on His part that would not let people be lost without a struggle and without a personal sacrifice to do all that He could to save them.

Grace has several aspects. Two of the most important in the process of salvation are forgiving grace and keeping grace. David exemplified these two aspects of grace when he prayed for God to "cleanse" him and to "keep" him from committing "presumptuous sins" (Ps. 19:12, 13, KJV).

Reinhold Niebuhr has expressed these two aspects of grace in terms of "grace as power and grace as pardon."[8] That wording clearly reflects that God's grace not only forgives rebellion among His subjects, but provides them with strength to break the bonds of sin in daily living. *Power* is a key word in the dynamics of salvation. According to Paul, individuals in their natural state "are under the *power* of sin," but "the gospel . . . is the *power* of God for salvation" (Rom. 3:9; 1:16).

The Greek word he uses for power in Romans 1 is *dynamis*. It is the root word behind the name of the explosive we call dynamite. God's grace as power is like dynamite in the Christian's life. And just as a mighty explosion of dynamite can change the face of the earth, so God's grace as power can transform our lives through the work of the Holy Spirit. Thus E. Glenn Hinson can speak of God's grace "as the living God invading our lives and transforming us."[9] We shall return to that topic repeatedly in the remainder of this book.

One of the most remarkable things about grace is that it is free. *Free*, however, must not be interpreted as *cheap*. We must never forget the high price paid on Calvary to make God's forgiveness and empowerment available to sinners.[10]

In spite of the high cost, however, people can contribute nothing to their own salvation. "All that man can possibly do toward his own salvation," Ellen White penned, "is to accept the invitation."[11] That acceptance, please note, is important. Salvation is not automatic or universal, as some teach, but must be received by individuals. That idea brings us to the topic of faith.

### Grabbing Hold of What We Don't Deserve

*The Nature of Faith*

While God through His grace (unmerited gift) made provision for salvation for every person, not all will be saved. Why? Because, as John Stott notes, "God does not impose his gifts on us willy-nilly; we have to receive them by faith."[12] According to Jesus, "whoever *believes* in him" will "have eternal life" (John 3:16). And Paul wrote that we are saved "by grace . . . through faith" (Eph. 2:8).

For the Bible writers, faith is the one essential condition of salvation. On the cross God *provided* salvation for every person, but each person must *accept* it before the provision becomes effective.

That point is illustrated in the apocryphal book of 2 Maccabees, in which we read of seven Jewish brothers captured by King Antiochus Epiphanes (second century B.C.). Syrian soldiers tortured the brothers one by one in front of the others and their mother because they would not submit to tasting swine's flesh. After he had six of them put to death, Antiochus called the seventh and promised to "make him rich . . . if he would give up the ways of his forefathers." The king next summoned the young man's mother in to enlist her aid in persuading him. After being "labored with . . . for a long time," she agreed to cooperate, but when she went in to her son, she urged him to stand fast, saying: "'Do not be afraid of this butcher, but show yourself worthy of your brothers, and accept death, so that by God's mercy I may get you back again with your brothers.'" The story concludes with the death of the seventh son, who endured torture "worse than the others."[13]

My point in using that Maccabean story is to illustrate that for a pardon to be effective, it must be accepted. That holds true for God's pardon of sinners also. It is imperative that we accept God's grace by faith. But what is faith?

Faith is several things. Central to the biblical concept of faith is *trust in God.* Trust, of course, implies belief in a person's trustworthiness. Morris Venden was correct when he wrote that "Christianity and Salvation are not based on what you do but on whom you know."[14] And Jesus has told us that "this is eternal life, that they know thee the only true God, and Jesus Christ" (John 17:3).

Faith is not blind—it is based on a knowledge of God's character. Out of that knowledge flows trust. Thus Hebrews 11 pictures the Old Testament faithful as living for God because they knew and trusted Him. Abraham, Moses, Rahab, David, and Samuel were individuals who illustrated faith because they trusted God and lived their lives on the basis of that confidence.

Venden tells the story of the tightrope walker who crossed Niagara Falls. After crossing, he asked the spellbound crowd, "How many of you believe I could cross the tightrope again, this time pushing a wheelbarrow with someone riding in it?"

The crowd applauded, certain he could do it. But then he called for volunteers to ride in the wheelbarrow.

There was, writes Venden, "a vast silence." He goes on to note that the story illustrates the difference between belief and trust.[15]

I would like to suggest that biblical faith includes both belief and trust—a trust based on belief. Edward Vick caught the essence of faith when he wrote that "faith means trusting utterly. Faith in God means that we put ourselves so into His care that we accept His evaluation of our humanity, His judgment upon it, and His way of handling us in our sin. Faith means that in our lost condition we let God do anything He wants with us."[16]

*Just as the first step in sin was distrust of God (Gen. 3:1-6), so the first step toward Him is trusting faith.* Faith is coming to grips with the fact that we must trust God because He has our best interest at heart.[17] Faith is a confident expectation that God will fulfill His promises.

Biblical faith, we should note, is always absolute. It is never moderate. James Denney can therefore write that "*faith* is not the acceptance of a legal arrangement; it *is the abandonment of the soul*, which has no hope but in the Saviour, *to the Saviour. . . . It includes the absolute renunciation of everything else, to lay hold on Christ.*" Faith is a "*passion* in which the whole being of man is caught up and abandoned unconditionally to the love revealed in the Saviour."[18]

P. T. Forsyth drives at the same point when he notes that Greek and philosophic wisdom uplifts the values of moderation, but not Christianity. "We cannot love God too much, nor believe too much in His love, nor reckon it too holy. *A due faith in Him is immoderate, absolute trust.*"[19]

A second aspect of biblical faith is that *it is a relationship with God.* Faith, as we have already noted, is much more than belief in a set of propositions respecting God or Jesus. Faith is trust in a Person. Because faith is trust in a Person, faith implies a relationship with that Person. It is a relationship of fidelity between two individuals. For Paul, faith was not faith "'in something'" but faith "'in someone,' in God, in Jesus Christ" (Gal. 2:16; Rom. 3:22, 26). The total Christian life is lived "in faith" to God.[20]

"Faith," penned Herbert Douglass, "is the opposite of rebellion."[21] If rebellion is at the heart of the sin relationship to God, then faith is at the core of the reconciled relationship to Him. And, we must remind ourselves, there are no other ways of relating to God outside of rebellion and faith.

A third aspect of biblical faith is that *it is a life of total commitment to God.* When Christ called Matthew from his post as tax collector and Peter from his fishing business, Dietrich Bonhoeffer points out, "only one thing was required in each case—to rely on Christ's word" by total commitment of their lives.[22]

Belief, trust, relationship, and commitment are four aspects of faith, with commitment forming the apex of what faith is all about. As a result, *the book of Hebrews regards "faith as something that one does rather than as something one has. It is an activity rather than a possession."* Thus Abel provided "a more acceptable sacrifice," Noah "constructed an ark," and Abraham "went out" (Heb. 11:4, 7, 8). Their belief in, trust in, and relationship with God led to total commitment and action. Without the last step, their faith would have been incomplete. Jürgen Moltmann summed that point up when he penned that "Christian faith can only mean committing oneself without reserve to the 'crucified God.'"[23]

Because faith is active in terms of trust and commitment, H. Wheeler Robinson has suggested that it is "primarily an act of the will."[24] That is, a person makes a choice to believe in, trust in, relate positively to, and commit himself or herself to God in Christ.

### The Role of the Will

But, we might ask, if the human will is fallen and the natural person has a bent toward evil, how is it that an individual can choose a faith relationship with God?

The answer is twofold. First, it is important to note that even though the image of God in human beings has been fractured and grossly distorted, it has not been destroyed (Gen. 9:6; 1 Cor. 11:7; James 3:9). A residue of the image continued to exist in humanity after the Fall. Therefore, although people are twisted and lost as a result of the Fall, they are still human. Thus individual human lives are the constant scene of a great struggle between the forces of good and evil as both sides seek to sway people either toward or away from God.[25]

Second, the Holy Spirit still operates in the lives of fallen beings as He seeks to inspire them to choose the good. The will, therefore, although naturally bent toward evil, receives the possibility of making a choice for God through the work of the Holy Spirit. God takes the first step. We respond. Jesus said, "No one can come unto me unless the Father who sent me draws him" (John 6:44; cf. 12:32).

John Wesley called this work of the Spirit "prevenient" grace. Prevenient grace, H. Orton Wiley writes, "is that grace which 'goes before' or prepares the soul for entrance into the initial state of salvation." In prevenient grace God acts to offer salvation and to make the person able to respond, yet the decision is that of the individual. God does not force the human will into faith. At most it is persuaded into faith by the demonstrated love of God.[26]

While Ellen White does not use the term "prevenient grace," her writings are permeated by that concept. She wrote: "The sinner cannot bring himself to repentance, or prepare himself to come to Christ. . . . The very first step to Christ is taken through the drawing of the Spirit of God; as man responds to this drawing, he advances toward Christ in order that he may repent."[27]

Not only is the will of an individual influenced by the work of the Spirit, but even faith itself is a gift of the Holy Spirit. While God gives to each person a "measure of faith" (Rom. 12:3), each individual must decide what to do with the gift. Therefore, "nowhere does faith take on the guise of a work . . . of human achievement" that "effectuates justification." Rather, faith is a trust and commitment to God based on an admission of human impotency.[28]

A choice for faith is the ultimate admission that God's grace is the individual's only hope. A faith commitment, therefore, is the acceptance of God and His salvation. Faith is a response to God's gracious gift, but it is He who has initiated both the gift and the response. The only part a person plays is to choose to accept or reject the gift. In that limited sense, faith is an act of the will.

So central is faith in the plan of salvation that Ellen White can say, "Faith is the only condition upon which justification can be obtained."[29] But if that is true, then what about such topics as repentance and the crucifixion of the self? After all, doesn't the New Testament tell us to "repent, and be baptized . . . for the forgiveness of . . . sins" (Acts 2:38), and to take up our cross if we hope to find life in Christ (Matt. 16:24, 25)? Are not these also conditions of salvation? It seems that they are, but that we should regard them as aspects of genuine faith.

### Repentance

Repentance can be viewed as the negative aspect of coming to Christ. If we see faith as a turning to Christ, then repentance is a simultaneous turning away from sin. We can translate the Greek words for repentance as "to change one's mind," "to regret," or "to be converted."[30] As people turn to God in faith, they are at the same time repenting of or turning from their previous way of life.

Repentance takes place when people see two things—the holiness of God and their own selfishness. It includes not only a heartfelt acknowledgment of our rebellious breaking of God's law, but also an admission that sin is a personal affront to our Creator. Thus P. T. Forsyth can write that "saving confession is not merely 'I did so and so,' but 'I did it against a holy, saving God.'"[31]

David's heartfelt cry in the wake of his disastrous adultery with Bathsheba and the multiple murder of her husband Uriah the Hittite and his men (see 2 Sam. 11:1-12:23) was that he had sinned against God—"Against thee, thee only, have I sinned" (Ps. 51:4). While it is true that adultery and murder are against people, in the ultimate sense, all sin targets God, the Creator of those offended in our acts against other people.[32]

David's prayer is a model of repentance:

"Have mercy on me, O God,
  according to thy steadfast love. . . .
For I know my transgressions,
  and my sin is ever before me.
Against thee, thee only, have I sinned. . . .
Hide thy face from my sins,
  and blot out all my iniquities.
Create in me a clean heart, O God,
  and put a new and right spirit within me. . . .
Restore to me the joy of thy salvation,
  and uphold me with a willing spirit. . . .
Deliver me from blood guiltiness, O God,
  thou God of my salvation,
  and my tongue will sing aloud of thy deliverance" (Ps. 51:1-14).

Not only did David's plea recognize the depth of his sin and the goodness of God, but it also called for the Lord to forgive and restore him, and, beyond that, to give him power to straighten out his daily life. In response to God's mercy, he would praise God and "teach transgressors thy ways" (verses 15, 13). David's was truly the repentance of "a broken spirit; a broken and contrite heart" (verse 17). Brunner was correct when he wrote that "we only really repent when we know that we can never be penitent enough."[33]

David's prayer exhibited both a change of mind and a desire to alter his actions. It coupled both faith and repentance. As he turned from his sin, he turned to his God—he rejected a sin relationship with God for a faith relationship.

Before moving away from the topic of repentance, we should note two things. First, that repentance is not a human "work." It "is no less the gift of God than are pardon and justification, and it cannot be experienced except as it is given to the soul by Christ."[34] Paul is clear that "the goodness of God leadeth thee to repentance" (Rom. 2:4, KJV). Our very ability to repent is another evidence of God's prevenient grace.

A second thing to consider is that repentance is not the work of a moment, but a way of life. Repentance is not merely a change of heart about the past or the present, but it includes the future. It is the Christian way of life. Marvin Moore caught the ideal when he noted that "repentance means recognizing God's way of life and desiring to make it one's own."[35]

### Self-crucifixion

Closely tied to repentance in both its role at the beginning of the Christian life and in its continuation throughout the life of a Christian is the crucifixion of the self. Christ set the stage for that radical and distasteful teaching at Caesarea Philippi, when He told His disciples: "If any man would come after me, let him deny himself and take up his cross and follow me. For whoever would save his life will lose it, and whoever loses his life for my sake will find it" (Matt. 16:24, 25).

To fully understand that statement, we need to put ourselves in the place of the disciples. The idea of being crucified does not do much to our twenty-first century imaginations. We have never seen a crucifixion. To us it is a dead word. But not for the disciples. When they saw a knot of Roman soldiers escorting a person through town carrying or dragging part of a cross, they recognized that it was a one-way trip. They knew the cross to be the cruelest and most humiliating of deaths. To Jesus and the disciples, the cross symbolized death.

What is it that must be put to death, we ask? The New Testament answer is the life centered on self. To understand Christ's meaning, we need to remember what sin is all about. Sin, in its most basic sense, is putting our self and our will rather than God and His will at the center of our life. It is rebellion against God in that we choose to become ruler of our own life. Sin is saying no to God and yes to self.

It is the self-centered life principle that is so natural to us that has to die. Bonhoeffer spoke to the heart of what it means to be a Christian when he wrote that "when Christ calls a man, he bids him come and die."[36]

Jesus pointed to the essential human problem when He claimed that "no one can serve two masters" (Matt. 6:24). The bottom line is: Who will I put on the throne of my life? My self or God? My will or God's? I cannot serve both at the same time. *When I come face to face with the claims of Christ, I must either crucify Him or let Him crucify me. There is no middle ground.*

At the center of the struggle is the individual human will, "the governing power in the nature of man." Sin originated in self-centered willfulness. Thus Ellen White can write that "the warfare against self is the greatest battle that was ever fought. The yielding of self, surrendering all to the will of God, requires a struggle; but the soul must submit to God before it can be renewed in holiness." As Denney put it: "Though sin may have a natural birth it does not die a natural death; in every case it has to be morally sentenced and put to death."[37] That sentencing is an act of the will under the impulse of the Holy Spirit. Christ called it a crucifixion.

Unfortunately, my self does not like to remain dead. The Pharisee in me wants to rise up and suggest that now that the crucifixion is past and done with, I have turned out to be a pretty good person after all. I love to trumpet my self. Self-glorification, of course (even if it focuses on my good deeds), is a sign that crucifixion is not a once-for-all operation. For that reason, Paul claimed that he had to die daily (1 Cor. 15:31). Or, as hymnist Frank Belden put it: "Self is worse than a nine-life cat, and must be killed by the Word *daily*."[38]

Christianity, fortunately, is more than a death of the old attitudes and ways. It is, as we shall see later in this chapter, a positive life based on a faith-relationship to Christ (see Gal. 2:20). Repentance and self crucifixion are the entryway to that faith relationship. Martin Luther showed a great deal of insight into the entire process when he wrote: "It is God's nature to make something out of nothing. This is why God cannot make anything out of him who is not yet nothing."[39]

## Justification and Related Topics

### Justification

The New Testament has many word pictures for salvation. Among them are such terms as *redemption, reconciliation,* and *propitiation.* The first takes us to the language of the marketplace, the second and third to that of the family and the sacrificial altar.[40]

However, one of the most significant metaphors of salvation in the New Testament is *justification*—a word that takes us to the language of the law court. Its essential meaning is to be declared righteous.

To Martin Luther, justification was the central scriptural doctrine. It was "the master and ruler, lord, governor and judge over all other doctrines," it is the unique Christian doctrine that "distinguishes our religion from all others."[41] Paul also put justification by faith at the center of his gospel (Rom. 1:16, 17; 3:24-26; Gal. 2:16-21).

Part of the reason Luther and Paul saw justification as central to the plan of salvation was undoubtedly due to the judgment theme that runs throughout Scripture (e.g., Eccl. 12:14; Dan. 7:10, 26; Matt. 25:31-46; Rom. 2:5; Rev. 14:7). But beyond the judgment imagery were the personal experiences of those two men. Both were Pharisees at heart. Each hoped to win the favor of God through amassing merits on the scale of judgment. But that attempt, as both learned, was an impossible task.

Luther's failure left him in a fearful state. He understood Paul's phrase "'the justice of God'. . . to mean that justice whereby God is just and deals justly in punishing the unjust." Thus God's righteousness was His terrible retributive justice and punishing righteousness. Luther knew he was lost to eternal hellfire because, even though he was "an impeccable monk," he stood before God the unmerciful judge as a lost sinner.

In that state of mind he could not understand what Paul meant by the phrase "The just shall live by faith" (Rom. 1:17, KJV). He pondered the passage for its meaning. "Then," he penned, "I grasped that the justice of God is that righteousness by which through *grace* and *sheer mercy* God justifies us through faith. *Thereupon I felt myself to be reborn and to have gone through open doors into paradise. The whole of Scripture took on a new meaning,* and whereas before the 'justice of God' had filled me with hate, now it became to me inexpressibly sweet in greater love. This passage of Paul became to me a gate to heaven."[42]

For Luther, the cruel judge had become the loving Father. Justification was for him, as it had been for Paul, the good news of salvation.

Paul and Luther in their Pharisaic days were not altogether wrong. After all, righteousness does demand perfect law keeping. The automatic penalty for failure is death and the wrath of God (see Rom. 6:23; 4:15). They also were correct about their shortcomings in obeying the law as God demanded.

What they neglected to realize is that Christ has kept the law perfectly for those who believe in Him. "The righteousness of God," therefore, "is embodied in Christ. We receive righteousness by receiving Him" rather than through wearisome toil. As a result, we are "justified [counted as though we are righteous] by his [God's] grace as a gift" which we receive by faith (Rom. 3:22, 24, 25). Thus we have righteousness "apart from law" (Rom. 3:21). Christ is "our righteousness" (1 Cor. 1:30). "The only thing we could really be said to contribute to our justification," Alister McGrath notes, "is the sin God so graciously forgives."[43]

Luther referred to the transaction in which Christ becomes sin for us, while we receive His righteousness (2 Cor. 5:21), as the "wonderful exchange." Puritan John Flavel rejoiced in the fact that "Christ is made unto us righteousness. . . . Instead of our own, we have His, we have gold for dung."[44]

*Justification* in Paul's general usage does not mean "to make righteous," but rather "to declare righteous." "The root idea in justification," George Eldon Ladd writes, "is the declaration of God, the righteous judge, that the man who believes in Christ, sinful though he may be, . . . is viewed as being righteous, because in Christ he has come into a righteous relationship with God."

An extension of a person's being viewed *as* righteous is that God treats them as if they *were* righteous. Relationship, Ladd suggests, is the key to understanding justification. "The justified man has, in Christ, entered into a new relationship with God," who now views him as righteous and treats him accordingly. The new relationship that brings justification, we should note, does not make a person intrinsically righteous, but it is *"real righteousness"* because a person's relationship to God in Christ is real. *Justification is the opposite of condemnation.* "It is the decree of acquittal from all guilt and issues in freedom from all condemnation and punishment."[45]

Biblical justification is not a mere legal transaction of forgiveness. Peter Toon points out that "while forgiveness is primarily concerned with cancelation of guilt, justification is primarily concerned with an external change in one's personal standing before God, a right relationship with him under the covenant of grace."[46]

We see that point illustrated in the parable of the prodigal son, in which the father not only forgives him but welcomes him fully back into the family at the very instant of confession. "Quick!" the father exclaimed, "bring the best robe" (Luke 15:22, NIV).

The fact that justification includes a declaration of righteousness and a treatment of sinners as if they were righteous on God's part has led some influential biblical scholars, such as William Sanday and A. C Headlam, to view it as a legal fiction.[47] That interpretation of justification appears to make God guilty of deception.

### Regeneration and Conversion

The accusation of deception might hold if justification by faith could stand by itself as an isolated Christian experience. The plain fact, however, is that justification does not exist by itself in real life. At the same time that individuals are justified by faith, they are also "born anew" (John 3:3, 7) or regenerated (see Titus 3:5). *This new birth is a real change in the converted per-*

*son.* If in justification God does something *for* us, in regeneration He does something *in* us through the power of the Holy Spirit. Just how the Spirit accomplishes His work in us, Jesus claimed, is beyond our comprehension, but everyone will be able to see the objective results (John 3:8).

Paul likened the conversion experience expressed in regeneration to a total change in the person. "Do not," he penned, "be conformed to this world but be transformed by the renewal of your mind" (Rom. 12:2). The word Paul used for "transformed" comes from a Greek word that we use in English as *metamorphosis.* Metamorphosis is that mysterious process by which an ugly, sluglike caterpillar transforms into an elegant and beautiful butterfly. It denotes a change so radical that unless people knew better, they wouldn't even realize it was the same life. That is what God wants to do for His children. Little wonder, then, that J. C. Ryle exclaimed that a Christ who only forgave but did not transform would be "only a half Saviour."[48]

Christians are new creations (2 Cor. 5:17; Gal. 6:15). As a result, they "walk in newness of life" (Rom. 6:4), serve in newness of spirit (Rom. 7:6), and their "inner nature is being renewed every day" (2 Cor. 4:16). In summary, they have not only put on a new nature, but they are being remade in the image of their Creator (see Col. 3:10). Whereas the natural man or woman is dead in sin, the Christian is alive in Christ (see Eph. 2:1-6). And whereas unconverted persons are "hostile to God" and His law, after regeneration they can "delight in the law of God" in their "inmost self" (Rom. 8:7; 7:22).[49]

One of the Puritan divines nicely illustrated the Christian's change of attitude toward sin and how that attitude affects action when he wrote: "He throws it [sin] away with abhorrence, as a man would a loathsome toad which in the dark he had hugged fast to his bosom and thought it had been some pretty and harmless bird."[50]

Conversion, as represented by baptism, is not only death to the old way of life, but resurrection to a new life in Christ (Rom. 6:1-4; Gal. 2:20; cf. John 15:4). The new birth represents a reorientation of one's *agapē* (love) from self to God and other people.[51] It is at the new birth that the law of God gets written on the "fleshy tables of the heart" (2 Cor. 3:3, KJV; Heb. 8:10).

Ellen White highlighted the crucial importance of the renewing experience of regeneration or the new birth when she wrote: "*Without the transforming process* which can come alone through divine power, *the original propensities to sin are left in the heart* in all their strength, to forge new chains, to impose a slavery that can never be broken by human power."[52]

80

Some Adventist writers and teachers have taught that certain people are "'born again' at the time of" their "natural birth just as Christ was," and thus are not "'alienated, separated from God'" in the same way that an unconverted sinner is.[53] But such a teaching finds no support in Scripture. It is based on an inadequate view of the power and universality of sin and sinful propensities in human nature and a faulty conception that tends to evaluate wrongly the "greater sins" as being those of adultery and murder rather than such "nice sins" as self-sufficiency and pride.

Such advocates, like the Pharisees of old, run the risk of destructive (and almost invisible) spiritual pride. While it is true that some may not be able to point to the exact point of their conversion,[54] that does not prove that as babies they were not self-centered and demanding or did not need to be converted from putting their self at the center of their life.

*The bottom line of the "some people are born as good as Christ" thesis is that there might be people in heaven who did not need a Savior to get there.* Of course, if sin is atomized to mean a few specific acts rather than an inbred bent or propensity to sin (as Ellen White suggests), then such individuals would probably need to be forgiven for an isolated sin here and there, but they certainly would not need to be born again. From the biblical perspective, such a teaching is strange theology at best.

As Gustav Aulén noted, "Individual and specific acts of sin are not isolated and unrelated to each other but are rooted in the inclination of man's will. . . . Sin does not refer to something external and peripheral in man nor to something 'accidental'; it has its 'seat' in his inner being."[55]

This reality led Christ to say that whatever defiles a person "proceeds from the heart" (Matt. 15:18). It is the natural heart, the New Testament repeatedly teaches, that needs to be transformed and regenerated. And it was that heart with its inborn "bent to evil" and "original propensities to sin" that so concerned Ellen White. "The Christian's life," she wrote, "is not a modification or improvement of the old, but *a transformation of nature*. There is a death to self and sin, and a new life altogether. This change can be brought about only by the effectual working of the Holy Spirit."[56]

Theologians and biblical scholars have argued throughout the ages as to whether justification and the new birth are one or two experiences. Luther and Wesley both held that one could not separate the two. Luther, who could use the term *justification* in various ways, wrote: "For we perceive that a man who is justified is not yet a righteous man, but is in the very movement or journey towards righteousness." Again, "Our justification is not yet complete. . . . It is still under construction. It shall, however, be completed in the resurrection of the dead."[57]

But it was Luther's chief lieutenant, Philipp Melanchthon, "who made the great mistake," Carl Braaten points out, "of narrowing justification down to the declaration that sinners are righteous on account of the external merits of Christ." Melanchthon's lead in restricting justification to the legal declaration that a sinner is reckoned as righteous has, unfortunately, been accepted uncritically by a fair number of Seventh-day Adventist authors.[58]

Ellen White, by way of contrast, stands with Luther and Wesley. "God's forgiveness," she wrote, "is not merely a judicial act by which He sets us free from condemnation. It is not only forgiveness *for* sin, but reclaiming *from* sin. It is the outflow of redeeming love that transforms the heart."[59]

In the end we can agree with J. Gresham Machen, who observed that the fine points of difference between justification and regeneration are not all that important, since "in reality they are two aspects of one salvation."[60]

### Adoption Into the Covenant and Assurance of Salvation

Also inextricably intertwined with justification and the new-birth experience is the New Testament teaching of adoption. We naturally associate birth with being in a family. One of the great Bible pictures of salvation is reconciliation, the reuniting of God with His children.

The need for reconciliation has its roots in the broken relationships caused by sin. Sin, Brunner suggests, "is like the son who strikes his father's face in anger, . . . it is the bold self assertion of the son's will above that of the father."[61]

Having become alienated from God, human beings are reconciled to Him at the point of their faith-choice to put Him and His will at the center of their lives. At the moment in which they turn from sin (repentance/conversion) and to God (faith) He declares them righteous (justified) and born again (regenerated). The reconciliation, as we noted with the prodigal son, is both complete and immediate at that very moment (Luke 15:19-24; cf. 18:14). "Beloved," writes John, "we are God's children now" (1 John 3:2). God is "our Father," and believers are called the "children of God" (Matt. 6:9; 1 John 3:1). "To all who received him [Jesus], and believed in his name, he gave power to become children of God" (John 1:12). Those who accept Christ will eventually "make" their "home with him" (John 14:23). And those who accept Christ by faith, says Paul, "receive adoption as sons" (Gal. 4:5; Eph. 1:5).

But isn't everyone a child of God, Christian or not? queries J. I. Packer. "Emphatically no!" he replies. "The idea that all men are children of God is not found in the Bible anywhere. The Old Testament shows God as the Father, not of all men, but of His own people, the seed of Abraham." And the New Testament plainly states that we are of Abraham's seed if we have accepted Christ (Gal. 3:26-29). "Sonship to God is not, therefore, a universal status upon which everyone enters by natural birth, but a supernatural gift which one receives through receiving Jesus. . . . '*As many as received Him*, to *them* gave He power to become the sons of God, . . . which were born, not of blood, nor of the will of the flesh, nor of the will of man, but of God' (John 1:12 f.)." Thus adoptive sonship or daughtership is a gift of grace that a person accepts at the moment of conversion.[62]

We need to understand and live the entire Christian life in terms of adoption. For one thing, being healed in our relationship to God means being healed in our attitude toward those Jesus called His brothers and sisters (Mark 3:35). Just as the entrance of sin led to alienation between human beings (Gen. 3:12; 4:1-16), so adoption into God's family means a healing of those relationships. Love to God and love to other people, therefore, are two prongs of God's great commandment, something that Christians are to extend to those who are still alienated from God and His adopted family (Matt. 22:36-40; Luke 6:27-36). Adoption should affect every part of Christians' lives as they seek to imitate the Father, glorify His and the family's name, and live a life pleasing to Him.[63]

Closely tied to adoption is the biblical concept of covenant. "Covenant," writes Karl Barth, "is the Old Testament term for the basic relationship between the God of Israel and His people."[64] He is their God, and they are His people whom He has chosen. A covenant is a compact or agreement between two parties, binding them mutually to the terms of a contract. In the Old Testament God agreed to bless Israel on the condition that they fulfill the terms of the agreement, which were faith and obedience (Deut. 7:6-16; 28:1, 15). After the crucifixion, the blessings and obligations of the covenant were transferred from Israel as a nation to those who have accepted Christ by faith, (Matt. 21:33-43; 1 Peter 2:9, 10; Gal. 3:28, 29).

The covenant relationship is central to all of Scripture. When we accept Christ, we are justified, regenerated, and adopted into the covenant relationship. At that time, God says, "I will put my laws into their minds, and write them on their hearts" (Heb. 8:10; cf. 2 Cor. 3:3). Thus the way of obedience becomes the path of the converted Christian.

J. A. Ziesler and Alister McGrath help us see that "righteousness" was a covenant word for the Hebrews. To be righteous meant that a person was in a right relationship with God. In the Old Testament, McGrath notes, righteousness is much more than an impersonal standard of justice— it "is a *personal* concept: it is essentially the *fulfillment of the demands and obligations of a relationship between two persons. . . .* To be 'right with God,'" therefore, "is to trust in his gracious promises and to act accordingly."[65]

Thus Abraham, upon being called into covenant relationship with God, not only believed Him, but responded accordingly in his daily life. For that reason, various Bible writers, in quite different contexts, can claim that Abraham was counted righteous because of both faith (Gen. 15:6; Rom. 4:3, 5, 9) and works (James 2:21). My point is that while we might separate faith and works for purposes of academic discussion, in daily life you cannot have one without the other, since both are a part of the same covenant relationship. (We will have more to say on that topic in chapter 5.) Because of regeneration, which takes place at the time a person is declared righteous, a justified Christian is in harmony with God's principles. Faith may be the way into the righteous relationship, but deeds or acts in harmony with God's will are the result of that relationship. Thus to be justified in the biblical sense means that a person is no longer in a sin relationship (in rebellion) to God, but in a faith relationship. Such a person belongs to the covenant family.

Because of their covenant relationship to God, Christians can have *assurance* of their salvation. Those who have accepted Christ by faith "have been saved" (Eph. 2:8; cf. Luke 7:50; 19:9; John 3:36; 5:24; 6:47). Salvation, however, is a continuing process rather than being a once-saved-always-saved event. That means that to retain the assurance of salvation, one must continue to remain in covenant relationship with God through Christ.

If a person sins, however, that does not mean that he or she ceases to be a son or daughter of the covenant (1 John 2:1). That only takes place if individuals refuse to repent of their rebellion. The deliberate choice of an ongoing rebellious attitude (sin relationship) toward God will nullify the assurance of the covenant, but one does not bounce in and out of the covenant relationship on the basis of individual sinful acts. As long as we choose to remain "in Christ," we may be confident of our accomplished salvation.[66]

We can summarize what we have said about justification thus far by noting that it is the legal declaration of forgiveness and the restoration of a healthy relationship between God and the sinner. The ground of justification, as Paul points out, is Christ's death (see Rom. 5:9; 3:24, 25). The means by which it becomes effective for the individual is faith (see Rom. 5:1; 3:25; Gal. 2:16, 20; Phil. 3:9). At the same time that individuals are justified, they are regenerated (born from above), adopted into the family of God, enter a covenant relationship with Him, and have assurance of their salvation so long as they choose to remain in a faith relationship. All of those blessings of grace, we should emphasize, take place at the *moment* one accepts Christ by faith.

**The Issue of Universal Justification**

Before moving away from the topic of justification, we need to examine one more of its aspects—the universal justification of every person. That topic has emerged from time to time down through Christian history, sometimes staying within the biblical perspective and sometimes wandering beyond it. Universalism, for example, takes the position that everybody will be saved because Christ died for all people.[67]

That teaching, of course, leaves the all-important condition of faith in Christ out of its reckoning. The Bible clearly states that "whoever believes" in Christ will not perish but has eternal life (John 3:36, 16; cf. 1 John 1:9; Gal. 2:16). God will not save people against their will. Faith is *the* condition of salvation.

But not all Adventists agree with that position. Back in the 1890s, for example, Ellen White rebuked A. T. Jones more than once for claiming that "there were no conditions implied in our receiving the righteousness of Christ." More recently, Jack Sequeira has stated that "I believe the Bible teaches that God actually and unconditionally saved all humanity at the cross so that we are justified and reconciled to God by that act (see Romans 5:10, 18; 2 Corinthians 5:18, 19). I believe that the only reason anyone will be lost is because he or she willfully and persistently rejects God's gift of salvation in Christ." In a similar vein, Donald K. Short writes disapprovingly of "some Christians I'm acquainted with [who] do not believe that the whole human race was legally saved, justified, and glorified independent of a personal faith commitment to Jesus as Savior and Lord."[68]

On the other side of the Adventist ledger on the topic is Ellen White, who wrote that "the *provisions* of redemption are free to all; the *results* of redemption will be enjoyed by those who have complied with the conditions" (the italics are hers). Again, she penned in the same month she rebuked Jones on the topic that "faith is the only condition upon which

85

justification can be obtained." On another occasion she wrote in the context of her approval of the 1888 message of Jones and E. J. Waggoner on justification that Christ died to provide the "benefits" of salvation "for every soul who should *believe* on Him."[69]

A text that some Seventh-day Adventists[70] have interpreted as teaching universal justification ("everyone is born legally justified") is Romans 5:18: "As one man's [Adam's] trespass led to condemnation for all men, so one man's [Christ's] act of righteousness leads to acquittal and life for all men." Of course, if a person chooses to employ the parallelism in the passage to prove universal justification, then he or she must also use 1 Corinthians 15:22 in its context ("For as in Adam all die, so also in Christ shall all be made alive.") to prove universal resurrection to salvation (see verse 23). And with that stroke a person arrives at universalism.

It seems that C. E. B. Cranfield is correct when he suggests that the gift is truly provided for all, but that Romans 5:18 "does not foreclose the question whether in the end all will actually come to share it." In a similar vein, John Murray differentiates between potential and actual justification. Verse 19 answers the question when it says that "*many* will be made righteous" through Christ (cf. verse 15). The "many," of course, are those who have complied with the faith condition that Paul has so aggressively argued for in Romans up to this point.[71]

Without doubt Christ died for the sins of "everyone" (see Heb. 2:9), but that does not imply universal justification. Another text often used to teach universal justification is 2 Corinthians 5:19, which notes that "in Christ God was reconciling the world to himself, not counting their trespasses against them." But the intent of that clause is to point out that "the plan of salvation does not consist in reconciling God to men, but in reconciling men to God." The real meaning concerning who is justified in 2 Corinthians 5 is that it is those who are "in Christ" (verses 17-20).[72]

Some of those Adventists teaching that people are "born justified" are often careful to distinguish between being "legally justified" and being "justified by faith" (saving justification), but the texts used do not substantiate the teaching.[73]

The reason for the entire argument of universal legal justification on the part of Robert Wieland and others seems to be to discover how the Adventist 1888 message of righteousness by faith is distinct from that held by other Protestants, in spite of the fact that the main proponents of the doctrine at Minneapolis (Ellen White and E. J. Waggoner) claimed that it was merely the same gospel that Paul, Luther, and Wesley preached.[74]

The argument regarding universal justification runs against the traditional Protestant/Adventist teaching that legal justification is provisional until accepted by faith. Rather than its being *provisional*, the Adventist proponents of universal legal justification hold that justification was *accomplished* for every human being at the cross. Thus Robert Wieland writes: "The common idea is that the sacrifice of Christ is only *provisional*, that is, it does nothing for anyone unless he first does something and 'accepts Christ.' Jesus stands back," the caricature goes, "with His divine arms folded, doing nothing for the sinner until he decides to 'accept.'. . . The true Good News is far better than we have been led to think. According to the 'precious' 1888 message, our salvation does not depend on our taking the initiative; it depends on our *believing* that God has taken the initiative in saving us."[75]

If that is part of the core of the 1888 message, then the Wesleyans with their view of prevenient grace have had it since the eighteenth century, and Jacobus Arminius (1560-1609) and others possessed it before that. One of the clear teachings of the Bible is that God did two things for the guilty Adam. First, He let Adam continue to live so that he could repent. We might call that general grace—a blessing that continues to the present. God has given probationary time to Adam's posterity to decide for Christ. During that time, God's gifts fall on the just and unjust alike so that they might see His goodness (see Matt. 5:45; Rom. 1:19, 20; John 1:9). God's general grace also suggests that He does not hold sins against people until they reach the age of accountability. Thus the salvation of those who die in infancy becomes a distinct possibility.

Second, beyond general grace, God extended prevenient grace to Adam. As a result, He sought out the guilty Adam in the garden, and He has sought out sinners ever since. One of the primary functions of the Holy Spirit is to search us out and convict us of sin so that we might be driven to Christ (John 16:7-15). Thus, Leo Cox writes, "no man will be sent to hell because he has no grace, but because he fails to use the grace he has."[76] The most important issue any person can ever face is accepting or rejecting what God has done for him or her in the person of Christ (John 3:36).

## Now, What About Justification Being the Work of a Lifetime and Sanctification Being the Work of a Moment?

It should be clear from the bulk of this chapter that justification takes place at the very instant that a sinner takes hold of God's grace by faith. Thus justification is primarily the work of a moment.

That is well and good, but the problem is that Christians continue to sin. They therefore stand in need of continuous justification, since "man has stored up no treasury of merit to offer for sin." Hans LaRondelle correctly suggests that we are in need of "*daily justification* by faith in Christ, whether we have consciously transgressed or unknowingly erred."[77]

Daily justification is closely tied to Christ's ministry in the heavenly sanctuary. "He always lives to make intercession" for "those who draw near to God through him" (Heb. 7:25; cf. 9:24). Christ, "who is at the right hand of God, . . . intercedes for us" (Rom. 8:34). "If any one does sin, we have an advocate with the Father, Jesus Christ the righteous" (1 John 2:1).

"Jesus," Ellen White wrote, "is represented as continually standing at the altar, momentarily offering up the sacrifice for the sins of the world. . . . A daily and yearly typical atonement is no longer to be made, but the atoning sacrifice through a mediator is essential because of the constant commission of sin. . . . Jesus presents the oblation offered for every offense and every shortcoming of the sinner."[78]

Some scholars prefer to think of ongoing justification as "continued forgiveness,"[79] since their standing with God was corrected at the time of their conversion and initial justification, but in essence the difference is largely semantic. Day by day Christ continues to mediate for His earthly brothers and sisters and to declare them righteous before the heavenly mercy seat.

Not only is there a sense in which justification is the work of a lifetime, but the major biblical use of the word *sanctification* indicates that it takes place in an instant. The fundamental meaning of the Hebrew word translated as "sanctify" is "to dedicate," "to consecrate," or "to set apart."[80] God told Moses to "sanctify" ("consecrate," RSV) the entire people of Israel to the Lord (Ex. 19:10, KJV). Not only were the Israelites sanctified or set apart for holy use and consecrated purposes, but so were the tabernacle and the instruments employed in the sanctuary service (Ex. 30:25-29; 40:9-11; Lev. 8:10-13).

The New Testament word translated as "sanctify" means "to make holy."[81] A saint (one who has been sanctified) is a person set apart for holy use by God.

The New Testament often speaks of sanctification as an accomplished fact. Thus the book of Hebrews says that "by a single offering he [Christ] has perfected for all time those who are sanctified" (Heb. 10:14; cf. verse 29). Again, Paul can write of the Corinthians as "those sanctified in Christ

Jesus, called to be saints" (1 Cor. 1:2; cf. Acts 20:32). Christians have been "sanctified by faith" in Christ (Acts 26:18) through the agency of the Holy Spirit (see Rom. 15:16; cf. 1 Thess. 5:23).

Paul even indicates the moment in people's lives when they become sanctified. "You were washed," he penned to the Corinthians, "you were sanctified, you were justified in the name of the Lord Jesus Christ" (1 Cor. 6:11). In short, people are initially sanctified at the time they are justified, regenerated, and adopted into God's covenant family. Persons become sanctified at the point in time that they believe in Jesus Christ. Thus *initial sanctification* signifies not a moral concept but a new relationship to God. Converts to Christ have been set apart to God and for His use in the same way that the priests and tabernacle were set apart for holy purposes in the Old Testament.[82]

Being sanctified is living in a state of dedication to God. Such dedication in the New Testament, suggests Anthony Hoekema, "means two things: (1) separation from the sinful practices of this present world and (2) consecration to God's service."[83]

Ellen White shares this perspective. "Genuine conversion is needed," she wrote, "not once in years, but daily. This conversion brings man into a new relation with God. Old things . . . pass away, and he is renewed and sanctified. But this work must be continual."[84]

That quotation brings us to the fact that sanctification is not only the work of a moment, it is also the result of a lifetime of letting God use us for His purposes. People who have been made holy at the new birth are called upon to be holy in daily living (see 1 Thess. 4:3-7; Rom. 6:19). As Donald Guthrie puts it, although the sanctification of Christians is an accomplished fact in the sight of God, "it still needs to be worked out in the lives of believers."[85]

It is helpful to think of sanctification at three levels: (1) initial sanctification, when a person comes to Christ and is justified and regenerated (born from above); (2) progressive sanctification, as individuals live for Christ and grow in grace in their daily lives; and (3) final sanctification or glorification, which takes place at the second coming of Christ, when Christians will be "changed, in a moment . . . at the last trumpet" (1 Cor. 15:52). We will have more to say on the final two phases of sanctification in chapters 5 and 10.

I might add, before passing on to another topic, that I am well aware of the fact that Ellen White wrote that "there is no such thing as instantaneous sanctification." She was not arguing against Paul and the other Bible writers, but against the excesses of certain holiness believers in her day who claimed that they had been completely sanctified and perfected in a moment by the Holy Spirit and were thereafter incapable of sin. That same extreme situation explains her suggestion that people should never say that they are sanctified.[86]

To take those statements out of their historical context is to pit her against Paul, who went so far as to claim sanctification for even the Corinthian believers. The threefold view of sanctification as being past, present, and future should enable us to understand better the many statements on sanctification we read in the Bible and in various Christian writers.

## Justification and Sanctification
## Can Be Relatively Meaningless Terms

G. C. Berkouwer indicates that one of the ongoing battles in theological history concerns the relative importance of justification and sanctification. "In this controversy one accuses the other of allowing justification to be assimilated by sanctification, only to be told that he, on the other hand, through his preoccupation with justification, crowds out sanctification." That discussion has certainly been at the center of the disruptive Adventist debates on righteousness by faith that came to a head in 1888 and have been in a state of constant agitation since about 1956.[87]

Berkouwer, after raising the issue, goes on to state that one really cannot talk about justification while ignoring sanctification and vice versa. James Denney was speaking to that point when he wrote that "*it has sometimes [been] forgotten that the great matter is not the distinction of justification and sanctification, but their connection, and that justification or reconciliation is a delusion unless the life of the reconciled and justified is inevitably and naturally a holy life.*" These two aspects of salvation are "*the indivisible and all-inclusive response of the soul to Christ.*"[88]

The great sixteenth century Reformers saw that truth clearly. Calvin could therefore write that "Christ justifies no one whom he does not at the same time sanctify. . . . You cannot possess him [Christ] without being made partaker in his sanctification, because he cannot be divided."[89] Luther also regarded salvation as a unified experience. As we noted earlier, it was his chief disciple (Philipp Melanchthon) who put an unhealthy overemphasis on forensic (legal) justification. Unfortunately, much post-Reformation theology followed Melanchthon here rather than Luther. That has led to serious distortions that still affect the thinking of some.

On the other hand, distortion also can go the other direction. William

Hulme points to that problem when he notes that "it is as artificial to separate justification and sanctification as it is hazardous to confuse them."[90]

We should note that the distinction does have roots in Scripture. Paul, for example, speaks of justification as being without works of law (Rom. 4:6), yet in the same letter he is obviously referring to progressive sanctification when he entreats believers to present their bodies "as a living sacrifice, holy and acceptable to God" (Rom. 12:1). The book of Romans moves from justification by faith in the early chapters to living the sanctified life in its later chapters.

For theoretical purposes, we can isolate justification and sanctification from each other, but in daily living they are intricately linked together. John Macquarrie helps us arrive at a balanced synthesis when he writes: "We are not to think of a sharp separation, but rather only of distinguishable aspects of a unitary process."[91]

The Bible is not nearly as concerned with discussing the fine lines of distinction between justification and sanctification as it is in speaking to meaningful Christianity. The New Testament does not argue whether sanctification is more important than justification or whether one comes before the other. The real issue, from its perspective, is whether a person is in a faith relationship to Jesus Christ. Sin is breaking a relationship with God, while faith is entering into and maintaining that relationship.

Paul is especially clear that a person is either "in Adam" or "in Christ" (1 Cor. 15:22; Rom. 5:12-21). Those who are "in Christ" are justified, sanctified, and are being progressively sanctified and perfected. "In Christ" occurs 164 times in Paul's writings, including 11 times (counting pronouns and synonyms) in one of the great opening sentences of Ephesians (1:3-14).

James Stewart points out that "the heart of Paul's religion is union with Christ. This, more than any other conception . . . is the key which unlocks the secrets of his soul." Both justification and sanctification lose all reality for Paul if separated from the concept of union with Christ. Justification should be viewed as uniting with Christ through faith. Thus Paul can say: "There is therefore now no condemnation for those who are in Christ Jesus" (Rom. 8:1). Sanctification is the continuation of people's lives in Christ and His life in them (Gal. 2:20). "Only when union with Christ is kept central," Stewart writes, "is sanctification seen in its true nature, as the unfolding of Christ's own character within the believer's life; and only then can the essential relationship between religion and ethics be understood."[92]

The realization of the importance of union with Christ helps Christians remember that "the resources for victory lie not in the individual but in Christ. Christians do not serve out of strength but out of yieldedness." God, through the power of the indwelling Spirit and the grace of Christ, enables them to live as loving Christians. P. T. Forsyth espoused this central Christian truth when he wrote that "we do not gain the victory; we are united with the Victor."[93]

Christians naturally bear fruit when they abide in Christ (see John 15:4). Because Christian living is living in union with Christ, it can never be cold, austere, or hard. Union with Christ means not only communion with God but also with our fellow creatures.[94] "Whoever keeps his word, in him truly love for God is perfected. By this we may be sure that we are in him: he who says he abides in him ought to walk in the same way in which he walked" (1 John 2:5, 6). The next two chapters will treat that majestic topic. Meanwhile, individuals who are "in Christ" can rest assured of their salvation.

---

[1] Barclay, *Matthew*, vol. 1, pp. 146, 147. See also, *The Oxford Dictionary of the Christian Church*, 2d ed., s.v. "Antony, St., of Egypt"; Kenneth Scott Latourette, *A History of Christianity*, rev. ed. (New York: Harper & Row, 1975), vol. 1, pp. 225, 226.

[2] Latourette, *A History*, vol. 1, p. 228; Earle E. Cairns, *Christianity Through the Centuries*, rev. and enl. ed. (Grand Rapids: Zondervan, 1981), pp. 152, 153.

[3] Carl E. Braaten, *Justification: The Article by Which the Church Stands or Falls* (Minneapolis: Fortress, 1990), pp. 96, 97.

[4] *Ibid.*, p. 97.

[5] *Ibid.*, p. 88. Cf. J. I. Packer, *Knowing God* (Downers Grove, Ill.: InterVarsity, 1973), p. 120; Alan Richardson, ed. *A Theological Word Book of the Bible*, (New York: Collier Books, 1950), pp. 100-102.

[6] Denney, *Christian Doctrine of Reconciliation*, p. 16.

[7] Luther, quoted in Gustaf Aulén, *Christus Victor*, trans. A. G. Hebert (New York: Macmillan, 1966), p. 105.

[8] Niebuhr, *Nature and Destiny of Man*, vol. 2, p. 107.

[9] E. Glenn Hinson, "A Contemplative Response," in *Christian Spirituality*, p. 46.

[10] See Knight, *The Cross of Christ*, pp. 44-58.

[11] White, *Selected Messages*, book 1, p. 343.

[12] John R. W. Stott, *The Cross of Christ* (Downers Grove, Ill.: InterVarsity, 1986), p. 71.

[13] 2 Maccabees 7:1-41 (Goodspeed).

[14] Morris L. Venden, *95 Theses on Righteousness by Faith* (Boise, Idaho: Pacific Press, 1987), p. 23.

[15] *Ibid.*, p. 47.

[16] Vick, *Is Salvation Really Free?*, p. 56.

[17] See Jack W. Provonsha, *God Is With Us* (Washington, D.C.: Review and Herald, 1974), p. 128.

[18] Denney, *Studies in Theology*, p. 155; Denney, *Christian Doctrine of Reconciliation*, p. 303; cf. pp. 163, 164.

[19] Forsyth, *Justification of God*, p. 126.

[20] Brunner, *Romans*, p. 142; John Murray, *Redemption Accomplished and Applied* (Grand Rapids: Eerdmans, 1955), pp. 110, 111; Aulén, *Faith of the Christian Church*, p. 278.

[21] Herbert Douglass, *Faith: Saying Yes to God* (Nashville: Southern Pub. Assn., 1978), p. 76.

[22] Dietrich Bonhoeffer, *The Cost of Discipleship* (New York: Collier, 1963), p. 87.

[23] Erickson, *Christian Theology*, p. 938; Jürgen Moltmann, *The Crucified God* (New York: Harper & Row, 1974), p. 39. (Italics supplied.)

[24] Robinson, *Redemption and Revelation*, p. 284.

[25] See Knight, *Philosophy and Education*, pp. 204-208. Cf. White, *Education*, pp. 15, 29; Calvin, *Institutes*, 2.2.12,13.

[26] H. Orton Wiley, *Christian Theology* (Kansas City, Mo.: Beacon Hill Press of Kansas City, 1952), vol. 2, pp. 344-357; Toon, *Justification and Sanctification*, pp. 106, 107. Cf. Harald Lindström, *Wesley and Sanctification* (Grand Rapids: Zondervan, 1980), pp. 44-50; Wesley, *Works*, vol. 6, pp. 511-513.

[27] White, *Selected Messages*, book 1, p. 390.

[28] Berkouwer, *Faith and Justification*, pp. 80, 86.

[29] White, *Selected Messages*, book 1, p. 389.

[30] Erickson, *Christian Theology*, pp. 934-938; *The New International Dictionary of New Testament Theology*, s.v. "Conversion, Penitence, Repentance."

[31] Forsyth, *Work of Christ*, pp. 151, 152.

[32] Derek Kidner, *Psalms 1-72*, Tyndale Old Testament Commentaries (Downers Grove, Ill.: InterVarsity, 1973), p. 190.

[33] Brunner, *The Mediator*, p. 534.

[34] White, *Selected Messages*, book 1, p. 391.

[35] Moore, *Refiner's Fire*, p. 87.

[36] Bonhoeffer, *Cost of Discipleship*, p. 99.

[37] White, *Steps to Christ*, pp. 47, 43; Denney, *Christian Doctrine of Reconciliation*, p. 198. Cf. F. W. Dillistone, *The Significance of the Cross* (Philadelphia: Westminster, 1944), p. 155.

[38] F. E. Belden to E. G. White, Sept. 26, 1895.

[39] Luther, quoted in Helmut Thielicke, *How the World Began*, trans. J. W. Doberstein (Philadelphia: Muhlenberg, 1961), opposite title page.

[40] See Knight, *The Cross of Christ*, pp. 62, 63, 68, 74.

[41] Luther, quoted in Alister E. McGrath, *Justification by Faith* (Grand Rapids: Zondervan, 1988), p. 147; Luther, quoted in Althaus, *Theology of Martin Luther*, p. 224.

[42] Luther, quoted in Roland H. Bainton, *Here I Stand: A Life of Martin Luther* (New York: New American Library, 1950), pp. 49, 50. (Italics supplied.)

[43] White, *Mount of Blessing*, p. 18; McGrath, *Justification by Faith*, p. 132.

[44] Luther, quoted in Althaus, *Theology of Martin Luther*, p. 213; Flavel, quoted in Ball, *English Connection*, p. 54. Cf. White, *The Desire of Ages*, p. 25.

[45] Ladd, *Theology of the New Testament*, pp. 437, 443, 445, 446. Cf. McGrath, *Justification by Faith*, p. 26.

[46] Peter Toon, *Born Again: A Biblical and Theological Study of Regeneration* (Grand Rapids: Baker, 1987), p. 64.

[47] William Sanday and Arthur C. Headlam, *The Epistle to the Romans*, 5th ed., The International Critical Commentary (Edinburgh: T. & T. Clark, [1902]), p. 36.

[48] Ryle, *Holiness*, p. 16.

[49] See Alan Richardson, *An Introduction to the Theology of the New Testament* (New York: Harper & Row, 1958), pp. 34-38.

[50] Joseph Alleine, quoted in Ball, *English Connection*, p. 75.

[51] David F. Wells, *Turning to God: Biblical Conversion in the Modern World* (Grand Rapids: Baker, 1989), pp. 41-43.

[52] Ellen G. White, *Evangelism* (Washington, D.C.: Review and Herald, 1946), p. 192. (Italics supplied.)

[53] E.g., Moore, *Refiner's Fire*, p. 132, n. 6. To be fair, this idea in Moore does not seem to be central to his theology, as it is to some, but he has conveniently and concisely stated the position.

[54] White, *Steps to Christ*, p. 57.

[55] Aulén, *Faith of the Christian Church*, pp. 240, 242.

[56] White, *Education*, p. 29; White, *Evangelism*, p. 192; White, *The Desire of Ages*, p. 172. (Italics supplied.)

[57] Luther, quoted in Toon, *Justification and Sanctification*, pp. 58, 59. See also, Althaus, *Theology of Martin Luther*, pp. 226-228; Braaten, *Justification*, p. 13; Cox, *Wesley's Concept of Perfection*, p. 136.

[58] Braaten, *Justification*, p. 13; Toon, *Justification and Sanctification*, p. 63. Among the Adventist authors who have followed Melanchthon's lead are Desmond Ford, David P. McMahon, and the later Robert Brinsmead. See also, Geoffrey J. Paxton, *The Shaking of Adventism* (Grand Rapids: Baker, 1978).

[59] White, *Mount of Blessing*, p. 114. Cf. White, *The Desire of Ages*, pp. 555, 556; Robert W. Olson, "Ellen G. White on Righteousness by Faith," in *Toward Righteousness by Faith: 1888 in Retrospect*, ed. Arthur J. Ferch (Wahroonga, Australia: South Pacific Division of SDA, 1989), pp. 102, 103.

[60] J. Gresham Machen, *Christianity and Liberalism* (Grand Rapids: Eerdmans, 1946), p. 140.

[61] Brunner, *The Mediator*, p. 462.

[62] Packer, *Knowing God*, p. 181.

[63] See *ibid.*, pp. 181-208, for an excellent discussion of adoption.

[64] Karl Barth, *Church Dogmatics*, trans. G. W. Bromiley (Edinburgh: T. & T. Clark, 1956), 4.1.22.

[65] Ziesler, *The Meaning of Righteousness in Paul*, pp. 38, 39; McGrath, *Justification by Faith*, pp. 24-28, 97, 98, 102, 107. See also *The Interpreter's Dictionary of the Bible*, s.v. "Righteousness in the NT."

[66] White, *Steps to Christ*, pp. 57, 58. See the last section of the present chapter for a fuller discussion of what it means to be "in Christ."

[67] See *Dictionary of Christianity in America*, s.v. "Universalism."

[68] E. G. White to A. T. Jones, Feb. 17, 1890; Apr. 9, 1893; Jack Sequeira, *Beyond Belief: The Promise, the Power, and the Reality of the Everlasting Gospel* (Boise, Idaho; Pacific Press, 1993), p. 8; Donald K. Short, *Signs of the Times*, May 2003, p. 3.

[69] Ellen G. White, *Patriarchs and Prophets*, p. 208, (italics in the original); White, *Selected Messages*, book 1, p. 389; Ellen G. White, *Testimonies to Ministers* (Mountain View, Calif.: Pacific Press, 1962), p. 92. (Italics supplied).

[70] Robert J. Wieland, *Grace on Trial* (Meadow Vista, Calif.: The 1888 Message Study Committee, 1988), p. 43; personal conversation with Dennis Priebe, Indianapolis, Ind., July 1990.

[71] C. E. B. Cranfield, *The Epistle to the Romans*, The International Critical Commentary (Edinburgh: T. & T. Clark, 1975), vol. 1, p. 290; Murray, *Redemption Accomplished and Applied*, p. 85. Cf. John Murray, *The Epistle to the Romans*, The New International Commentary on the New Testament (Grand Rapids: Eerdmans, 1959), vol. 1, p. 203.

[72] Francis D. Nichol, ed., *The Seventh-day Adventist Bible Commentary* (Washington, D.C.: Review and Herald, 1953-1957), vol. 6, p. 869.

[73] E.g., Wieland, *Grace on Trial*, pp. 43-48. On the agreement of Waggoner's understanding with that of the great reformers, see Knight, *Angry Saints*, pp. 40-43.

[74] Wieland, *Grace on Trial*, pp. 35, 36; Knight, *Angry Saints*, pp. 40-61.

[75] Wieland, *Grace on Trial*, pp. 43, 47.

[76] Cox, *Wesley's Concept of Perfection*, pp. 189, 190. Wallenkampf, *Justified*, pp. 37-43, presents a helpful discussion of prevenient and general grace under the heading of "Temporary Universal Justification."

[77] Leon O. Hynson, *To Reform the Nation: Theological Foundations of Wesley's Ethics* (Grand Rapids: Zondervan, 1984), p. 104; LaRondelle, *Christ Our Salvation*, p. 45.

[78] White, *Selected Messages*, book 1, pp. 343, 344.

[79] E.g., Erickson, *Christian Theology*, p. 963; Cox, *Wesley's Concept of Perfection*, p. 191.

[80] *Theological Wordbook of the Old Testament*, s.v. "*qadash.*"

[81] *Theological Dictionary of the New Testament*, s.v. "*hagios, hagiazo, hagiasmos, hagiotes, hagiosyne.*"

[82] See Ladd, *Theology of the New Testament*, pp. 519, 520.

[83] Hoekema, "Reformed Perspective," in *Five Views on Sanctification*, p. 63.

[84] White, *Our High Calling*, p. 215.

[85] Donald Guthrie, *New Testament Theology* (Downers Grove, Ill.: InterVarsity, 1981), p. 669.

[86] Ellen G. White, *The Sanctified Life* (Washington, D.C.: Review and Herald, 1937), p. 10; White, *The Great Controversy*, pp. 469-473; White, *Testimonies for the Church*, vol. 1, pp. 22, 23.

[87] Berkouwer, *Faith and Sanctification*, p. 9. Much of the Seventh-day Adventist discussion of "The 1888 Message" centers around the relation of justification and sanctification. For overviews, see Knight, *From 1888 to Apostasy* and *Angry Saints* and George R. Knight, *A User-friendly Guide to the 1888 Message* (Hagerstown, Md.: Review and Herald, 1998). For a survey that skews the whole issue toward the polar position of forensic justification, see Paxton, *The Shaking of Adventism*.

[88] Berkouwer, *Faith and Sanctification*, p. 9; Berkouwer, *Faith and Justification*, p. 100; Denney, *Christian Doctrine of Reconciliation*, pp. 297, 300. (Italics supplied.)

[89] Calvin, *Institutes*, 3.16.1.

[90] William E. Hulme, *The Dynamics of Sanctification* (Minneapolis: Augsburg, 1966), p. 47.

[91] Macquarrie, *Principles of Christian Theology*, p. 343.

[92] Stewart, *A Man in Christ*, pp. 147, 152, 153.

[93] Dieter, "The Wesleyan Perspective," in *Five Views on Sanctification*, p. 35; Forsyth, *Justification of God*, p. 221.

[94] Murray, *Redemption Accomplished and Applied*, pp. 170, 171.

Chapter 5

# More on Sanctification

"At last," says the Pharisee, "this book is getting to the 'real stuff' of sal-vation. We are finished with the milk for newborn babes in Christ, and are ready for the meatier stuff of mature Christian living. Now that we have examined the rather insignificant basement of salvation (justification and its related entities), we are ready to build the mansion of sanctification, and, better yet, perfection. God has done His part—now it is time to do ours."

All too often this type of thinking has dominated the attitude of sin-cere Christians. Thus, as Gerhard Forde puts it, "Sanctification enters the picture . . . to rescue the good ship Salvation from shipwreck on the rocks of Grace Alone." Pharisaic talk about sanctification can be dangerous, Forde suggests, because "it misleads and seduces the old being into think-ing it is still in control."[1] *Satan's master temptation, "You will be like God" (Gen. 3:5), still appeals to the human heart. Self has a hard time staying on its cross.*

Post-justification Christian living faces several major dangers. The first is antinomianism—the doctrine that Christ's death somehow did away with the law and thus the moral structure of the universe. In antinomian thinking the Christian has no obligation to keep the law, since he or she is not "under law" (Rom. 6:15).

The opposite danger is to make the gospel into a new law. For advo-cates of this way of thinking, the very essence of Christian life is some form of law keeping. For certain individuals it is monkish asceticism, while for others it may be dietary perfectionism, but for all the new law becomes a fetish that stands at the center of their religious experience. "Mankind," penned Leon Morris, "has a fiendish ingenuity in discovering ways of bringing itself into bondage."[2]

A third way to jump the track in thinking about sanctification is to emphasize total passiveness on the part of the Christian—"Jesus does it all."

I used to hold that position, but finally concluded that it could not account for the many imperatives sprinkled through the pages of the New Testament, such as "fight," "strive," "work," and so on.

A fourth way to misunderstand sanctification is to confound it with justification, as if it were an aspect of justification. People holding this position have generally confused the biblical texts that speak of instantaneous sanctification (being set apart by God for holy living) with the theological concept of progressive sanctification. In this way of thinking, sanctification (like justification) is a vicarious entity. Rather than being something that God does *in* us, sanctification is also something Christ did *for* us. To John Wesley, the teaching of vicarious holiness was "the masterpiece of Satan." He held that holiness is both inward and outward.[3]

The present chapter will seek to steer a safe course through the many shoals that beset the important topic of progressive sanctification. We will discuss such issues as the meaning and essence of sanctification in a Christian's daily existence, the role of the Holy Spirit in sanctification, the place of human effort and "works," the nature of "good" and "bad" works, the place of deeds in the final judgment, and the relationship of prayer and other "means of grace" to the sanctification process.

Before moving to a definition, we should remember a few cautions. First, we can never separate progressive sanctification from justification in real life. Second, at the heart of sanctification is union with Christ. Christian behavior flows out of a vital relationship with Christ. "Good" behavior not rooted in a faith relationship may be moral, but it is not Christian. Lastly, *living as a Christian in terms of lifestyle and behavior adds nothing to a person's salvation in Christ. At the very most, such living is a response to having been saved by Christ.*

### Growth in Christ

We noted in chapter 4 that the beginning of the Christian life is closely associated with being born from above (John 3:3, 7). Paul uses the same metaphor to discuss Christian living. His most complete discussion of the topic appears in Romans 6.

The first five chapters of Romans cover the depth of sin, the uselessness of the law to solve the sin problem, and the necessity of justification by faith as the sinner's only hope in the face of human helplessness and the condemning function of the law. At the beginning of Romans 6 Paul poses a question that naturally arises from his teaching that God graciously forgives people while they are still sinners. If grace is a good thing, he queries, then wouldn't it be good for Christians to continue to sin so that grace could multiply (Rom. 6:1)?

Paul's answer is emphatically negative: "By no means! How can we who died to sin still live in it?" Christianity, he continues, means more than merely a death to the old way of life. The very ordinance of baptism that symbolizes a person's outward acceptance of Christ has two implicit meanings: (1) A person who has crucified the self has buried the old way of self and sin, but (2) beyond the negative of death and burial of the old way is the resurrection to the new way of life in Christ Jesus. Thus Christians are to "walk in newness of life" (verses 1-4).

Union with Christ means having access to His resurrection power. Christians, therefore, no longer need to "be enslaved to sin" (verses 5-11). Because of God's empowering grace, they are free from the dominion of sin. They are to yield themselves to Him "as men who have been brought from death to life," and they are to surrender their "members [bodily parts] to God as instruments of righteousness" (verses 12-14).

Grace-empowered Christians are to be "obedient from the heart" and "slaves of righteousness" rather than slaves to sin. Just as they once gave themselves to impurity, they are now to submit themselves "to righteousness for sanctification" (verses 15-19).

Romans 6 presents a radical and revolutionary view of Christian living that affects every aspect of thought and behavior. James Stewart, in commenting on that chapter, writes that *"union to Jesus means an end and a beginning more absolute and clear-cut and radical than any other transformation in the world. . . . To be united with Christ means to be identified with Christ's attitude to sin.* It means seeing sin with Jesus' eyes, and opposing it with something of the same passion" as Christ at Calvary.[4]

Not only do born from above Christians have a new attitude toward sin, but they also possess a new perspective on righteousness. Luther made that point graphically clear when he wrote that as a Christian "you must have as great a desire for chastity as you had for fornication."[5]

Even though sanctification may begin with the heart, it cannot but lead to changes in a person's entire daily life. Peter summed it up nicely when he noted that Christ "bore our sins in his body on the tree, that we might die to sin and live to righteousness" (1 Peter 2:24).

The Bible pictures progressive sanctification as a dynamic growth process. *"Grow,"* admonishes Peter, "in the grace and knowledge of our Lord and Savior Jesus Christ" (2 Peter 3:18). Note that the text does not suggest that we are to grow *into* grace, but to progress *in* grace. One is infilled with empowering grace at the point of initial sanctification. Progressive sanctification is a continuous developmental experience through the aid of divine grace.

Peter can therefore write that "his divine power has granted to us all things that pertain to life and godliness, through the knowledge of him who called us to his own glory and excellence. . . . Make every effort to supplement your faith with virtue, and virtue with knowledge, and knowledge with self-control, and self-control with steadfastness, and steadfastness with godliness, and godliness with brotherly affection, and brotherly affection with love" (2 Peter 1:3, 5-8).

Paul presents the same dynamic process of maturation when he admonishes Christians "to grow up in every way into him who is the head" (Eph. 4:15). Christians are those "being changed into his likeness from one degree of glory to another" (2 Cor. 3:18). Their faith is to be "growing abundantly" (2 Thess. 1:3), and their love should "abound more and more" (Phil. 1:9). The dynamic process of sanctification is to affect every aspect of the Christian's life— "spirit and soul and body" (1 Thess. 5:23).

Sanctification's effects will manifest themselves in both the inner mind and outward behavior. One result will be a clearer understanding of our true condition. C. S. Lewis perceptively observed that "when a man is getting better, he understands more and more clearly the evil that is still in him. When a man is getting worse, he understands his own badness less and less."[6]

Sanctification also affects the Christian's total behavioral experience. "Luther," penned Dietrich Bonhoeffer, "had said that grace alone can save; his followers took up his doctrine and repeated it word for word. But they left out its invariable corollary, the obligation of discipleship." We must never forget that the confession of the primitive Christian church was not of Jesus as Savior but of Jesus as Lord. "To make Christ Lord," John Stott asserts, "is to bring every department of our public and private lives under his control."[7] Because we were "bought with a price," Paul claimed, we are to "glorify God" (1 Cor. 6:20).

Progressive sanctification is a vital step in the process of salvation. As Ellen White says, "The sinner is not saved *in* his sins, but *from* his sins." James Stalker implied much the same thing when he wrote that "St. Paul's whole teaching revolves between the two poles of righteousness through the death of Christ for us and holiness through the life of Christ in us."[8]

A great deal of theology has seen justification as providing "one's title to heaven" and sanctification as being a person's "fitness" for heaven. A second prominent theme is that justification saves from the guilt and penalty of sin, while sanctification delivers from the power of sin.[9]

One important question that has faced Christians for the past 2,000 years is, "If Christ won the victory for us on Calvary, why do we feel pulled and pushed toward both sin and righteousness in our daily lives? If we have been born again, shouldn't our thoughts and actions all be pure and holy?"

## The Tension in Christian Living Between the Ideal and the Real

That problem was highlighted for me a few years ago while teaching a course in philosophy. The class contained a Muslim graduate student under sponsorship from the government of Saudi Arabia. My student friend was beginning to talk about Christianity in my office on a regular basis. Then one week he reported to me that he had attended for the first time a Christian (Baptist, in this case) church, but had come away perplexed.

The source of his confusion was that he had seen the preacher "dunk" someone under the water and then declare him to be a "new person." My Muslim friend was not only astounded at the "dunking," but was even more concerned about the "new person" proclamation. After all, he claimed, the individual baptized looked like the same one who went under the water.

That experience highlighted for me the fact that it sometimes takes "alien eyes" for us to see into the deeper things that those raised in a Christian culture take for granted in their daily lives. The baptized person is in some respects a new person, but in other aspects she or he is the same old individual.

The Bible teaches that the new Christian has a new relationship to God and a new mind, heart, and set of attitudes toward sin and righteousness. But, on the other hand, the newly baptized person also continues to exist in the same body. He or she still has the same wife or husband and even retains his or her previous characteristics and personality. The new Christian is new, yet not new! And therein lies a problem—a tension between the old and the new.

As a result, the New Testament often sees the Christian as being in a state of war with the forces of evil. Thus Paul can admonish Timothy to "fight the good fight of faith" (1 Tim. 6:12, KJV). A Christian must struggle with both the temptation to follow the old habit patterns and the devil, who "prowls around like a roaring lion, seeking some one to devour"

(1 Peter 5:8). Christians are called upon to "resist the devil" (James 4:7; cf. Eph. 4:27).

Paul vividly describes the heart of the Christian's warfare in Galatians 5:16, 17: "Walk by the Spirit, and do not gratify the desires of the flesh. For the desires of the flesh are against the Spirit, and the desires of the Spirit are against the flesh; for these are opposed to each other."

The battle symbolism is a running motif throughout the New Testament. Paul refers to Timothy as "a good soldier of Christ Jesus" (2 Tim. 2:3) and suggests that Christians should be armed with "the weapons of righteousness" (2 Cor. 6:7) and clothed in the "whole armor of God" (see Eph. 6:10-17). The apostle John can likewise write of the rewards of those who "conquer" in the Christians' warfare (Rev. 2:7, 11, 17, 26; 3:5, 12, 21).

While it would be wonderful if the Christian life was one of instantaneous and total victory over every aspect of sin in one's life, that is hardly the biblical picture. Paul, therefore, could write that he was not "already perfect" (Phil. 3:12), and John could flatly state that any Christian who claimed to be without sin made God "a liar" (1 John 1:10). Because Christians continue to sin after baptism, they can rejoice that they have "an advocate with the Father" to continue to mediate forgiveness in the heavenly sanctuary (1 John 2:1).

Christ won the victory over Satan and sin on the cross for every person who accepts Him by faith. He conquered the devil through His life, death, and resurrection. The challenge for the Christian is not to win the victory that Christ has already won, but to stay united to the Victor.

John Stott put his finger on the heart of the problem we have been discussing when he observed that "though the devil has been defeated, he has not yet conceded defeat. Although he has been overthrown, he has not yet been eliminated. In fact he continues to wield great power. This is the reason for the tension we feel in both our theology and our experience." James M. Gustafson spoke to the issue when he wrote that "Christ has won the decisive battle." "Ultimate victory is no longer in doubt, but the 'mopping up' operations must continue until the end."[10]

Those "mopping up" operations take place not only in the universe at large, but in the life of every Christian believer. The first is the scene of the great conflict between Christ and Satan in macrocosm, while the second is the same battle in microcosm. "The warfare against self," the "greatest battle . . . ever fought," will continue until the second coming of Jesus.[11]

Fortunately, the Bible applies the victory to the individual Christian. Sin, notes Paul, no longer has "dominion" over believers (Rom. 6:14). They do not need to have sin "reign" in their mortal bodies as long as they stay yielded to God (verses 12, 13). For those "in Christ," sin has changed from a reigning monarch to an illegal alien with no rights, but it still is not easily removed. As John Murray put it, "There is a total difference between *surviving sin* and *reigning sin*, the regenerate in conflict with sin and the unregenerate complacent to sin. . . . *It is one thing for the enemy to occupy the capital; it is another for his defeated hosts to harass the garrisons of the kingdom.*"[12]

Justification, regeneration, and initial sanctification provide believers with a new attitude toward sin, but do not alter established traits of character or habits.

Ellen White reinforces the Bible writers by stating that as Christians "we may make mistakes, but we will hate the sin that caused the sufferings of the Son of God." Again, she wrote, "the Christian will feel the promptings of sin, but he will maintain a constant warfare against it."[13]

Those "promptings of sin" are closely related to what Ellen White referred to as "propensities to evil" or a "bent to sin" and Paul thought of as the pull of "the flesh." What takes place at conversion is a complete change of spiritual direction, rather than an immediate transformation of habit patterns. That shift is a gradual process. R. N. Flew helps us at this point when he writes that "for most believers their sins are not fleeting visitations, but expressions of some habit."[14]

Maxie Dunnam claims that while "habits that have been years in the making may be put aside by a transforming experience of Christ," "these habits sometimes [often, is probably more accurate] have a residual hold on us." When we are in trial or when things get tough or frustrating, "we are tempted [often below the level of conscious choice] to turn back to the old ways" as we respond to a situation.[15]

One of the functions of progressive sanctification is to bring a Christian's habit patterns into line with his or her attitude toward sin. That is the constant work of a lifetime. John Wesley referred to the process as a gradual mortification (putting to death) of the old ways.[16] Paul is referring to that gradual process when he writes that a person who has "put on the new nature . . . *is being renewed* in knowledge after the image of its creator" (Col. 3:10).

Because sin continues in believers, so must confession, sanctification, and justification. The mind and will are changed through God's grace immediately at the time of a person's acceptance of Christ, the habits and character are progressively transformed throughout a Christian's life, and the sinful nature will finally be dealt with at the resurrection (chapter 10 will treat this last topic at some length).

## Moving Beyond "Clothesline" Sanctification

In this section we will examine the essence of sanctified living—one of the most confused topics in most people's thinking.

Before examining the central core of the sanctified life, we should look at some dangerous misconceptions about it. The first views sanctification as following a list of dos and don'ts. Thus, for some Christians, the essence of sanctified living is a matter of not eating between meals or not wearing certain types of clothing. Christian living for such people degenerates into rigidly following a list of rules much like those kept by the Pharisees of old.

Closely related to the list approach is another favorite of the Pharisees—looking at the sanctified life in the negative. That is, people become "holy" by what they avoid. Edward Heppenstall puts us right on that point when he writes that "the most important thing is not what we are saved from but what we are redeemed for. Redemption in Christ is never an escape from life. We are saved from sin in order to live for Christ."[17]

For too many, Christian living consists in seeking to be "good by not being bad" and by building moral fences so that they will have the security of knowing just where to stop in their approach to what might be considered a sin.[18] Such a view of sanctification is much closer to the mentality of the Pharisees than it is to New Testament Christianity.

At the heart of all false avenues to sanctified living is a trivialization of righteousness through a breaking up of the righteous life into manageable blocks of behavior. Such an approach is directly related to the atomization of sin that we discussed earlier. It lends itself nicely to "clothesline preaching" and making such items as dietary reform and a person's outward dress the things to focus on in discussions of living the Christian life. That type of "sanctification" has an excellent historic pedigree, having been at the center of Pharisaic Judaism.

*The "benefit" in the trivialization of sanctification and negative approaches to the topic is that they lower the standard to the place where it is conceivably possible to perfectly obey the law.* Jesus, however, did a "hatchet job" on trivialization in the Sermon on the Mount, in which He highlighted the depth and unity of the law by relating it to the law's underlying principles. When He told His listeners that their righteousness must exceed that of the scribes and Pharisees

(Matt. 5:20), He was advancing them to a higher standard than that provided for by the atomization of righteousness and a list of dos and don'ts.

Christianity is a "recasting of the soul," rather than merely a way of life or a set of new habits. As a result, Christianity is "salvation from selfishness," even from the selfishness of feeling proud about our good deeds and lifestyle improvements.[19] *Thus Christianity represents salvation from SIN and not merely salvation from sins.*

According to the Bible, the essence of sanctification is a total transformation of heart that leads to a change of life that includes the way we treat and view ourselves, our neighbors, and God. Progressive sanctification is the process by which the Holy Spirit turns selfishness and self-love into love to God and other people in daily living.

*Sanctification is nothing less than the process by which Christians become progressively more loving.* It is therefore not surprising to find Jesus claiming that the whole of the Old Testament legal structure is really built upon the principles of love to God and love to other people (Matt. 22:34-40). Likewise, the only two men who ever asked Jesus what they needed to do to be saved were told to love their neighbor in Christian service without reserve (Matt. 19:21, 22; Luke 10:25-37). Our Lord even went so far as to claim that the only way people will know if they are His disciples is if they "have love for one another" (John 13:35).

Paul hammered home Christ's message again and again. He advised the Colossians above all things to "put on love, which binds everything together in perfect harmony" (Col. 3:14). "The whole law," he wrote to the Galatians, "is fulfilled in one word, 'You shall love your neighbor as yourself'"(Gal. 5:14; cf. Rom. 13:8, 10). He then went on to contrast the works of the flesh and the fruit of the Spirit. The first set is built on selfishness, while the characteristics of the second (being in the singular— "fruit") all flow out of *agapē* love (Gal. 5:22, 23).

With those Bible passages in mind, it is not surprising to find Vincent Taylor defining sanctification as "perfect love," Wesleyan theologians suggesting that sanctification is "love in action," or Ellen White informing her readers that "true sanctification means perfect love, perfect obedience, perfect conformity to the will of God."[20] In tying perfect love to perfect obedience, she is following the lead of Paul and Jesus in pointing out that one who loves fulfills the law in all its aspects.

Mildred Wynkoop appears to be on track when she writes that the *agapē (self-giving) love of the Christian "is a quality of a person. . . . It is a principle by which one orders life." The Christian who is being sanctified comes more and more to live by the two great principles of God's law. Love to God and neighbor become the spring from which flow the rest of life's activities. Obedience not based on love, Ellen White suggests, is founded on selfishness.*[21]

Christian freedom is never freedom in an irresponsible sense, but rather the opportunity "through love [to] be servants of one another" (Gal. 5:13). John Stott asserts that not only does discipleship to Jesus bring every part of a Christian's life under His control, but that such discipleship is a call to service. Thus "no Christian can live for himself any longer."[22]

Unfortunately for the cause of truly balanced sanctification, Edward Heppenstall observes, "it is easier to sacrifice oneself on the altar of religious extremism than to love God and to love the unlovable."[23]

*The call to the present age is not for a lower level of righteousness, but a higher. Itemized and trivialized righteousness is no more adequate today than when Christ upbraided the Pharisees for aiming too low in His Sermon on the Mount.*

When love becomes *the* principle of life, it will not be divorced from "good works." To the contrary, Leon Morris suggests, Christian love becomes the foundation of good works.[24] It is to that topic we now turn. After examining the role of the Holy Spirit in the daily outworking of the Christian life, we will explore the human aspect and the part played by works, or deeds, in the developing Christian experience.

### The Holy Spirit's Task in Sanctification

The New Testament leaves little doubt that sanctification is the responsibility of the Holy Spirit. Peter writes that Christians are "sanctified by the Spirit for obedience to Jesus Christ" (1 Peter 1:2), and Paul tells us that it is God who sanctifies (1 Thess. 5:23; cf. Rom. 15:16). It was in the context of the promise of the gift of the Spirit that Jesus said, "Apart from me you can do nothing" (John 15:5). And the greatest human accomplishments are called the "fruit of the Spirit" (Gal. 5:22, 23).

With those teachings in mind, Carl Henry could write that "the Spirit is the dynamic principle of Christian ethics, the personal agency whereby God powerfully enters human life and delivers man from enslavement to Satan, sin, death, and law. The Spirit of God is not listed under 'others' in the *dramatis personae* of redemption. He is a main character whose role is crucial for the life of holiness in all its phases."[25]

Those born of the Spirit also live their developing and growing Christian lives in the power of that same divine Person. Progressive sanctification is best viewed as a continuation of the work begun by the Holy Spirit in regeneration.

Speaking of persons who do not understand the ongoing activity of the Spirit, Ellen White wrote that "many have an idea that they must do some part of the work alone. They have trusted in Christ for the forgiveness of sin, but now they seek by their own efforts to live aright. But every such effort must fail."[26]

Human effort is doomed to failure. If individuals do not succeed, they will become spiritually discouraged, but if they do have some success, they face the temptation of spiritual pride—the most hopeless of all sins. Thus it is both dangerous and impossible for Christians to work out their own holiness.

Paul discovered a basic secret of Christian living when he learned that God's power was "made perfect in weakness." The apostle could say that he was strong when he was weak because it was then that he let God's power work in his life (2 Cor. 12:9, 10). The apostle had a similar thought in mind when he wrote that "it is no longer I who live, but Christ who lives in me" through the gift of His Holy Spirit (implied in Gal. 2:20). Again, when he admonished the Philippians to "work out your own salvation," he quickly added that God was at work in them "both to will and to work for his good pleasure" (Phil. 2:12, 13).

G. C. Berkouwer, in commenting on Philippians 2:12, 13, notes that "progress in sanctification never meant working out one's own salvation under one's own auspices; on the contrary, it meant working out one's own salvation with a rising sense of dependence on God's grace."[27]

Berkouwer's point is a crucial one for Christians to understand, since there are two ways to view a person's relationship to the Spirit in progressive sanctification. One leads to an increasing independence from Christ's grace as a person becomes more and more like God. Such a model suggests that sanctified Christians will someday be able to stand on their own without Christ because they have become like God.

The second way of relating to the Holy Spirit in sanctification implies an ever-increasing dependence upon Him. The more people in this category realize their helplessness and weakness, the more they pray for God's power in their lives. This second model is the one found in the Bible. On that point, Ellen White suggests that "all our good works are dependent on a power outside of ourselves. . . . Only by constant renunciation of self and dependence on Christ can we walk safely."[28]

The continual outpouring of the Spirit reflects a major aspect of Christ's heavenly ministry. A first function is continuous forgiveness through His mediation. The second is continuous empowerment through the gift of the Spirit so that forgiven and born from above Christians can live Christian lives. Both are God's grace to us. Failure in Christian living is in a large measure a failure to appropriate the gift of the Holy Spirit.

At this point we are led to wonder about the human part in the plan of salvation. What about "works" and human "effort"? It is to those topics that we now turn.

## What About Works?

A story tells of the Lutheran pastor who based his deathbed confidence that he would be in heaven on the fact that "he could not remember ever having done a good work in his life!"[29]

His point, of course, was that he had been totally saved at justification. While such a statement would not seem altogether strange coming from a Lutheran pastor, it would be quite out of the thinking of many Adventist ministers, some of whom have tended toward the opposite extreme.

We will come back to our Lutheran friend, but first we need to examine a few Bible texts on the topic.

Paul, the great apostle of salvation by grace through faith without works of the law, clearly indicates that faith, far from overthrowing the law, actually establishes it (Rom. 3:31). The book of Romans, in fact, leads its readers through the entire process of being saved, all the way from being forensically justified (legally being counted righteous) to living out the principles of the law in their daily lives. The great ethical chapters of Romans 12-14, with all their advice on Christian living and fulfilling the law, are actually the climax to the book. God saves and empowers individuals so that they can live truly Christian lives in the daily world.

In like manner, the great salvation passage in Ephesians 2 goes out of its way to point out that we are saved "by grace . . . through faith" and not of works ("lest any man should boast"), and continues on to claim that Christians are "created *in* Christ Jesus *for* good works . . . that we should walk in them" (verses 8-10).

James, of course, is notorious for having declared that "a man is justified by works and not by faith alone" (James 2:24). Luther, coming out of works-oriented medieval Catholicism, could not see how James's book could be a part of the biblical canon. The apostle was not on Luther's list of approved theologians.

Modern scholars, however, generally see no conflict between James and Paul. Rather, they suggest that the two apostles were speaking to different audiences and placed their emphases on different parts of a shared gospel. Both saw an integral connection between the way a Christian believes and the way he or she lives. "Faith alone justifies," Peter Toon writes, "but the faith that justifies is not alone." Thus J. H. Ropes tells us in his important commentary on James that faith not matched by works is an "incomplete faith." Works show "that the faith had always been of the right kind, and so 'completed' it."[30] The apostle James summed up the New Testament teaching on the topic nicely when he wrote that "faith by itself, if it has no works, is dead" (James 2:17, cf. verse 26).

The sixteenth-century Reformers also saw the unity of faith and works—even Luther when he was not overreacting against his own works-oriented monkhood. Thus he could declare in his preface to Romans that "it is a living, busy, active, mighty thing, this faith; and so it is impossible for it not to do good works incessantly. . . . It is impossible to separate works from faith, quite as impossible as to separate heat and light [from] fires."[31]

John Calvin wrote in a similar vein that "Christ justifies no one whom he does not at the same time sanctify. . . . He bestows both of them at the same time, the one never without the other. Thus . . . it is that we are justified not without works yet not through works."[32]

As a result, although Calvin and Luther taught justification by faith alone, they never advocated justification by faith without works—an impossibility. According to William Barclay, "One of the most dangerous of all religious tendencies is to talk as if faith and works were entirely different and separate things. There can be no such thing as a faith which does not issue in works."[33]

Thomas Oden also helps us on this topic when he points out that "classical Christianity has concerned itself not merely with toothless talk of God's pardon, but more so with a supportive community and a structure for moral development by which that pardon might become appropriated in the life of responsible love."[34]

That thought brings us back to the Lutheran pastor whom we met at the beginning of this section—the one who "knew" he would be in heaven because "he could not remember ever having done a good work in his life." Lutherans traditionally have had a difficult time relating works with faith—sanctification with justification—because they have followed those of Luther's statements that were reactions or overreactions to salvation by works. Thus they placed their emphasis on the sum total of salvation being encapsulated in forensic or legal justification. Some Adventists, in the tradition of those who think they are following Desmond Ford, have taken the same path.

The argument of Lutheran scholar Gerhard Forde is therefore quite meaningful. After pointing out that Lutherans have too often found no bridge between redemption and Christian living (i.e., justification and progressive sanctification), he suggests that the problem rests in their "knee-jerk" overemphasis on the metaphor of forensic (legal) justification. While that metaphor is of utmost importance, Forde claims that it can never be discussed without the complementary metaphor of death and life. If justification is defined as "death before life," he argues, then sanctification is a "life beyond death." That is, works are a natural result of being born again in Christ at the point of forensic justification. Through the combination of those salvational metaphors, Forde brings both sides of Luther into balance in much the same way that we need to approach our reading of Paul.[35]

It is all too easy to have a "knee-jerk" reaction to the Pharisees of our own day who still follow the path of the ancient Jews and the medieval church in seeking to make works a part of the "pay" for our salvation. Beyond that, most of us probably also react against the residual Pharisee in our own skin. The answer, however, is not to swing from one metaphorical extreme to another, but to find the balance between them. *Salvation is by grace through faith without works, but salvation is never without works.*

## "Good" Works and "Bad" Works

OK, you may be saying by this time, if works are so good, why does the New Testament have so much to say against them? The answer is that it does not view all works from the same perspective. Rather it is especially set against at least three types of works: (1) works of the flesh (Rom. 8:3-10), which are the outworkings of the sinful nature; (2) works of the law (Rom. 3:28; Gal. 2:16; Eph. 2:9), which people carry out in the hope of gaining salvation; and (3) "dead works" (Heb. 6:1), which are the activities of individuals "out of relationship with the living God" and hence "devoid of the quickening power of grace."[36]

Over against those less-than-sanctified works, the New Testament places works of faith. Paul speaks approvingly of "faith working through love" (Gal. 5:6). He commends the Thessalonians' "work of faith and labor of love" (1 Thess. 1:3; cf. 2 Thess. 1:3). And part of his task was to call the Gentiles to "the obedience of faith" (Rom. 1:5; 16:26).

Jesus also made it plain that there were "good" works and "bad" works. For example, in Matthew 7, He tells of rejecting some in the final judgment who had done "many mighty works" in His name. But in the same passage He also says that "he who *does* the will" of His Father would be in the kingdom (verses 21, 22).

109

Paul clarifies the distinction between "good" and "bad" works when he says that "whatever does not proceed from faith is sin" (Rom. 14:23). Faith, remember, is being in a right relationship with God through Jesus.

A legalistic work is one done out of our own resources in an attempt to gain favor or salvation from God. On the other hand, works of faith flow out of a saving relationship with Jesus, are energized by the Holy Spirit, and are shaped and softened by the love of the Father. Works of faith flow out of justification and being born from above, while works of law seek to make a person right with God.

There is all the difference in the world between those two types of works. One is a self-conscious struggle to earn God's favor, while the other is a spontaneous reaction of the "saved" person. Luther helps us when he notes that "it is impossible for it [faith] not to do good works incessantly." Faith "does not ask whether there are good works to do, but before the question rises, it has already done them, and is always at the doing of them."[37]

An understanding of the correct relationship between works and justification (being put right with God), the new birth, and initial sanctification is crucial. A saved person does not work to get saved any more than "a tree produces fruit to prove that it is alive. A tree produces fruit because it is alive, not to prove that it is alive."[38]

"Good" works take no credit for themselves. They "should be quite as natural and spontaneous," Gerhard Forde writes, "as a parent running to pick up and comfort a child. . . . One doesn't stop to think about it ('Let me see now, should I do this or shouldn't I? Is it necessary?'); one doesn't even worry about whether it is a good work or not—one just does it. And after it is over, one forgets about it completely."[39] On the other hand, those involved in dead works and works of law are always desiring credit, recognition, and reward.

Ellen White highlights the importance of works of faith when she writes that "in order for man to retain justification, there must be continual obedience, through active, living faith that works by love and purifies the soul. . . . In order for man to be justified by faith, faith must reach a point where it will control the affections and impulses of the heart; and it is by obedience that faith itself is made perfect."[40]

The sequence of grace and deeds is crucial in the distinction between "good" and "bad" works. Both testaments constantly picture God as supplying the grace before expecting a response (e.g., Ex. 20:2, 3; Deut. 7:6-12; 1 Cor. 6:20; Gal. 5:1). Because of what He has done for them,

110

Christians are impelled and empowered to spread His love to their neighbors.[41]

The faith relationship is a dynamic one that motivates the Christian to serve others in the spirit and strength of Christ. The Christian life is one of service expressed in "faith working through love" (Gal. 5:6). Thus it is not one of monkish seclusion but a life for others. John Wesley picturesquely claimed that "'Holy Solitaries' is a phrase no more consistent with the Gospel than holy adulterers."[42] Works of faith are an integral part of the Christian's daily life.

That topic brings us to the issue of human effort in works of faith. Does God do it all, or do human beings somehow cooperate with Him in Christian works?

**What About Human Effort?**

Some Christian writers seem to imply that "Jesus does it all." All we have to do is surrender our lives to God, and He contributes all the effort. All our striving is striving to stay surrendered. That was the teaching of many of the holiness preachers of the past century, and one certainly gets that general impression from some of the writings of Morris Venden.[43]

I used to teach that the sum total of human works was striving to stay surrendered. While I still believe that the concept has much truth in it, I have come to the conclusion that it fails to do justice to either the richness of the biblical language on the topic or to daily experience.

The Bible is laced with words and stories that imply human effort beyond that required to stay surrendered. Moses, for example, (1) is commended for having "refused to be called the son of Pharaoh's daughter," (2) chosen to share the plight of the Israelites, (3) "suffered" for Christ, (4) "left Egypt," and (5) "endured" one problem after another (Heb. 11:23-28).

In addition, Jesus told the disciples to "seek" the kingdom of God (Matt. 6:33), and Paul tells us to "put to death" the works of the body, to present our bodies as a living sacrifice, and to "walk by the Spirit" while refusing to gratify the desires of the flesh (Rom. 8:13; 12:1, 2; Gal. 5:16). John, meanwhile, tells us that we should "keep" God's commandments (Rev. 14:12; cf. John 14:15; 15:10).

The New Testament is full of action words. The Bible picture is not one of the saints being carried to heaven on beds of ease. Neither does Scripture teach the efficacy of human effort separated from God's empowerment. "Apart from me," Christ said, "you can do nothing" (John 15:5). The picture is rather one of cooperation between God and human beings.

*Sin and Salvation*

Thus Paul can write, "I also labour, striving according to his working, which worketh in me mightily" (Col. 1:29, KJV), and "I can do all things in him who strengthens me" (Phil. 4:13).

The picture of cooperation also appears in the Old Testament. In Leviticus 20:7 the Lord tells the people of Israel to "sanctify" themselves, whereas the next verse claims that it is He who sanctifies His people (see 2 Cor. 7:1; cf. 1 Thess 5:23). Similarly, when the children of Israel were ready to cross the Red Sea, Moses instructed them to "'*stand firm,* and *see the salvation of the Lord, which he will work for you today.* . . . The Lord will fight for you, and *you have only to be still.*'" But then God commanded the people to "*go forward*" (Ex. 14:13-15). While He opened the way, He didn't carry the people. They crossed the dry seabed using their own effort.

*Thus there is a passive and an active element in our walk with God. First comes surrender, then comes Spirit-empowered action that requires human effort.*

Perhaps the clearest text on the interaction of God's working and human effort is Paul's admonition to the Philippians: "Work out your own salvation with fear and trembling; for God is at work in you, both to will and to work for his good pleasure" (Phil. 2:12, 13). That passage shows the active role of the Christian in putting forth effort, but it places human effort in the context of God's grace. John Murray makes that point clear when he writes that "*because* God works we work." Our working is not suspended because God works, nor does His work cease because we work, but Christian effort can take place only in the context of God's prior working in our heart and mind and in continuous union with the Holy Spirit. "Sanctification," writes Anthony Hoekema, "is a work of God in us that involves our responsible participation."[44]

With those thoughts in mind, it is no longer impossible (as it once was) for me to understand how the Revelator could refer to the fine-linen clothing of the saints at the end of time as "the righteous deeds of the saints" (Rev. 19:8). In commenting on that text, Robert Mounce claims that "this does not deny the Pauline doctrine of justification based on the righteous obedience of Christ (Rom. 5:18, 19), but suggests that a transformed life is the proper response the call of the heavenly bridegroom." George Eldon Ladd notes that "while the wedding garment is a divine gift," the Christian's relationship with salvation is a dynamic one. "The saints who are summoned to the Lamb's feast are those who have exercised steadfast endurance, who have kept the commandments of God, and have persevered in their faith in Jesus (Rev. 14:12)."[45]

"Conversion," J. C. Ryle explains, "is not putting a man in an arm-chair and taking him easily to heaven. It is the beginning of a mighty con-flict, in which it costs much to win the victory." The Christian life is a challenge to effort as long as life shall last. "Those who are waiting to be-hold a magical change in their characters without determined effort on their part to overcome sin," Ellen White penned, "will be disappointed." That effort, however, must always be in cooperation with God's empow-ering grace and within the faith relationship if it is to succeed. "All that man can do without Christ is polluted with selfishness and sin; but that which is wrought through faith is acceptable to God."[46]

In summary, human effort is important and needed. While such effort does not lead to salvation, it certainly flows from it. Bonhoeffer empha-sized that point when he suggested that "only those who obey believe." Bishop Ryle put it graphically when he wrote that one who holds that a Christian need not practice God's precepts in daily life "is really little bet-ter than a lunatic."[47]

Thus far in this chapter we have spent a great deal of time on human effort and "good" works. We will now examine the role of those works and efforts in the final judgment.

**Works in the Judgment**

Judgment has never been a popular subject with "normal" people, but, for better or worse, it is a fact of existence just as much as illness or death. Those topics, of course, have not been overly popular either, but denying their reality does not solve the threat they pose.

Now, it is not too difficult to see why nonbelievers find the idea of judgment distasteful, but for a Christian to get upset over the topic shows a lack of understanding concerning the purpose of divine judgment. It in-volves their vindication through confirmation that they are "in Christ." The good news is that there is "no condemnation for those who are in Christ Jesus" (Rom. 8:1). "If God is for us, who is against us? . . . It is God who justifies [counts righteous]; who is to condemn?" Christ "is at the right hand of God" to intercede "for us." Nothing can separate those "in Christ" from the love of God (verses 31-39; cf. Zech. 3:1-5). The Christian, therefore, can look forward to the final acts of judgment with peace and joy.

The fact of the final judgment is a pervasive scriptural teaching. My present point is to note that the intent of the final judgment is to deter-mine who is "in Christ." "He who has the Son," John wrote, "has life;

he who has not the Son of God has not life" (1 John 5:12; cf. John 5:24). "Everyone who looks to the Son and believes in him," claimed Jesus, "shall have eternal life, and I will raise him up at the last day" (John 6:40, NIV).

Being "in Christ," as we noted earlier, is a biblical phrase indicating a person's total relationship to God. It includes both justification (being counted righteous and put into a right relationship with God) and sanctification (being set aside for holy use and responding to God's love in ethical living through the empowerment of the Holy Spirit). All people are either in a faith relationship to God or in a sin (rebellion) relationship to Him.

Thus being "in Christ" as a focus of judgment is a relational evaluation. A person in Christ has accepted *both* His forgiving grace and His way of life. Those two items, as we noted in chapter 4, can never be separated.

The New Testament makes it clear that a person's daily life provides evidence for the final judgment. The Revelator tells us that the dead will be judged "by what they had *done*" (Rev. 20:12). Doing is important because a person "in Christ" will exhibit His actions. The fine linen of the saved, wrote John, "is the righteous *deeds* of the saints" (Rev. 19:8). For deeds to be righteous, of course, they have to be done within a faith relationship with Christ. The wedding garment of Matthew 22:1-14 should be thought of in terms of total salvation. Those who have put on Christ will be living the Christ life. In other words, in real life (as opposed to isolated theological speculation) justifying grace can never be separated from sanctifying grace. The person "in Christ" must have both. Thus, William Johnsson indicates, the judgment is essentially a pronouncement that men and women are righteous, that they are in a faith relationship to God.[48]

Both faith and obedience are central to the judgment. According to the Gospel of John, "He who *believes* in the Son has eternal life; he who does not *obey* the Son shall not see life, but the wrath of God rests upon him" (3:36).

Isolated belief does not indicate a saving relationship, nor do isolated works. Many of those lost will have done "many mighty works" in His name (Matt. 7:22). As Donald Bloesch points out, "We are to be judged according to our works," but not saved by them. Those "in Christ" will have both a relationship with their Lord and a life that reflects that relationship. "Works of faith" are the inevitable outgrowth of faith. "It is an evidence that a man is *not* justified by faith," Ellen White penned, "when his works do not correspond to his profession."[49]

Leon Morris notes that one of the great paradoxes of salvation is that salvation does not depend on anything we do, yet no one is saved without a faith response that includes "godly living."[50]

At this juncture it is important to highlight the fact that the judgment does not evaluate works from the perspective of the Pharisaic definitions of sin and righteousness or modern fundamentalism's clothesline approach to sanctification. Sin and righteousness, we noted earlier, are ways of relating to God and the principles of His character and law. The big mistake of the Pharisees was to atomize sin in such a way as to define it as an action rather than a total attitude and relationship to God. Once again, we remind ourselves that both the Pharisees and their modern heirs have tended to view God's law as a set of discrete negative prohibitions rather than a positive principle of love that must pervade every aspect of a person's being and life.

That whole approach has led to a view of judgment that itemizes sins and good acts in a misleading manner. As a result of that misconception, Ellen White can write of "many today [who] claim to obey the commandments of God, but . . . have not the love of God in their hearts to flow forth to others."[51]

Jesus definitely pictured the judgment as related to works. The sequence in Matthew 24 and 25 is of crucial importance here. Matthew 24 is His fullest presentation of the Second Coming, while chapter 25 consists of three parables integrally related to His return.

The first parable is that of the 10 virgins (Matt. 25:1-13). It alerts all Christians that they must watch and be ready for the Second Advent. The next parable, that of the talents (verses 14-30), suggests that Christians must work and use their talents as they watch in readiness for Christ's return.

The last parable (verses 31-46), that of the judgment of the sheep and the goats, indicates the *kind of works* that God will be looking for in the final judgment. Shockingly, at least from the perspective of the Pharisees and others with legal orientations to works and atomized views of sin in His audience, Jesus fails to uplift flawless Sabbath keeping or dietary rigidity. Rather, His focus in the judgment will be on whether people have internalized *agapē* love in their hearts—whether they have actively cared for their neighbors when they were hungry, sick, and in prison. That is *the* point of the judgment.

Ellen White makes the same point crystal clear when, in commenting on the parable of the sheep and the goats, she says that Jesus represented the decisions of the judgment "as turning upon *one point*. When the nations

115

are gathered before Him, there will be but two classes, and their eternal destiny will be determined by what they have done or have neglected to do for Him in the person of the poor and suffering."[52]

That judgmental process is not salvation by works, but an evaluation of a response to God's love. A lack of a response indicates no reception of that love, no transformation of the character by love through the power of the Spirit.

Sanctification begins with the renewing of a person's heart at the time of initial salvation. The progressive aspects of sanctification center on an internalization of the loving, serving, caring character of Christ and a gradual eradication of the old characteristics that reflected such attributes as selfishness, Pharisaic hardness of heart, and judgmentalism.

The spirit of our daily actions, therefore, is important, because "actions repeated form habits, habits form character, and by the character our destiny for time and for eternity is decided."[53]

**Sanctification and the "Means of Grace"**

The means of grace are the avenues through which earthlings receive God's grace. Some have thought of them as a sort of "magical" event, as when a baby is baptized and immediately is freed from the guilt it was supposedly born with or when the saying of a mass confers special blessings regardless of the recipient's attitudes and life.

Partaking of communion, being baptized, reading the Bible, praying, or hearing the Word of God being preached have no inherent merit or magic in them. Yet, when *coupled with faith*, each of those activities becomes a means by which God reaches out and imparts His grace to His people.

Spiritual growth is no more automatic than physical growth. Just as on the physical plane one must eat, drink, and exercise to maintain health and growth, so certain activities on the spiritual plane promote vitality. "Grace," Ellen White points out, "can thrive only in the heart that is being constantly prepared. . . . The thorns of sin will grow in any soil; they need no cultivation; but grace must be carefully cultivated."[54]

God's primary means of grace is the Bible, from which we derive our knowledge of Christ. Thus Peter can plead with the recipients of his letters to "grow in grace, and in the knowledge of our Lord and Saviour Jesus Christ" (2 Peter 3:18, KJV). Again, he wrote, "Desire the sincere milk of the word, that ye may grow thereby" (1 Peter 2:2, KJV; cf. Col. 1:10; John 17:17). When received in faith, the message of the Bible "will regulate the desires, purify the thoughts, and sweeten the disposition. It quickens the faculties of the mind and the energies of the soul. It enlarges the capacity for feeling, for loving."[55]

It is impossible to grow in Christ without imbibing the Word of God through personal study, hearing the Word being preached, and meditating upon it.

God has chosen the Bible in relationship to the enlightening guidance of the Holy Spirit to be the primary means of grace. John wrote his book in order that his readers "may believe that Jesus is the Christ, the Son of God, and that believing" they "may have life in his name" (John 20:31; cf. 2 Tim. 3:15). Those who have the Word possess "the keys of the kingdom of heaven" (Matt. 16:19; cf. Luke 11:52; John:17:3). Bible reading, preaching, and evangelism are therefore channels of grace.

Another important means of grace is prayer—defined by some as the breath of the soul. "Prayer," Ellen White penned, "is the key in the hand of faith to unlock heaven's storehouse."[56] No one can be strong in Christ without a regular devotional life. Such devotional life is a special time when we not only meditate upon God and His love, but daily reconsecrate ourselves to Him.

Other avenues of grace include participating meaningfully in the Lord's Supper and other symbolic events of the church and fellowshipping with other Christians in worship, outreach, and certain forms of recreation. God communicates His truth, knowledge, and love in many ways, and He wants His children to receive all the benefit they can.

But we must never forget that it is possible to pray long, study the Bible diligently, and be "fanatics for the church" and still be lost. Such was the case with the Pharisees of old. They rigorously studied both the Bible and the "straight testimony" of their oral tradition without ever coming to know God or His softening love. Such practices failed to be a means of grace to them because they were not received in the context of a humble and receptive faith relationship. That possibility still exists.

We should also note that God's means of grace do not function when their focus is merely inward. Bible reading and prayer become dysfunctional when the reason for such activities is that we can feel secure (if not proud and self-satisfied) that we have daily chalked up our "faithful hour" in meditating upon the life of Christ or bettered last year's "record" of "spiritual" accomplishment.

For God's means of grace to be effective, they must not only soften our hearts and transform our lives, but they must also lead to a life of service for others. Stagnant Christians are an impossibility, a contradiction in terms.

The means of grace only function as means of grace within a faith relationship enlivened and empowered by God's Spirit. Outside of that dynamic and that relationship, they are merely the reading and saying of good words and the doing of moral actions. Inside of that dynamic relationship, however, such activities are necessary ingredients to spiritual growth in progressive sanctification.

---

[1] Gerhard O. Forde, "The Lutheran View," in *Christian Spirituality*, pp. 15, 16.

[2] Morris, *The Atonement*, p. 126.

[3] Wesley, *Works*, vol. 10, p. 367.

[4] Stewart, *A Man in Christ*, pp. 192, 196. (Italics supplied before ellipsis points, but not after.)

[5] Luther, quoted in Althaus, *Theology of Martin Luther*, p. 140.

[6] C. S. Lewis, quoted in Wallenkampf, *Justified*, p. 81.

[7] Bonhoeffer, *Cost of Discipleship*, p. 53; John R. W. Stott, *Basic Christianity*, 2d ed. (Downers Grove, Ill.: InterVarsity, 1971), p. 113.

[8] Ellen G. White, *Faith and Works* (Nashville: Southern Pub. Assn., 1979), p. 31; James Stalker, *The Example of Jesus Christ* (New Canaan, Conn.: Keats, 1980), p. 11. (Italics supplied.)

[9] See, for example, Ryle, *Holiness*, p. 30; Ball, *English Connection*, p. 63; Ellen G. White, *Messages to Young People* (Nashville: Southern Pub. Assn., 1930), p. 35; Forsyth, *Work of Christ*, p. 221; Wesley, *Works*, vol. 2, p. 509; Hoekema, "The Reformed Perspective," in *Five Views on Sanctification*, p. 61.

[10] Stott, *Cross of Christ*, pp. 239, 240; Knight, *The Cross of Christ,* pp. 96-100; James M. Gustafson, *Christ and the Moral Life* (Chicago: University of Chicago Press, Phoenix edition, 1979), p. 21.

[11] White, *Steps to Christ*, p. 43.

[12] Murray, *Redemption Accomplished and Applied*, p. 145. (Italics supplied.)

[13] White, *Selected Messages*, book 1, p. 360; White, *The Great Controversy*, pp. 469, 470.

[14] Flew, *The Idea of Perfection*, pp. 395, 396. Cf. Venden, *95 Theses*, p. 92.

[15] Maxie D. Dunnam, *Exodus*, The Communicator's Commentary (Dallas: Word, 1987), p. 173. Cf. Thomas A. Davis, *How to Be a Victorious Christian* (Washington, D.C.: Review and Herald, 1975), p. 127.

[16] Wesley, *A Plain Account of Christian Perfection*, p. 90.

[17] Edward Heppenstall, *Salvation Unlimited: Perspectives on Righteousness by Faith* (Washington, D.C.: Review and Herald, 1974), p. 248.

[18] Venden, *95 Theses*, p. 25; Coleman, *Pharisees' Guide*, p. 16.

[19] H. D. McDonald, *The Atonement of the Death of Christ* (Grand Rapids: Baker, 1985), p. 16; W. L. Walker, *What About the New Theology?*, 2d ed. (Edinburgh: T. & T. Clark, 1907), pp. 155-164.

[20] Vincent Taylor, *Forgiveness and Reconciliation*, 2d ed. (London: Macmillan, 1946), pp. 170-179; Dieter, "The Wesleyan Perspective," in *Five Views on Sanctification*, p. 27; Wilber T. Dayton, "Entire Sanctification," in *A Contemporary Wesleyan Theology*, ed. Charles W. Carter (Grand Rapids: Zondervan, 1983), vol. 1, pp. 521-523; Ellen G. White, *The Acts of*

*the Apostles* (Mountain View, Calif.: Pacific Press, 1911), p. 565. Cf. White, *Christ's Object Lessons*, p. 360; White, *Selected Messages*, book 1, p. 337; White, *Signs of the Times*, May 19, 1890, pp. 289, 290.

[21] Mildred Bangs Wynkoop, *A Theology of Love* (Kansas City, Mo.: Beacon Hill Press of Kansas City, 1972), p. 33; White, *The Great Controversy*, pp. 467, 469; White, *The Desire of Ages*, p. 28.

[22] Stott, *Basic Christianity*, p. 113.

[23] Edward Heppenstall, "Let Us Go on to Perfection," in *Perfection: The Impossible Possibility* (Nashville: Southern Pub. Assn., 1975), p. 87.

[24] Leon Morris, *Testaments of Love: A Study of Love in the Bible* (Grand Rapids: Eerdmans, 1981), pp. 235-239.

[25] Carl F. H. Henry, *Christian Personal Ethics* (Grand Rapids: Eerdmans, 1957), p. 437.

[26] White, *Steps to Christ*, p. 69.

[27] Berkouwer, *Faith and Sanctification*, p. 112.

[28] White, *Christ's Object Lessons*, p. 160.

[29] Gerhard O. Forde, *Justification by Faith—A Matter of Death and Life* (Philadelphia: Fortress, 1982), p. 39.

[30] Berkouwer, *Faith and Justification*, pp. 130-139; Toon, *Justification and Sanctification*, p. 34; J. H. Ropes, *The Epistle of St. James,* The International Critical Commentary (Edinburgh: T. & T. Clark, 1916), p. 220.

[31] Martin Luther, *Commentary on Romans*, trans. J. T. Mueller (Grand Rapids: Kregel, 1976), p. xvii.

[32] Calvin, *Institutes*, 3.16.1.

[33] Barclay, *Romans*, p. 38.

[34] Thomas C. Oden, *After Modernity . . . What?* (Grand Rapids: Zondervan, 1990), p. 138.

[35] Forde, *Justification by Faith*, pp. 42, 19, 21, 39-59.

[36] Hugh Montefiore, *The Epistle to the Hebrews,* Harper's New Testament Commentaries (San Francisco, Harper & Row, 1964), p. 105.

[37] Luther, *Commentary on Romans*, p. xvii.

[38] Wallenkampf, *Justified*, p. 107. Cf. Taylor, *Forgiveness and Reconciliation*, p. 145.

[39] Forde, *Justification by Faith*, p. 55.

[40] White, *Selected Messages*, book 1, p. 366.

[41] For helpful discussions on the relationship between the indicative and the imperative in Paul, see Ridderbos, *Paul*, pp. 253-258; Ronald Y. K. Fung, *The Epistle to the Galatians*, The New International Commentary on the New Testament (Grand Rapids: Eerdmans, 1988), pp. 278-283.

[42] Wesley, *Works*, vol. 14, p. 321.

[43] E.g., Andrew Murray, *Absolute Surrender* (New York: Fleming H. Revell, 1897); Robert Pearsall Smith, *Holiness Through Faith* (New York: Anson D. F. Randolph & Co., 1870); Morris L. Venden, *Salvation by Faith and Your Will* (Nashville: Southern Pub. Assn., 1978).

[44] Murray, *Redemption Accomplished and Applied*, pp. 148, 149; Hoekema, "Response to Horton," in *Five Views on Sanctification*, p. 139.

[45] Robert H. Mounce, *The Book of Revelation*, The New International Commentary on the New Testament (Grand Rapids: Eerdmans, 1977), p. 340; George Eldon Ladd, *A Commentary on the Revelation of John* (Grand Rapids: Eerdmans, 1972), p. 249.

[46] Ryle, *Holiness*, p. 67; White, *Selected Messages*, book 1, pp. 336, 364. Cf. White, *Christ's Object Lessons*, p. 56.

[47] Bonhoeffer, *Cost of Discipleship*, p. 76; Ryle, *Holiness*, p. 26.

[48] William G. Johnsson, *Religion in Overalls* (Nashville: Southern Pub. Assn., 1977), p. 63. For a helpful discussion of judgment by works, see Berkouwer, *Faith and Justification*, pp. 103-112.

[49] Donald Bloesch, *Essentials of Evangelical Theology* (New York: Harper & Row, 1978), vol. 1, p. 184; White, *Selected Messages*, book 1, p. 397. (Italics supplied.)

[50] Leon Morris, *The Cross in the New Testament* (Grand Rapids: Eerdmans, 1965), pp. 390, 391. Cf. Edward Heppenstall, *Our High Priest* (Washington, D.C.: Review and Herald, 1972), p. 132.

[51] White, *Christ's Object Lessons*, p. 279.

[52] White, *The Desire of Ages*, p. 637. (Italics supplied.) Cf. Ellen G. White, *The Ministry of Healing* (Mountain View, Calif.: Pacific Press, 1942), pp. 104, 105.

[53] White, *Christ's Object Lessons*, p. 356.

[54] *Ibid.*, p. 50.

[55] *Ibid.*, p. 101.

[56] White, *Steps to Christ*, p. 94.

# Chapter 6

# Sanctification, Perfection, and the Example of Jesus

"Pharisaic athletes" are still alive and active in the twenty-first century. Of course, they no longer concern themselves with the size of a rock one can lawfully carry on the Sabbath day as did the historic Pharisees, nor are they following the pattern of Saint Simeon Stylites, who avoided temptation by having himself buried up to his neck in sand for several months and later by sitting atop a pole for several decades. But I can assure you that the program still exists.

Through the years I have heard reports of many of the modern variety. One has been so faithful in health reform (a nice area for accomplishment, since we can view both its sins and its righteous acts in terms of easily achieved, "bite-sized" chunks) that even though he is nearly six feet, six inches tall, he weighs less than 140 pounds. He is finding more and more things not to eat on his road to perfection. Even "pole-sitting Simeon" would have to be impressed with this person's accomplishment. I can personally identify with him, since in the first year after my conversion I went from 165 pounds to 120 in my striving to be the first perfect Christian since Christ.

It is often the paradox of *rigid* health reform that the better you get at it the less healthy you look. Many of the "spiritual athletes" I've met around the country look both yellow of skin and weak of body. I even heard of one who claims she has been so faithful that the healing processes of her body have slowed down significantly because of dietary rigor. An injury that should have healed in a few weeks has taken months to mend. One could certainly commend her for her faithfulness to an ideal, even though one may wonder what it has to do with health reform or Christianity. I have been under the "strange" impression that health reform should make persons stronger so that they can serve Christ better.

Other achievements relate to eating between meals. Some circles apparently view this vice as one of the ultimate sins. For example, a story tells of the lay pastor who faithfully took communion to shut-ins but refused to partake of the emblems with them, since that would be eating between meals. That particular bit of "faithfulness" especially intrigued me since Webster's definition of "communion" implies a sharing or a common participation in an event.

If one were to ask such individuals the rationale for such activity, they would probably reply that they were seeking to develop Christlike characters. Some might even indicate that when they have "perfectly reproduced" the "character of Christ," He will come again.[1] At any rate, that is what I used to tell people a few years back when I was more fully on that particular road to "Christlikeness."

Of recent years I have been somewhat troubled concerning how the biblical Jesus, who came "eating and drinking" and fellowshipping with "tax collectors and sinners" (Luke 7:34; 15:1, 2) in His reaching out "to seek and to save the lost" (Luke 19:10), could possibly be the model for such "spiritual" attitudes and activities as those listed above. I have also been perplexed over how to line up such approaches to Christianity with the apostle Paul, who flatly stated that "the kingdom of God is not food and drink but righteousness and peace and joy in the Holy Spirit" (Rom. 14:17).

The very word *joy* used in that text is remarkable, since I can often tell whom in a camp meeting audience is working hardest at perfection by the sullen expression on their faces. I get the message that being perfect is a frightfully serious business. Like the elder son (representing the Pharisees) in the parable of the prodigal, they can't bear too much joy, and they usually turn out to be just as critical as he was (Luke 15:25-32). To many such people, the word *celebration* is the most diabolical entry in the dictionary,[2] in spite of Paul's words in Romans 14:17 above and Jesus' repeated emphasis on joy and celebration in Luke 15 (see, for example, Luke 15:5, 6, 7, 9, 10, 20, 22, 23, 24, 25, 27, 30, 32). If we were to remove all the texts expressing joy and celebration in that chapter, its heart would be gone. The same appears to be true in the experience of many people. They think that because they live in the antitypical day of atonement, they have no right to rejoice. But if they are "in Christ" they ought to rejoice in their assurance of salvation—though, of course, if they are unsure whether they are living a life in Him, their lack of joy and celebration is understandable.

## Moving Beyond the Bad News Interpretation of the Good News

One of the tragedies of Christian history is the blaming of grotesque Christian living characteristics on being like Jesus and as being the way to overcome sin. Beyond the spiritual contortions of the early monks, we find those of the Middle Ages. Even in the twentieth century we find such "spiritual athletes" as Jesuit William Doyle inflicting upon himself great personal discomforts, including the wearing of a hair shirt, exposure to nettles and to freezing water at midnight, and lying on cold chapel stones. Of course, he had to deal with his healthy appetite—a perennial area of perfectionist concern across history. Doyle's notebook records in detail his many temptations with sugar, cake, honey, jam, and other delicacies: "Violent temptation to eat cake, resisted several times. Overcame desire to take jam, honey, and sugar. Fierce temptation to take cake, etc." "God has been urging me strongly all during this retreat to give up butter entirely."[3]

"Monasticism," R. N. Flew observes, "is the boldest organized attempt to attain to Christian perfection in all the long history of the Church." The motivation for such heroic endeavors was the imitation of Christ. Keeping their eyes on Christ was all-important, even if it destroyed human feelings. Cassian (ca. 360-430), for example, approvingly reports how a monk, after living in seclusion for 15 years, received a packet of letters from his parents and friends, but threw it into the fire unopened because the letters would draw his attention from heavenly things.[4]

The general spirit of such ideals has not restricted itself to the ancients and Roman Catholics. Evangelical Protestants have often reflected the same mentality, even though they may explain it in somewhat different terms. Stan Mooneyham, former president of World Vision, reports his own growing up in a fundamentalistic church, noting that he meets those who have had "a legalistic and judgmental gospel inflicted upon them early in life" almost everywhere he goes. Mooneyham aptly calls that religious approach "the 'bad-news' interpretation of the good news." The "bad news" mentality is seemingly obsessed with the "haunting fear that somebody, somewhere, is having a good time."[5]

Unfortunately, many people assume that that mentality is God's. C. S. Lewis relates the story of the schoolboy asked what he thought God was like. "He replied that, as far as he could make out, God was 'The sort of person who is always snooping round to see if anyone is enjoying himself and then trying to stop it.'"[6]

I can speak as an authority on this topic, because a few weeks after being baptized I met some zealous Adventists who helped me reach the same conclusion. It took several years and a desperate attempt to escape from the oppressiveness of my "Christianity" before I saw that my dismal judgmentalism and negativity were not related to the Jesus of the Bible. I, of course, had interpreted my attitude and outlook as being like that of Christ. Since then I have concluded that to live with that kind of Jesus throughout the ceaseless ages of eternity might be a better definition of hell than the fiery perdition described in the Bible.

When Peter and other New Testament writers said that Jesus is "our example," they used the Greek word *hypogrammos,* which literally means "to write under." It alludes to the elementary classroom, in which the teacher writes letters on one line and asks the child to copy them on the next line. Thus the New Testament, suggests Sinclair Ferguson, "is urging Christians to write the biography of their own lives with one eye on the lifestyle which Jesus had written. Imitation of the incarnate Savior is the essence of continuing sanctification."[7]

While it is true that God wants us to follow Christ's example, it is also true that He desires us to look to the Bible to find what that pattern consists of. And in following Christ, the Father would have us move beyond Pharisaic negativism and judgmentalism to the good news interpretation of the good news.

### Imitating Jesus: A New Testament Imperative

The New Testament is consistent in its insistence that the Christian should reflect Christ in holy living. Peter wrote that Jesus left an "example" so that others could "follow in his steps" (1 Peter 2:21). Elsewhere Peter added, "as he who called you is holy, be holy yourselves in all your conduct; since it is written, 'You shall be holy, for I am holy'" (1 Peter 1:15, 16). Jesus encouraged the attitude of imitation when He referred to Himself as "the way" (John 14:6). In fact, the first name for the Christian religion was "the Way" (see Acts 9:2; 19:9, 23; 22:4; 24:14, 22). After washing the disciples' feet, Jesus said: "I have given you an example, that you also should do as I have done to you" (John 13:15). To reflect the example of Jesus became an important part of "the Way." Christians were those who walked "in the same way in which he walked" (1 John 2:6). Thus Paul could urge the Corinthians to have "the mind of Christ" (1 Cor. 2:16) and commend the Thessalonians for being "imitators . . . of the Lord" (1 Thess. 1:6).

G. C. Berkouwer ties the imitation of Christ to progressive sanctification. "The imitation of Christ," he wrote, "is not merely a form of sanctification, one among several, but a description of its essence."[8] If that is so, it behooves us to explore the topic at this juncture in this book. First, however, it will be important to place imitation in the broader context of the plan of salvation.

We must never isolate imitation from God's justifying grace. Pelagius (died ca. 419) taught that Jesus was primarily an example of human perfection rather than a Savior from sin. He aimed at establishing a perfect church as an example to the sinful world. The possibility of developing that perfect church was based on the teaching that Adam's original sin had not bent the human will toward evil. Therefore, because people were born without a bias toward sin, they could live the sinless life by following the example of Christ. The Christian's task, Pelagius held, was to choose between the bad example of Adam and the good example of Jesus. Grace from that perspective was God encouraging and motivating one to do the right.[9] The central ideas of Pelagianism not only tended to encourage monasticism, but are still alive, as I earlier pointed out, in sectors of the Adventist community.

Those following the rationale of Pelagius not only downplay the magnitude of sin and its effects, but also overplay unaided human ability. Christianity, points out James Orr, is "distinctively a religion of Redemption." Following the example of Christ is not like following that of Buddha. Christianity is not the achieving of victory through prolonged striving for righteousness, but a religion of salvation, in which the death of Christ frees individuals from the guilt and penalty of sin in justification and from the power of sin in sanctification.[10]

Christ is an example for the Christian, but He is much more than that. He is first and foremost a Savior. Because Christians have been saved, they can follow His example through the gift of the Holy Spirit. As Luther put it, "Imitation does not make sons, but sonship makes imitators."[11]

The Bible leaves us in no doubt that Christians are to conquer as Christ did (Rev. 3:21), that they are to attain "to the measure of the stature of the fulness of Christ" (Eph. 4:13), and that faith "is the victory that overcomes the world" (1 John 5:4).

Ellen White was of the same mind. "God," she penned, "calls upon us to reach the standard of perfection and places before us the example of Christ's character. In His humanity, perfected by a life of constant resistance of evil, the Saviour showed that through co-operation with Divinity, human beings may in this life attain to perfection of character. This is God's assurance to us that we, too, may obtain complete victory."[12]

That oft-noted statement nearly always gets quoted without the qualifying statement in the topic sentence at the head of the paragraph that each Christian is to develop "perfection of Christian character" "in his sphere." This suggests that Christ's "sphere" might he different from ours (we will return to this concept in chapter 8).

In another place, Ellen White wrote that Christ came with our heredity "to share our sorrows and temptations, and to give us the example of a sinless life." We could easily multiply such statements.[13]

Before moving on to the nature of the imitation of Christ, it is important to note that while other human beings are like Christ in many ways, they are dissimilar from Him in others. For example, the Bible refers to no other child as "the holy one . . . the Son God" (Luke 1:35, NIV). Christ was not just another person. He was born holy—"born from above" from His very birth. As a result, He never had a bent toward evil like other children.

Following up on that thought, Ellen White penned that "it is not correct to say, as many writers have said, that Christ was like all children. . . . His inclination to right was a constant gratification to His parents. . . . He was an example of what all children may strive to be. . . .

"No one, looking upon the childlike countenance, shining with animation, could say that Christ was just like other children." "Never," she said in another connection, "in any way, leave the slightest impression upon human minds that a taint of, or inclination to corruption rested upon Christ." On yet another occasion she wrote that Christ "stood before the world, from His first entrance into it, untainted by corruption." That cannot be said of any other human being.[14]

By way of contrast, she commented that other humans (including children) have "a bent to evil."[15] And Paul emphasizes that "all have sinned and fall short of the glory of God" (Rom. 3:23).

Human children can get their "bent" corrected only through coming to Christ and being "born from above" (John 3:3, 7, margin) and by accepting the power of the Holy Spirit into their lives. As a result, they become partakers of the divine nature that Christ experienced at birth.

Even then, however, they are still not exactly like Christ in His humanity, because they have brought into their new life their past sinful habits and well-developed tendencies. Thus all human children, unlike Christ, need to be justified (counted righteous), regenerated (born from above to get their inclinations running in the right direction), and progressively sanctified (a rerouting of their ingrained habits).

126

Christ, of course, had to go through none of those procedures. He did not need to be justified, because He never sinned. Nor did He need to he regenerated, because He was born with an "inclination to right." And He did not need to be sanctified, because He never had evil habit patterns to modify.

On the other hand, Jesus was like the rest of humanity in many ways. Ellen White claimed, for example, that Christ "took upon him our sinful nature." Since, as we noted above, she repeatedly stated that Jesus did not have a fallen moral nature, her statements regarding His "sinful nature" must refer to His physical aspects. Thus she penned, "Jesus accepted humanity when the race had been weakened by four thousand years of sin. Like every child of Adam He accepted the results of the working of the great law of heredity."[16]

Another way in which Christ in His humanity was like us is that He chose not to use His divine power on his own behalf during His incarnation. Having "emptied himself" (Phil. 2:7), God the Son lived in dependence upon God the Father while on earth, as must all other God-fearing people (John 5:19, 30; 8:28; 14:10). He did not come to earth to live as God, but to live in obedience to God as a human being and to overcome where Adam and Eve fell (Rom. 5:15-19; Phil. 2:8). As Ellen White put it, "The power of the Saviour's Godhead was hidden. He overcame in human nature, relying upon God for power." Not only had He "endured every trial to which we are subject," but "He exercised in His own behalf no power that is not freely offered to us." We may have the dynamic power of the Holy Spirit to overcome sin just as Christ had.[17]

Thus He was like us in some ways and different in others. When Paul claims that God sent His Son "in the likeness of sinful flesh" (Rom. 8:3; cf. Phil. 2:7), he meant similar, not exact. The gospels use the same Greek word to suggest that the kingdom of God is "like" a mustard seed or a treasure hid in a field (Luke 13:19; Matt. 13:44). The idea is similarity, not absolute likeness.[18]

With that concept in mind, it is easier to see why Ellen White suggested that our human victory over sin would not be exactly like Christ's. "Christ," she stated, "is our pattern, the perfect and holy example that has been given us to follow. *We can never equal the pattern; but we may imitate and resemble it according to our ability.*"[19] Thus Christ has His sphere, and we have ours.

Another point to keep in mind regarding the imitation of Christ is that it is all too easy to overly literalize the example motif. Thus some become celibate, while others tote a wooden cross from place to place in their attempt to "be like Jesus."

T. W. Manson seems to have the correct idea when he writes that the imitation of Christ is "not a slavish copying of his acts but the working of his mind and spirit" in daily life. The fundamental principles of His life are to become normative for us.[20]

We now need to examine the "fundamental principles" of Christ's life central to His victory over sin and that are at the center of His character. Those chief characteristics are the heart of His being, the essence out of which radiated His daily actions.

Those core characteristics are all-important in following the example of Christ. Without them, all outward activities are less than Christian. It appears that the center of Christ's life contained two elements: (1) a surrendered will and (2) a heart of love that led to a life of loving actions.

### The Essence of Christ's Temptation and Victory

To hear some people talk, one would guess that temptation has to do with whether one should wear a wedding ring, eat cheese, or steal a car. Those things may or may not be temptations, but they are not TEMPTATION.

Christ's life illustrates the nature of the TEMPTATION that is the parent of all temptations. That TEMPTATION was to "do His own thing," to live His own life, and to avoid His cross.

The key to understanding Christ's TEMPTATION is Philippians 2:5-8: "Have this mind among yourselves," Paul wrote to the believers, "which is yours in Christ Jesus, who, though he was in the form of God, did not count equality with God a thing to be grasped, but *emptied himself* taking the form of a servant, being born in the likeness of men. And being found in human form *he humbled himself and became obedient unto death, even death on a cross.*"

Note that Christ the God-man "emptied himself" of something when He became a human being. While the apostle does not define the full meaning of these words, it seems clear from a study of the rest of the New Testament that part of what Jesus did in becoming human was to strip Himself voluntarily "of the insignia and prerogatives of deity." Thus Paul seems to be saying that Christ voluntarily gave up the independent use of His divine attributes and submitted to all the conditions of human life.[21]

In other words, as we noted above, Jesus remained God but voluntarily chose not to use His divine powers on His own behalf. Like other people, He remained dependent upon the Father and the Holy Spirit's power during His earthly existence. He met Satan's challenge that obedience to the law was impossible. In His perfect life of obedience, Jesus overcame where Adam failed, but He did so as a human being rather than as God. In His reliance upon His Father and the power of the Holy Spirit for daily strength, He had the same help that we may have in our daily lives.[22]

Because Jesus had voluntarily emptied Himself, He could resume divine power at any moment He chose to do so. Unlike other human beings, Jesus could have used His awesome abilities as God at any split second. To do so, however, would have broken the plan of salvation, in which Jesus came to disprove Satan's claim that God's law could not be kept by human beings.

It is at the point of Christ's voluntary self-emptying that we find the focus and strength of His temptations throughout His life. If the enemy had been able to persuade Jesus to "unempty" Himself even one time and get Him to use His "hidden" power in anger or on His own behalf, the war would have been over.

The item to note is that Christ was not only tempted "in every respect . . . as we are" (Heb. 4:15), but that He was tempted far beyond the point where ordinary humans can ever be tempted, since He actually had the power of God *in* (rather than *at*) His fingertips. The great struggle of Christ was to stay emptied.

That is the significance of the temptation to "command . . . stones to become loaves of bread" (Matt. 4:3). Such a thing would be no temptation to me, because I can't do it. I could go out to the beach and command all day and never have a loaf for lunch. But Jesus could have. As the agent of creation of all that exists, He had the ability to make bread out of nothing.

Christ had been without food for more than a month when the temptation concerning the bread came to Him. Certainly it must have been an attractive suggestion, but we miss the point if we see it merely as a way to satisfy His appetite. The real TEMPTATION was to reverse the self-emptying of Philippians 2 by using His divine power to meet His personal needs. That, of course, would have meant that He was not facing the world like other people. Underlying the TEMPTATION was the subtle insinuation that, *if* He were truly God (Matt. 4:3), He could use His special powers for Himself instead of relying upon the Father.

Some circles engage in a great deal of discussion regarding what it meant for Jesus to be tempted "in every respect . . . as we are, yet [be] without sin" (Heb. 4:15). It seems from a simple reading of the Bible that Jesus, irrespective of the constitution of His human nature, endured temptations far beyond the point that any other person can ever be tempted. Most of His temptations are not even temptations to us, because we lack the ability to respond to them successfully.

I demonstrated in *The Cross of Christ: God's Work for Us* that "all Christ's temptations . . . centered on having Him give up His dependency on the Father—to take control of His own life by becoming 'un-emptied.'"[23]

Closely related to that issue was the enticement to follow His own will rather than that of the Father, especially as God's will led to humbling Himself to becoming "obedient unto death, even death on a cross" (Phil. 2:8). As Raoul Dederen has written, Christ's special temptation throughout His life was "to depart from the accomplishment of His mission as Redeemer and turn from the path of suffering and death that His Messianic mission necessarily entailed."[24]

That issue explains the forcefulness of Christ's rejection of Peter's suggestion that Jesus did not need to "suffer many things from the elders and chief priests and scribes, and be killed." "'Get behind me, Satan!'" was Christ's unparalleled rebuke of His disciple (Matt. 16:21, 23).

Jesus had seen crucifixions in His travels, and, like any normal human being, He had no longing to exit the world through the excruciating death of the cross. It would have been much easier to become the political Messiah the Jews (including the disciples) anticipated (see Matt. 4:8-10; Isa. 2:2; Jer. 3:17; John 6:1-15).[25] Beyond that, Jesus had no desire to bear the judgment of the world by becoming sin for all humanity in the great sacrifice on Calvary (see John 12:31-33; 2 Cor. 5:21). The thought of separation from God while bearing the sins of the world on the cross was abhorrent to Him.

The TEMPTATION to do His own will by avoiding the cross reached its climax in Gethsemane as He came face to face with the full meaning of the cross. At that time Christ was "greatly distressed and troubled" and asked that "if it were possible, the hour might pass from him" (Mark 14:33, 35).

Fighting the temptation to do His own will and back off from the cross, Christ underwent duress that we can understand only faintly. In great agony and dread, Jesus finally made His decision. "My Father," He repeatedly prayed, "if this cannot pass unless I drink it, thy will be done" (Matt. 26:42).

On the cross itself Jesus faced the combined force of the two aspects of His TEMPTATION: to do His own will by coming down from the cross and to use His power for His personal benefit.

A major difference between Christ's crucifixion and that of other Roman crucifixions is that Christ did not have to stay on the cross. As D. M. Baillie put it, "Jesus did not die as a helpless victim: He could have escaped."[26] As the man who was God, He could have "unemptied" Himself and ended the ordeal.

Jesus, however, had *chosen* to die on the cross. His crucifixion was a voluntary act of obedience to God's will. "I lay down my life. . . . No one takes it from me, but I lay it down of my own accord." "The good shepherd lays down his life for the sheep" (John 10:17, 18, 11). Thus Christ *could* have come down from the cross, but He *would* not.

All through Jesus' life Satan tempted Him away from the cross, and he continued that same program during the crucifixion itself as he sought to lure Jesus to "unempty" Himself and do His own will. This time the tempter used the very persons that Christ was dying for. Passersby derided Him, taunting that He had made great statements about what He could do. If you are who you claim to be, they challenged, "save yourself, and *come down from the cross!*" The chief priests and scribes also got into the action, ridiculing Him to one another and saying: "He saved others; he cannot save himself. Let the Christ, the King of Israel, *come down now from the cross*, that we may see and believe." Meanwhile, some of the Roman guard "also mocked him" (Mark 15:29-32; Luke 23:36).

How would you have responded to such challenges and treatment if you had had access to the power of God? I would have been mightily tempted to get off my cross and give such ungrateful people exactly what they deserved. I would have demonstrated exactly who I was. They would certainly be sorry that they had exhausted *my* patience when I was trying so hard to do *them* a favor.

Fortunately for the universe, Christ did not fall for Satan's ploy. *He resisted the TEMPTATION to get off His cross, to put His own will and authority at the center of His life, and thereafter to do "His own thing." Thus He overcame where Adam failed.* Not only did His death cancel the penalty for sin, but His life provided an example for Christians to emulate. The cry, "It is finished" (John 19:30), in part meant that *He had lived a life of surrendered obedience, proving once for all to the universe that it could be done.* He stayed on His cross to the end and thus could utter His words as a shout of victory.[27]

The cross stands just as much at the center of TEMPTATION in our lives as it did in Christ's. Remember that Adam and Eve fell when they rebelled against God and put their wills at the focus of their lives and put their own selves in the commanding position that belonged to God. SIN is a rebellious, broken relationship with God. Out of that broken relationship flows a series of sinful actions (sins).

The New Testament imperative is the crucifixion of self-centeredness for every individual disciple of Christ, coupled with a new life to be lived in resurrection power (Rom. 6:1-11). "If any man would come after me," Jesus said, "let him deny himself and take up his cross and follow me" (Matt. 16:24). "I have been crucified with Christ," Paul claimed. "*It is no longer I who live, but Christ who lives in me; and the life I now live in the flesh I live by faith in the Son of God, who loved me and gave himself for me*" (Gal. 2:20).

The crucifixion of the self-centered, willful self stands at the very heart of Christianity. The imitation of Christ is much more than the development of a set of moral habits. As the Pharisees of all ages have proved, a person can be morally upstanding yet still be self-centered and proud. Martin Luther discovered that. When he entered the monastery, notes Bonhoeffer, "he had left everything behind except his pious self." But when he met Christ, "even that was taken from him."[28]

The gospel call is for crucifixion and transformation rather than a gradual improvement of the self-centered life (Rom. 12:1, 2). To pass from the self-centered spirit that is natural to humanity to the spirit of Christ, H. H. Farmer indicates, is not a matter of gentle growth or natural evolution. Rather, "it is an uprooting, rending, tearing, splitting and breaking, surgical-operation kind of thing, a . . . crucifixion."[29]

The center of the struggle is the individual human will, "the governing power in the nature of man." Thus Ellen White can write that "the warfare against self is the greatest battle that was ever fought. The yielding of self, surrendering all to the will of God, requires a struggle; but the soul must submit to God before it can be renewed in holiness."[30]

As James Denney put it: "Though sin may have a natural birth it does not die a natural death; in every case it has to be morally sentenced and put to death."[31] That sentencing is an act of the will under the impulse of the Holy Spirit.

As with Christ, the struggle to go to our cross will be the severest of our lives. That is because, P. T. Forsyth points out, "our will is our dearest life, the thing we cling to most and give up last." "God alone," Ellen White penned, "can give us the victory" in this struggle with our willful self. But He cannot and will not force our wills. "The stronghold of Satan" is only broken as the "will" is "placed on the side of God's will." But the strength for victory comes from God. "If you are 'willing to be made willing,' God will accomplish the work for you"[32] (cf. Phil. 2:12, 13).

Please note that Christians do not *give up* their wills. Rather they *give over* their wills to the transforming power of God's Spirit. The will still remains the controlling power in their lives, but the converted will is now in harmony with God's principles. Thus Christians do not become automatons in the hands of God, but responsible agents who share His viewpoint. The born from above Christian's heart and mind will be so in harmony with God's will "that when obeying Him" they "shall be but carrying out" their "own impulses."[33]

Christ had His cross, and we have ours. He died on His for our sins, in which He had no share; and we die on ours to all pride and self-reliance, that we might partake of His life. At the cross of Christ all intellectual and moral independence finally shatters, and we freely admit our dependence on God in every aspect of our lives. From the viewpoint of the cross the words of Christ take on new meaning: "Whoever would save his life will lose it," but "whoever loses his life for my sake . . . will save it" (Luke 9:24).

If we can view coming to Jesus for justification and regeneration as initial crucifixion, then we should see the sanctified life as living the life of the cross. Thus Christ told His disciples to take up their crosses "daily" (Luke 9:23), and Paul asserted: "I die every day" (1 Cor. 15:31).

Just as TEMPTATION in Christ's life was first to depend on Himself and not go to the cross and second to come down from the cross, so it is with His followers. The TEMPTATION is always present to step down from our crosses and give people what they "deserve," to "do our own thing," to become the gods of our own lives, to make the Adam choice rather than the Christ choice.

*To follow the example of Christ means not only to go to the cross, but to live the life of the cross. "Let this mind be in you,"* wrote the apostle, *"which was also in Christ Jesus: Who, being in the form of God . . . made himself of no reputation, and took upon him the form of a servant, . . . and . . . humbled himself, and became obedient unto death, even the death of the cross"* (Phil. 2:5-8, KJV).

## The Character of Christ

Not only will Christians following Christ die the death He died, but they will also live the life He lived. Death without resurrection is not the gospel pattern. Christianity is primarily a positive force, not a negative one.

133

The death of self as the center of existence opens the way and sets the stage for Christian living.

The life of the cross is one of self-sacrificing love and service to other people. Just as "God is love" (1 John 4:8) and "so loved the world that he gave his only son" (John 3:16), so Christ "came not to be served but to serve, and to give his life" (Matt. 20:28). Love and service to others form the very foundation of Christ's character and were the attributes continually in evidence in His earthly ministry.

The same elements are the foundation of the life lived after the example of Jesus. In contrasting the principles of the world with those of the cross, Jesus told His disciples that in the unconverted world the great exercised authority over others. "But," He commanded them, "it shall not be so among you; . . . whoever would be great among you must be your servant. . . . For [because] the Son of man came . . . to serve, and to give his life" (Mark 10:43-45).

Christ's life was to be the pattern for His followers. "In the Saviour's life," Ellen White noted, "the principles of God's law—love to God and man—were perfectly exemplified. Benevolence, unselfish love, was the life of His soul." Jesus "lived only to comfort and bless."[34]

Luther also zeroed in on the essence of living after the example of Christ. "I should," he penned, "become a Christ to my neighbor and be for him what Christ is for me." The Christian, Anders Nygren suggested, is to be "the channel of God's down-pouring love."[35]

As in the life of Christ the Exemplar, so it must be in our lives. *If we are following His example, love to God and our neighbors will be the principle of action that informs and guides our daily activities. That concept and the life it leads to are at the heart of both progressive sanctification and perfection.*

John Wesley put it nicely when he wrote that "'faith working by love' is the length and breadth and depth and height of Christian perfection. . . . And in truth, whomsoever loveth his brethren, not in word only but as Christ loved him, cannot but be 'zealous of good works.' He feels in his soul a burning, restless desire of spending and being spent for them. . . . At all possible opportunities he is, like his Master, 'going about doing good.'"[36]

Having the "mind of Christ" will not only lead to loving actions in our daily lives, but will also help us hate sin as Christ did, because we now realize that it destroys the lives of God's children. Thus the principle of love to God and our fellow beings will affect *every aspect* of our daily living. Nothing in our lives is outside the reach of the principle of love. The follower of the example of Christ is one who lives a radically transformed life. In this chapter we have examined the meaning of imitating Christ. First and foremost, we have discovered, following Christ's example means the crucifixion of the principle of selfishness central to the "natural person" and the living of a life of loving service to those in the world around us.

We will now turn to the topic of perfection, an important issue, since Jesus commanded His followers to be "perfect, even as your Father which is in heaven is perfect" (Matt. 5:48, KJV).

---

[1] White, *Christ's Object Lessons*, p. 69. Chapter 9 will treat this quotation in detail.

[2] One certainly gets that impression from the videotapes that John Osborne put out on celebration worship.

[3] William Doyle, quoted in Menninger, *Man Against Himself*, p. 123.

[4] Flew, *The Idea of Perfection*, pp. 158, 168; LaRondelle, *Perfection and Perfectionism*, pp. 304, 305.

[5] Stan Mooneyham, *Dancing on the Straight and Narrow* (San Francisco: Harper & Row, 1989), pp. 12, 13.

[6] Lewis, *Mere Christianity*, p. 69.

[7] Sinclair B. Ferguson, "The Reformed View," in *Christian Spirituality*, p. 66.

[8] Berkouwer, *Faith and Sanctification*, p. 135.

[9] See *The Westminster Dictionary of Christian Theology*, s.v. "Imitation of Christ, The"; *Evangelical Dictionary of Theology*, s.v. "Pelagius, Pelagianism."

[10] See Orr, *Christian View of God*, pp. 287, 288; Stalker, *Example of Jesus*, pp. 15, 16.

[11] Luther, quoted in Hinson, *To Reform the Nation*, p. 162, n. 17.

[12] White, *Acts of the Apostles*, p. 531.

[13] *Ibid.*; White, *The Desire of Ages*, p. 49. Cf. White, *Testimonies to Ministers,* p. 173; White, *The Great Controversy*, p. 623.

[14] E. G. White, *The Youth's Instructor*, Sept. 8, 1898, pp. 704, 705; E. G. White to Brother and Sister Baker [Feb. 9, 1896]; E. G. White, *Seventh-day Adventist Bible Commentary*, vol. 7, p. 907.

[15] White, *Education*, p. 29. For more on this topic in the context of the 1888 General Conference session, see Knight, *From 1888 to Apostasy*, pp. 132-150.

[16] E. G. White, *Review and Herald*, 15 Dec. 1896, p. 789; White, *The Desire of Ages*, p. 49.

[17] E. G. White, *The Youth's Instructor*, Apr. 25, 1901, p. 130; White, *The Desire of Ages*, p. 24.

[18] *A Greek English Lexicon of the New Testament* (Arndt and Gingrich), s.v. "*homoiōma*."

[19] E. G. White, *Review and Herald*, Feb. 5, 1895, p. 81. (Italics supplied.)

[20] T. W. Manson, quoted in E. J. Tinsley, *The Imitation of God in Christ* (Philadelphia: Westminster, 1960), p. 179.

[21] See *The Interpreter's Bible Dictionary*, s.v. "*Kenosis*"; Edward Heppenstall, *The Man Who Is God* (Washington, D.C.: Review and Herald, 1977), pp. 67-80.

[22] See White, *The Desire of Ages*, p. 24.

[23] Knight, *The Cross of Christ*, p. 86. That book, pp. 82-91, provides a much fuller treatment of Christ's temptation.

[24] Raoul Dederen, "Atoning Aspects in Christ's Death," in *The Sanctuary and the*

*Atonement: Biblical, Historical, and Theological Studies,* Arnold V. Wallenkampf and W. Richard Lesher, eds. (Washington, D.C.: General Conference of SDA, 1981), p. 307.

[25] See Knight, *The Cross of Christ,* pp. 85-88.

[26] D. M. Baillie, *God Was in Christ* (New York: Charles Scribner's Sons, 1948), p. 182.

[27] William Barclay, *The Gospel of John,* 2d ed., Daily Study Bible (Edinburgh: The Saint Andrew Press, 1956), vol. 2, p. 301.

[28] Stott, *Basic Christianity,* 111; Bonhoeffer, *Cost of Discipleship,* p. 51.

[29] H. H. Farmer, quoted in Dillistone, *Significance of the Cross,* p. 155.

[30] White, *Steps to Christ,* pp. 47, 43.

[31] Denney, *Christian Doctrine of Reconciliation,* p. 198.

[32] P. T. Forsyth, *The Cruciality of the Cross* (Wake Forest, N.C.: Chanticleer, 1983), p. 92; White, *Mount of Blessing,* p. 142.

[33] White, *The Desire of Ages,* p. 668.

[34] White, *Steps to Christ,* p. 28; White, *The Desire of Ages,* pp. 57, 70.

[35] Luther, quoted in Althaus, *Theology of Martin Luther,* p. 135; Anders Nygren, *Agape and Eros* (Philadelphia: Westminster, 1953), p. 733.

[36] Wesley, *Works,* vol. 14, pp. 321, 322.

# Chapter 7

# The Bible on Perfection and Sinlessness

Early in my Christian experience I arrived at the "Pharisaic paradox of perfection." Having set out to be the first sinlessly perfect Christian since Christ, I eventually came to the ultimate frustration of my life: The harder I tried, the worse I became.

Unfortunately, those who had to work around me or live with me saw the paradox much sooner than I did. As I look back, I blush at the thought of how my "spiritual superiority" made me harsh, judgmental, exacting, condemning, and negative. Because human nature has not changed across the ages, the spirit of Pharisaism is today what it was in Christ's time.

D. M. Baillie helps us unlock the secret of the paradox of Pharisaic perfection when he notes that certain types of perfectionism and character development keep us "thinking about ourselves. It is self-centered, and self-centeredness is the very thing from which we need to be saved, because it is the essence of sin. . . . The very worst kind of self-centeredness . . . [is] self-righteousness and pride. So instead of becoming saints, we become 'Pharisees.'"[1]

False approaches to perfection fail because they focus on self and personal progress. As we move through this chapter, we will discover that the essence of biblical perfection is far from the self-centeredness of Pharisaic perfectionism.

### Being Perfect: A Bible Command

"You . . . must be perfect, as your heavenly Father is perfect" (Matt. 5:48), Jesus told His hearers. In that text Jesus not only issued the command, but He set up God as the standard of perfection.

"Walk before me, and be thou perfect," God directed Abraham in reiterating the covenant (Gen. 17:1, KJV). The book of Hebrews tells us to "go on unto perfection" (Heb. 6:1, KJV), and Paul wrote to the Colossians that he desired to "present every man perfect in Christ Jesus" (Col. 1:28, KJV). God gave the various spiritual gifts "for the perfecting of the saints" (Eph. 4:12, 13, KJV).

With those and other texts in mind, Jean Zurcher can write that "the entire Bible is one ringing call to perfection," and R. Newton Flew can conclude that *"Christianity is not Christianity unless it is aiming at Perfection."* "The doctrine of Christian perfection . . . lies not merely upon the by-paths of Christian theology, but upon the high road."[2]

*The only thing one can conclude from the Bible is that perfection must be possible, or its writers would not have urged it upon believers.* Thus the issue is not the possibility of perfection, but what the Bible writers mean by "perfection." And do they suggest that we can achieve it during our earthly lifetimes?

Before examining the Bible to ascertain the meaning of the word, it will be helpful to look at several preliminary aspects of the topic. First, we can avoid a lot of confusion if we recognize that perfection has more than one meaning in a believer's life. Marvin Moore correctly notes that "in one sense, we are perfect in Jesus the moment we accept Him as our Saviour, because His righteousness covers our sins." In addition, however, "character perfection continues during one's entire lifetime."[3] Thus we find biblical concepts of perfection related to both justification and progressive sanctification. We will note in chapter 10 a third biblical concept of perfection related to glorification, when our bodily natures are transformed at the second coming of Christ (1 Cor. 15).

It is crucial to recognize that perfection as it relates to justification is *not* what the Bible is talking about in such texts as Matthew 5:48, Hebrews 6:1, and Ephesians 4:12, 13 (all quoted above). Those passages speak of a dynamic process of character development in which people really do become more and more like their "heavenly Father."

Paul refers to that aspect of perfection when he suggests to the Corinthians that they "make [their] holiness perfect" in the fear of God (2 Cor. 7:1). It is also in view when the author of Hebrews tells believers to "go on unto perfection" (Heb. 6:1, KJV) and when Paul reminds the Corinthians that they "are being changed into his likeness from one degree of glory to another" (2 Cor. 3:18; cf. Gal. 4:19; 2 Peter 3:18).

Vincent Taylor decries the fact that perfection is too often thought of as a "fixed" and "static" standard, "whereas the Christian ideal . . . must be conceived as capable of endless enrichment." Moore suggests the same thing when he urges us to think of perfection as a line rather than a point to be achieved. "The word *point*," he perceptively suggests, "is too limiting. Perfection is more a state of being, more a relationship with Jesus, more a way of life, than it is a 'point' that one can measure to know when he has reached it." Mildred Wynkoop speaks of perfection as a depth of relationship "relative to one's spiritual capacity at any one time."[4]

The biblical picture, of course, is that people's capacity continually increases if they are perfect (that is, being perfected). That increase, as we shall see in chapter 10, will continue throughout eternity. The dynamic "line" of character development is infinite. "Perfect Christians" always become more and more like God without ever becoming just like Him. Heaven will be a place of infinite spiritual growth.

It is unfortunate that down through history unbiblical teachings related to perfection and sinlessness have repeatedly led to excesses and fanaticism. Thus John Wesley, a man who spent his life teaching the possibility of perfection, referred to some perfectionists who "made the very name of Perfection stink in the nostrils."[5]

Perverted theories of perfection have led to several aberrations among Christians. One distortion of the doctrine surrenders the clear distinction between the believer's will and that of the Holy Spirit. Thus because a person is "perfect" by definition, whatever he or she does is right and sanctified. Such teaching in the 1840s led to "spiritual wifery" and other perversions among ex-Millerite Adventists and other Christians.[6]

A second misguided approach to perfection leads in a materialistic direction. Thus the 1890s saw some holiness and Adventist groups believing that their gray hairs would regain their natural color. And such preachers as E. J. Waggoner taught that one who truly had Christ's righteousness would never get sick.[7]

A third misdirection of perfectionism is a moralism that uplifts external conformity to law. In moralistic perfection every human act becomes regulated by laws that become increasingly complex and cover every aspect of diet, recreation, dress, and so on. Holiness through celibacy, flagellation, vegetarianism and other dietary restrictions, and even self-castration, have not been uncommon among believers holding to moralistic views of perfection. Desperately in earnest, people of this persuasion develop long lists of rules, and the more they read the longer their lists become. The Pharisees and monks belonged to this camp of perfectionism, and Adventists and other conservative Christians in the modern world have often joined in.

A fourth misunderstanding of New Testament perfection substitutes the legal perfection of justification for the progressive perfection of character development. We are perfect in Christ, the theory runs, and that is all that is required. This theory teaches, writes Wynkoop, the fiction "that character can be transferred from one person to another." Thus Christ became our vicarious perfection. In this way "salvation terminates probation." "Though usually a good moral life is encouraged, it is not considered necessary to salvation." Such a belief, we should note, leads to logical antinomianism in thought if not in practice.[8] Seventh-day Adventists at times have found themselves caught up in this unbiblical form of perfection—a teaching directly related to the theory that justification can be separated from sanctification (discussed in chapter 4).

**Biblical Perfection**

One of the most serious problems among Christians with regard to perfection is that people bring their own definitions of perfection to the Bible rather than letting Scripture define perfection for them. That procedure usually leads people to view perfection in absolutist terms that may be in harmony with Greek philosophy but are not a part of the biblical use of the word.

In platonic thought, which greatly influenced the Christian church in its early centuries, something was perfect if it never had to change. We see that concept best represented in Plato's allegory of the cave, which reflects upon the perfection of those things beyond the realm of change.[9]

When we apply the concept to Christian theology, a person who never had to change would have to be absolutely sinless, since all sinners need to get rid of their sinful habits. It was the equation of perfection with absolute sinlessness that set the stage for monasticism in the early and medieval church. In spite of the fact that that definition of perfection was a part of the distortion that entered Christian theology through Greek philosophy, the sixteenth-century Reformation did not correct it.

Many modern Christians, including most Seventh-day Adventists, continue to operate with the Greek philosophic idea of perfection rather than with the biblical concept. Adventists have faulted most other Christians for imbibing the Greek philosophic contribution of innate immortality of the soul, but they have too often swallowed the error on the definition of perfection being sinlessness. The plain fact is, as we will see below, that *the Bible teaches both sinlessness and perfection, but it never equates them.* We need to view the recapturing of the biblical concept of perfection as a part of an ongoing reformation that began in the sixteenth century and will continue until the Second Advent. That progressive reformation seeks to get back to all of the Bible's teachings that became distorted during the church's early centuries.

The importing of extra-biblical meanings for perfection into the text has played havoc with the concept and has hindered understanding. In seeking to determine the biblical meaning of perfection, we need to let the context of the passage using the word be the true commentary on its meaning. Beyond that, we should seek to discover the biblical meaning of words used to translate our English word *perfection*.

Of the Gospel writers, only Matthew employs the term *perfect*, and he uses it only three times. The first two cases are in the frustrating saying of Matthew 5:48: "You, therefore, must be perfect, as your heavenly Father is perfect." While that text has sent people off on frenzied tangents of extremism in lifestyle and monastic discipline in the hope that separation from the world and sinners might enable them to be as perfect as God, the context suggests just the opposite course of action.

Being perfect as the Father is perfect, according to verses 43-47, means loving (*agapaō*) not only one's friends but also one's enemies. "*Love your enemies* and pray for those who persecute you, *so that you may be sons of your Father* who is in heaven" (verses 44, 45). The parallel passage in Luke reinforces that message. "Be merciful," Jesus commanded in the context of loving one's enemies (Luke 6:27-35), "even as your Father is merciful" (verse 36). Thus the Gospel writers equated being merciful with being perfect. Just as God sent Christ to die for His enemies (Rom. 5:6, 8, 10), so His children are to emulate His heart of love.

In commenting on Matthew 5:48, William Barclay nicely summarizes its message: "The one thing which makes us like God is the love which never ceases to care for men, no matter what men do to it. We . . . enter upon Christian perfection . . . when we learn to forgive as God forgives, and to love as God loves."[10]

The only other use of the word *perfection* in the Gospels occurs in Christ's conversation with the rich young ruler. You will recall that in his desire to gain eternal life, the man had come to Christ with a *list* of his accomplishments in commandment keeping. But he still felt that he had not *done* enough to gain the prize, so he asked Jesus what he still needed to do. The answer: "If you would be perfect, go, sell what you possess and give to the poor, and you will have treasure in heaven; and come, follow me"(Matt. 19:16-21).

Christ would not allow the young man to trivialize and itemize righteousness. Jesus not only once again tied being perfect to loving one's neighbor, but He placed that love in the context of a life-changing followership with Himself. "The real decision which Christ required from the rich young ruler," writes Hans LaRondelle, "was not primarily of an *ethical* [doing something] nature, but of a radical *religious* [relationship] nature: the complete self-surrender to God."[11] To relate to Christ includes assimilating and reflecting His character of love. Other Bible passages dealing with God's ideal for humans are in harmony with Jesus' Gospel statements (see, for example, 1 John 2:4-6; James 1:27; Micah 6:8).

At this juncture it is crucial to realize that biblical perfection is a positive rather than a negative quality. The essence of perfection is not refraining from certain things and actions, but of performing loving actions while in relationship to Christ. It is daily living and demonstrating Christlike love toward both other people and God. "Perfection," Zurcher writes, "is more than simply not doing wrong. It is the overcoming of evil with good in harmony with the basic principle laid down in the golden rule [see Matt. 7:12]." "Character perfection," suggests C. Mervyn Maxwell, "is nothing less than to 'live love.'"[12]

Love, therefore, defines both sin and Christian perfection. If, as we saw in chapter 2, sin is essentially focusing my love (*agapē*) on myself, biblical perfection is shifting that love back to God and my neighbor. That transformation, Paul indicates, will change every aspect of my everyday life (Rom. 13:8-10; Gal. 5:14).

Perfect love, Leo Cox asserts, is *not* "'perfect performance,' or 'perfect skill,' or 'perfect human nature.'" Rather, it is rendering obedience in relationship to both the God of love and the great principle undergirding His law.[13] Attempts at "becoming perfect" divorced from a living relationship with Jesus and the loving heart of His law are sterile, cold, dead, and often ugly—a truth frequently demonstrated by those of Pharisaic disposition.

It is now time to turn to the Bible words used to express the English word *perfection*. None of them mean sinlessness or have absolutist connotations. The key New Testament word translated as "perfection" is *teleios*, the adjective form of *telos*. The idea behind *telos* has entered the English language through our word *teleology*—"the fact or quality of being directed toward a definite end or of having an ultimate purpose," according to Webster.

That meaning is from the Greek, where *telos* means "an end," "a purpose," "an aim," or "a goal." Something is *teleios* if it fulfills the purpose for which it was created. People are therefore perfect *(teleios)* if they meet God's intent for them. The Bible leaves no doubt as to the purpose for which He created humans. "Let us make man in our image, after our likeness," reads the Genesis story (Gen. 1:26). It was only natural for Jesus to claim that the Christian ideal is that people should become *teleios* (perfect) in love, like their Father in heaven (Matt. 5:48; cf. 1 John 4:8). They were made to act in love rather than to behave like the devil, as humans have unfortunately done since the fall of Genesis 3.

The meaning of *teleios* is not "sinless" but "mature," "whole," or "undivided."[14] Christ could therefore say to the rich young ruler that if he wanted to be perfect *(teleios)* he must become totally committed to God (Matt. 19:21).

The idea of perfection as maturity is explicitly clear in Hebrews 5:13–6:1, in which we read that Christians should move beyond the nourishing milk of their Christian childhood to the solid food of the "mature [from *teleios*]." The mature are "those who have their faculties trained by practice to distinguish good from evil. Therefore let us . . . go on to maturity ["perfection" in the KJV, from *telos*]."

The perceptive reader may have noted that when I began my discussion of biblical perfection, nearly all my quotations came from the King James Version of the Bible, contrary to my usual practice of using the Revised Standard Version. That was because the RSV (and other modern versions) nearly always translates the *telos* word group as "mature" rather than "perfect."

According to the New Testament writers, the "perfect" Christian is the mature, whole, complete Christian. The same holds true for the Old Testament, in which the words translated as "perfect" generally mean "complete," "upright," or "blameless" in a spiritual sense.[15]

Thus Scripture could call Noah, Abraham, and Job "perfect" (Gen. 6:9; 17:1, KJV; Job 1:1, 8, KJV), even though they had obvious faults. The perfect Old Testament saint was the person of the "perfect heart" toward God as he or she "walked" in His way and will (1 Kings 8:61; Isa. 38:3; Gen. 6:9; 17:1). The perfect person, writes P. J. Du Plessis, is the one in "total submission to the will of God" and in complete "devotion to His service"; the one who has "an unimpeded relationship with Yahweh."[16]

In summarizing the biblical view of perfection, we can say that biblical perfection is not the abstract standard of flawlessness found in Greek philosophy, but "man's perfect relationship with God and his fellowman."[17] Biblical perfection involves ethical conduct, but it involves much more than mere behavior. It centers on maturing the relationships ruptured during the rebellion of the Genesis Fall.

John Wesley's definitions of biblical perfection deserve more study than they often receive by Adventists. Perfection, he concluded, is perfect love of God and our neighbor expressed in word and action. And love to God, he suggested, is "to delight in him, to rejoice in his will, to desire continually to please him, to seek and find our happiness in him, and to thirst day and night for a fuller enjoyment of him."[18]

Again, Wesley wrote, perfection "is purity of intention, dedicating all the life to God. It is the giving God all our heart; it is one desire and design ruling all our tempers. It is the devoting, not a part, but all, our soul, body, and substance, to God. In another view, it is all the mind which was in Christ, enabling us to walk as Christ walked. It is the circumcision of the heart from all filthiness, all inward as well as outward pollution. It is a renewal of the heart in the whole image of God, the full likeness of Him that created it. In yet another, it is the loving God with all our heart, and our neighbor as ourselves." It is hard to improve on such a definition, one that Wesley saw as describing "the whole and sole perfection."[19]

## Biblical Sinlessness

*The Bible explicitly teaches that we may be sinless in this life.* The apostle John in his first epistle is clear on that point. "No one who abides in him sins. . . . No one born of God commits sin; for God's nature abides in him, and *he cannot sin* because he is born of God" (1 John 3:6, 9). "We know that whosoever is born of God sinneth not; but he that is begotten of God keepeth himself, and that wicked one toucheth him not" (1 John 5:18, KJV).

Taken by themselves, these passages appear to describe and require sinless perfection for every Christian. On the other hand, other texts in this same epistle seem to imply just the opposite. For example, "if we say we have no sin, we deceive ourselves"; "if we confess our sins, he is faithful and just, and will forgive our sins"; "if we say we have not sinned, we make him a liar"; "I am writing this to you so that you may not sin; *but* if any one does sin, we have an advocate with the Father, Jesus Christ the righteous" (1 John 1:8-2:1).

In light of these two sets of texts, it is clear that John is either terribly confused or he is operating with a definition of sin that is more complex than generally acknowledged by those who glibly quote him as saying that "sin is the transgression of the law" (1 John 3:4, KJV) and give that text an interpretation based purely on outward behavior.

The fact that John has a complex definition of sin in mind is evident not only from the passages quoted above, but also from 1 John 5:16, in which he notes that some sin is "not unto death," while other sin is "unto death" (KJV).

The faultline between that sin which cannot be found in the believer ("sins unto death," 3:9; 5:16) and those sins open to mediation by Christ ("not unto death," 1:9; 2:1) is found in a person's attitude. It is important to note that in all the passages in 1 John demanding sinlessness, the Greek verbs describing people who sin are in the present tense, thereby denoting individuals who live in a state of continual or habitual sinning. On the other hand, in 1 John 2:1, in which John reminds us that if we sin we have a Mediator, the verb is in the aorist tense, indicating a definite past action that is not ongoing and therefore is not habitual.[20]

The picture in 1 John is the contrast between those who have an attitude of rebellion toward God and live in continual sin as a way of life and those who commit sins that they repent of as they turn to the Mediator for forgiveness and cleansing. The first category indicates those who have sinned "unto death," while the sin of those in the second category is "not unto death."

Those with sin "unto death" live in a state of "lawlessness" (1 John 3:4) and rebellion toward God, while those in line with the Mediator have been "born of God," abide "in him," and have become a part of the family of God through adoption (1 John 3:9, 6, 1).

Because Christians have been born from above and have had their minds transformed, they do not have a rebellious attitude toward God. Rather, they *"walk* in the light, as he is in the light" (1 John 1:7; cf. 2:6). On the other hand, some claiming to have "fellowship with him . . . walk in darkness" (1 John 1:6). "He who says 'I know him' but disobeys his commandments is a liar, and the truth is not in him" (1 John 2:4).

By his very use of the word *walk*, it is clear that John is speaking of two ways of life that harmonize with his use of verb tenses. One is the *SIN relationship* to God that leads to a life of ongoing lawlessness (sins) and eventuates in death. The other is the *faith relationship* with its born from above attitude toward sin and its use of the Mediator. *Those in this second group John defines as being sinless, even though they still commit specific acts of sin for which they need forgiveness.* Thus sinlessness is not only a possibility in the present life, but a biblical promise and demand. *The Christian "cannot sin* [live in a state of rebellion] because he is born of God" (1 John 3:9). On the other hand, those not born of God "are the children of the devil." In their rebellion they neither do God's will nor do they love their neighbor (verse 10).

The same basic pattern appears in Paul's discussion of sinlessness in Romans 6. That passage twice states that Christians have "died to sin" (verses 2, 11) and that they "have been set free from sin" (verse 22). Paul's real point, however, is not that Christians don't ever commit individual acts of sin but that they do not live lives controlled by sin. Thus they are "no longer . . . enslaved to sin," and sin does not have "dominion" over them (verses 6, 14).

The whole passage builds upon Paul's argument in Romans that a person is either in a SIN (rebellion) relationship with Christ or in a faith relationship. Those in a faith relationship are "united with him" in the death of their old mind-set and resurrected with newness of attitude toward God and His principles. Thus they "walk in newness of life" (verses 1-11). They do not let sin "reign" in their "mortal bodies," nor do they live lives yielded to sin (verses 12-14). As a result, they are sinless in the same sense that John claimed that Christians were sinless. That is, even though they have sins, of which they repent, they do not live in a state of SIN (rebellion toward God and His principles).

It is important to note, however, that Paul is quite clear that such Christians live out their faith relationship in "mortal bodies" (verse 12). Therein is an aspect of Christian life that made Paul and John differentiate between sinlessness and what we might call absolute sinlessness.

### Perfect But Not Yet Perfect, Sinless But Not Yet Sinless

The distinction between sinlessness and absolute sinlessness also appears in Paul's conception of perfection and absolute or ultimate perfection. In Philippians he describes himself and some of the Philippians as already "perfect," yet in the same passage he claims that he had not yet attained to perfection (Phil. 3:15, 12, KJV). The "already perfect" state refers to the Philippians' dedication of heart and mind to Christ, while the "not yet perfect" status suggests that Paul and his church were in a process of growth and development in their perfection. That is, they were already perfect (mature in their attitude to Christ), but they were on the way to a fuller perfection.

Thus being perfect is a dynamic state in which dedicated Christians continue to advance in Christian living.[21] Paul can therefore write to the Philippians that he is pressing on in his growing and developing perfection (Phil. 3:12-14). His heart, mind, and attitude toward God were perfect and right, but he had not developed absolute perfection. Paul could be perfect but not yet perfect in the same way that John's readers could be sinless but not yet sinless in the absolute sense. Bible readers too often pass over those scriptural distinctions.

Absolute sinlessness, when one begins to think about it, is a rather far-reaching state of being. Those who so glibly demand it of themselves and others usually define sin as merely avoiding conscious acts of rebellion against God, but sin also includes unconscious acts and acts of omission. In other words, absolute sinlessness (or absolute perfection) not only includes a complete forsaking of all conscious and unconscious sins, but it also implies that one never neglects doing good.

That distinction becomes especially clear when we note that Christ's portrayal of the final judgment did not condemn the Pharisees of old for sins of commission, but for sins of omission. That is, they failed the judgment, not because they had performed a sinful act, but because they had failed to feed their neighbor and visit the sick (Matt. 25:31-46).

God's emphasis on the invisible sins of omission stands in stark contrast to those who would define sin only as consciously rebellious acts of commission. The standard of God's character is much higher than either modern or ancient Pharisees have thought. One good reason to lower the standard by defining sin only as conscious rebellion, of course, is that it makes it easier to reach. Thus, the negative approach of the Pharisaic mind is understandable.

The claim to be totally free from sin in this life is based on a faulty definition of sin. Ellen White points us to a broader definition than we often hear when she writes that "none of the apostles and prophets ever claimed to be without sin. Men who have lived nearest to God, men who would sacrifice life itself rather than *knowingly* commit a wrong act, men whom God had honored with divine light and power, have confessed the sinfulness of their own nature."[22]

We should note at least two points in the above quotation. First, she reinforces the biblical concept between conscious and unconscious sins that we spent considerable space on in chapter 2. Those who never knowingly do wrong are still not without sin. A related point is that unconscious sin is rooted in human nature. That root, of course, will be with human beings until the second coming of Christ (see 1 Cor. 15:44, 51-53; Phil. 3:20, 21).

Because sin contains what Ellen White consistently referred to as conscious and unconscious aspects and Wesley called proper and improper sins, Wesley could claim that being perfect "in love" was consistent with "a thousand mistakes."[23]

Being "perfect" for Paul in Philippians and being "sinless" for John in his first epistle did not mean either absolute perfection or absolute sinlessness. But it did involve being free from an attitude of rebellion toward the Father and His principles set forth in the law of love.

Because of less-than-adequate bodies and flawed minds that don't know and understand everything (see 1 Cor. 13:12), Christians commit sins of ignorance and sins of infirmity.[24] As Wesley put it, there are those who "love God with all their heart. . . . But even these souls dwell in a shattered body, and are so pressed down thereby, that they cannot always exert themselves as they would, by thinking, speaking, and acting, precisely right. For want of better bodily organs they must at times think, speak, or act wrong; not, indeed, through a defect of love, but through a defect of knowledge. And while this is the case, notwithstanding that defect, and its consequences, they fulfill the law of love," but not perfectly. As a result of their shortfall of love in action, even though it is based upon ignorance and infirmity, they still "need the blood of atonement, and may properly for themselves . . . say, 'Forgive us our trespasses.' "[25]

Thus we can be perfect or sinless in attitude without being perfect or sinless in action. John, Paul, and Wesley agree on that point. They also agree, as we have noted above and in chapter 2, that even unconscious or improper sins still need confession and the blood of atonement. While the ethical concept of sin deals with a person's intentions, the legal concept of sin involves all infractions that fall short of Gods ideal. Both types of sin come within the forgiving grace of God.

Paul's dichotomy between being already perfect but not yet perfect (Phil. 3:9-15) and John and Paul's division between being sinless but not yet sinless (Rom. 6; 1 John 3:9; 1:9-2:1) must be seen in terms perfection of attitude versus perfection of action. The first should be the Christian's current possession while the second is an ideal aimed at in this life.

Leo Cox expressed the issue implicit in Paul's "mortal bodies" (Rom. 6:12), Wesley's "shattered bodies," and Ellen White's "sinfulness of human nature" concepts when he penned that "like a musician who has perfect skill would fail with a faulty instrument, so the pure in heart do often falter with their broken earthen vessels. But the 'sour notes' on the broken instrument do not disprove the perfection of the prompting love!" Edward Heppenstall spoke to the same point when he wrote that the Holy Spirit never "so overpowers man's limitations due to sin as to enable man to arrive at a state of [absolute] sinlessness."[26]

Perfection in the Bible, in terms of human beings in their mortal bodies, is perfection of the spiritual orientation and attitude rather than total perfection in all its aspects. Thus the tension within Paul's perfect but not yet perfect teaching. The heart and mind have been transformed so that the Christian no longer has a willful desire or conscious intention to go on sinning. Christians are not slaves to sin. Rather, they are servants of *agapē* love to both God and their fellow beings.

Because of that, it is possible, according to the Bible, for every Christian to live free from rebellion against God and His principles. Thus Jude writes that God is able to keep us "from falling" and "to present" us "without blemish before the presence of his glory" (Jude 24). As Ellen White put it, God's help enables a person "to overcome every temptation wherewith he is beset."[27]

Wesley held that "in the greatest temptations, a single look to Christ, and the barely pronouncing [of] His name, suffices to overcome the wicked one, so it be done with confidence and calmness of spirit."[28]

That approach to overcoming temptation sounds both naive and simplistic. But think about it for a moment. I have known for years that I cannot sincerely pray and commit a deliberate act of sin at the same time. I have experimented. Temptation can become sin at the point that I become conscious of the temptation. At that very point I can choose to do one of two things. I can reject the temptation through God's power, or I can dwell on the temptation and cherish it a bit. In other words, I can ask God into my life to help me overcome, or I can tell Him to "scram" for a while so that I can enjoy my private lust.

My point is that I have discovered that all desire for willful sin leaves me when I approach God in a state of prayer. It is His Spirit who comes to my aid in prayer not only to give me a distaste for my sinful desire, but also to enliven that Christian love in my soul for another person, myself, and God, so that I do not want to perform actions that hurt or destroy and put Christ on the cross.

My problem, however, is similar to that of Saint Augustine, who, in suffering with the major temptation of his life, would pray, "Make me chaste Lord, but not yet." The trouble is that I am not overly anxious for the victory quite yet. I want just this one more time to savor my sinful thought or act. Too often I really don't yet want God intruding into my thoughts. Because I don't want Him as Lord of my life right now, I have chosen my sinful thoughts and/or actions over Him. On the other hand, I have discovered that when I am in a state of prayer, I lose the enjoyment of my sin. The temptation ceases to have power over me. I may waver and need to pray more than once, but His power is there if I desire it.

In short, I have discovered through empirical testing in daily life that I cannot sin when I am consciously surrendered and in a state of prayer to God. Paul received a message of truth for each of us when God told him, "My grace is sufficient for you, for my power is made perfect in weakness"(2 Cor. 12:9).

The above discussion of temptation must be seen in the context of the undeniable power of the pull of sin in our "mortal flesh." It is a fatal mistake to underestimate the strength of sin in human lives. The point is that even though the sin-power is forceful and persistent, God's power is more than sufficient if a person really wants it.

*A major aspect of Christian perfection (or maturity) is the perfect desire to become perfect in love toward other people and God.* The immature (or less than perfect) response is to desire my sin regardless of the results in terms of broken relationships to God and other people, accompanied by the thought that I will pray about it later, since the God who forgives at least "seventy times seven" (Matt. 18:22) will forgive me yet again.

And He will forgive again when we pray in repentance and faith, but His real desire is that we advance beyond the pattern of defeat to one of victory through using the spiritual power He has placed at our command. As Wesley so aptly put it, "No man sins because he hath not grace, but because he does not use the grace that he hath."[29]

Please remember, however, that Christian perfection is not merely entering into a conscious faith relationship in which wrong acts become repulsive. Even more important, it is a reaching out in love to both God and one's fellow beings. Perfection is a life lived in outgoing love that demonstrates that the God of love has transformed both our hearts and our outward actions—two aspects of our life that can never he separated. Thus Christian perfection is not merely negative (what I don't do) and internal—it is also positive (what I do do) and external. As a result, the Christian makes a difference in the quality of his or her world.

### John Wesley and the Restoration of Biblical Perfection

Both the Wesleyan denominations and Ellen White in *The Great Controversy* picture John Wesley as a continuation of the Protestant Reformation. J. Kenneth Grider writes that Wesley's contribution "is the teaching which peculiarly completes Martin Luther's 16th-century attempt to reform Christian doctrine according to its New Testament pattern. While it belonged to the man from Wittenberg to reestablish the doctrine of justification by faith, it belonged to the man from Epworth, Mr. Wesley, to reestablish the doctrine that, once justified by faith, believers may be sanctified [or perfected] wholly by faith . . . in this life."[30]

The classical Reformers of the sixteenth century, in their reaction against works-oriented medieval Catholicism, bent over backward to emphasize God's work *for* human beings in justification. In the process, while not denying the necessity of transformation of Christian lives, they tended to downplay sanctification or God's work *in* people. By Wesley's time in the mid-eighteenth century the overemphasis on forensic justification had led many to some form of antinomianism (rejection of the moral law), and the church needed a course correction toward sanctification.[31]

Wesley saw himself as called to make that course correction. Noting that "many of the Reformers themselves complained . . . that 'the Reformation was not carried far enough,'" Wesley went on to suggest that the focus of the completed Reformation should not be on rites and ceremonies but "on an entire change of men's *tempers* and *lives*."[32]

Donald Dayton hit that same point from another angle when he penned that while the generation after the Reformation, in their devotion to clarifying the faith, left us the great Protestant creeds, "the Wesleyan tradition . . . has left us a legacy of works of love."[33]

An emphasis on sanctification and Christian perfection in the present life was the great contribution of John Wesley. Christian perfection, he noted, is "the grand depositum which God has lodged with the people called Methodist; and for the sake of propagating this chiefly he appeared to have raised us up."[34]

Any religion that did not restore the true holiness lost at the Fall was for Wesley "no other than a poor farce, and a mere mockery of God, to the destruction of our own soul. . . . By nature ye are wholly corrupted. By grace ye shall he wholly renewed."[35]

Wesley refused to define perfection as being sinless because of the distinction between deliberate sins and mistakes or improper sins. Rather, he defined perfection as "pure love filling the heart, and governing all the words and actions. If," he added, "your idea includes anything more or anything else, it is not Scriptural." *Many, he correctly points out, stumble because "they include as many ingredients as they please not according to Scripture but their own imagination, in their idea of one that is perfect; and then readily deny anyone to be such who does not answer that imaginary idea.*" Thus, Wesley admonishes, we must stay close to the biblical definitions. "*Pure love reigning alone in the heart and life,—this is the whole of Scriptural perfection.*" It was the ability to love that humanity lost at the Fall.[36]

Calvinist theologians have rejected Wesley's definition of perfection as perfect love and have insisted that perfection consists of absolutely sinless behavior, an impossibility, they claim, as long as people possess mortal bodies. Thus while Calvinism holds to perfection, it also claims that humans cannot he perfect until the second coming of Christ.[37]

John Wesley, on the other hand, with his insightful distinction between proper sins and "sin improperly so called," holds that perfection in the present life is a perfect attitude toward God and other people while one is in a faith relationship to God. While Wesley's understanding of perfection affects every aspect of a person's outward life, it does not demand absolutely perfect performance. Mistakes or unintentional sins are quite in harmony with Wesleyan perfection. Thus in talking of perfection, Wesley does not hold to a *legal* definition of sin that defines any deviation from the will of God as sin, whether voluntary or involuntary. Rather, he holds to an ethical-relational view of sin that sees it as intentional rejection of God's will. Thus being perfect is in harmony with many "mistakes" and other imperfections—Wesleyan perfection is not sinless perfection.[38]

His position, as we saw above, is in harmony with the Bible's position on sin, perfection, and sinlessness. The Bible knows nothing of the Greek absolutist definition of human perfection. Absolute perfection in the Bible is an attribute of God alone.

Thus Wesley is at one with Calvinistic theologians in holding that absolute sinlessness is an impossibility in the present life. Such perfection as he taught, for example, did not mean a Christian would never "think an useless thought" or "speak an useless word. I myself," he penned, "believe that such a perfection is inconsistent with living in a corruptible body." If Christian perfection implies perfect behavior, he asserted, "we must not expect it till after death." The perfection of love to God and other people that Wesley taught "is consistent with a thousand nervous disorders, which that high-strained perfection is not."[39]

Wesley made a crucial point when he noted that those who "overdo" perfection by defining it "too high (so high as no man that we ever heard or read of attained)" will eventually "undo" it, "driving it out of the world" by making it unbelievable.[40] That insight continues to he true to the present day, as exhibited in the often forceful and frustrated attitudes of those who seek to push non-biblical absolutes onto their neighbors as well as onto themselves. We must never forget that the sinless perfectionists of His day instigated Christ's death.

All too often, the least convincing demonstrations of perfection are by those who, in their legalistic (rather than relational) definition of sin, are striving for absolute perfection. Such were the Pharisaic goats who were totally surprised by God's true standard in the great judgment scene of Matthew 25:31-46. Many who have done "many mighty works" in Christ's name will be found wanting because they have failed to internalize the principles of His character as expressed in the great law of love (see Matt. 7:21-23; 5:48; 22:34-40; Luke 6:36).

In the fullest sense, they have not kept the law, even though they had totally dedicated their lives to upholding the legalistic bits and pieces of the law (Rom. 13:8, 10; Gal. 5:13, 14). The bits and pieces (the letter) of the law only have Christian meaning when infused with the spirit of the law (2 Cor. 3:6). And that spirit, internalized in the heart of the believer through the power of the Holy Spirit (Heb. 8:10), stands at the center of biblical perfection.

At this point it is important to realize that Ellen White was raised as a Wesleyan. Beyond that, the words she uses and the way she employs them fall into the Wesleyan tradition. As I have continued to study both Ellen White and Wesley I have become increasingly convicted that we cannot really understand Ellen White's use of terminology and concepts related to perfection until we examine the Wesleyan background that she grew up in. Her writings are permeated with those Wesleyan usages that are in harmony with the biblical teachings on sin, perfection, and sinlessness.[41]

On the other hand, in the area of perfection, Ellen White discriminated carefully (as she did when relating to concepts used by other people in other areas of her writing) between biblical and nonbiblical ideas. On that count she flatly rejected two Wesleyan ideas: (1) that a Christian could be instantaneously perfected at a point in time in his/her earthly experience and (2) that such perfected Christians could be conscious of their own perfection. Beyond those issues, however, she is largely in harmony with Wesley's understanding of biblical perfection. And, it seems to me, as noted above, that Wesley generally reflects the biblical position.

We will now turn to Ellen White's teachings on the topic of perfection. Chapter 8 will examine them in a general way, while the ninth chapter will look at the type of perfection one must have in order to be translated at the second coming of Christ.

[1] Baillie, *God Was in Christ*, pp. 205, 206.

[2] Jean R. Zurcher, *Christian Perfection: A Bible and Spirit of Prophecy Teaching* (Washington, D.C.: Review and Herald, 1967), p. 6; Flew, *The Idea of Perfection*, pp. 398, 397. (Italics supplied.)

[3] Moore, *Refiner's Fire*, pp. 106, 107.

[4] Taylor, *Forgiveness and Reconciliation*, p. 144; Moore, *Refiner's Fire*, p. 114; Wynkoop, *Theology of Love*, p. 295.

[5] John Wesley, *The Letters of the Rev. John Wesley, A. M.*, ed. John Telford (London: Epworth, 1931), vol. 5, p. 38.

[6] E.g., see Ronald G. Walters, *American Reformers, 1815-1860* (New York: Hill and Wang), pp. 54-60; George R. Knight, *Millennial Fever and The End of the World: A Study of Millerite Adventism* (Boise, Idaho: Pacific Press, 1993), pp. 247-257. Ellen White also faced this problem in her early experience.

[7] S. N. Haskell to E. G. White, Oct. 3, 1899; Virginia Lieson Brereton, *Training God's Army: The American Bible School, 1880-1940* (Bloomington, Ind.: Indiana University Press, 1990), p. 11; Ellet J. Waggoner, *General Conference Bulletin*, 1899, p. 53.

[8] Wynkoop, *Theology of Love*, pp. 279, 280.

[9] Plato *Republic* 7.514-517.

[10] Barclay, *Matthew*, vol. 1, p. 177.

[11] LaRondelle, *Perfection and Perfectionism*, p. 181.

[12] Zurcher, *Christian Perfection*, p. 25; C. Mervyn Maxwell, "Ready for His Appearing," in *Perfection: The Impossible Possibility*, p. 164; cf. p. 141.

[13] Cox, *Wesley's Concept of Perfection*, pp. 146, 145.

[14] *Theological Dictionary of the New Testament*, s.v. "*Teleios* in the New Testament"; *The International Standard Bible Encyclopedia*, 1977-1988 ed., s.v. "Perfect; Make Perfect; Perfection."

[15] *Theological Wordbook of the Old Testament*, s.v. "*Tāmam* [and derivatives]."

[16] Paul Johannes Du Plessis, *Teleios: The Idea of Perfection in the New Testament* (Kampen, Netherlands: J. H. Kok, [1959]), p. 241.

[17] LaRondelle, *Perfection and Perfectionism*, pp. 327, 38, 39, 43, 48, 49.

[18] Wesley, *Works*, vol. 11, p. 446; vol. 7, p. 495.

[19] Wesley, *A Plain Account of Christian Perfection*, pp. 117, 118.

[20] See Guthrie, *New Testament Theology*, pp. 666, 667; Taylor, *Forgiveness and Reconciliation*, pp. 163-165.

[21] See Ridderbos, *Paul*, p. 271.

[22] White, *Christ's Object Lessons*, p. 160. (Italics supplied.)

[23] Wesley, quoted in Dieter, "The Wesleyan Perspective," in *Five Views on Sanctification*, p. 23.

[24] See Cox, *Wesley's Concept of Perfection*, pp. 168-173.

[25] Wesley, *A Plain Account of Christian Perfection*, p. 84.

[26] Cox, *Wesley's Concept of Perfection*, p. 150; Heppenstall "Let Us Go on to Perfection," in *Perfection: The Impossible Possibility*, p. 76.

[27] White, *Our High Calling*, p. 48.

[28] Wesley, *A Plain Account of Christian Perfection*, p. 109.

[29] Wesley, *Works*, vol. 6, p. 512.

[30] White, *The Great Controversy*, pp. 253-264; J. Kenneth Grider, *Entire Sanctification: The Distinctive Doctrine of Wesleyanism* (Kansas City, Mo.: Beacon Hill Press of Kansas City, 1980), p. 11.

[31] See Thomas C. Oden and Leicester R. Longden, eds., *The Wesleyan Theological Heritage: Essays of Albert C. Outler* (Grand Rapids: Zondervan, 1991), pp. 76-95.

[32] Wesley, *Works*, vol. 6, p. 263.

[33] Donald W. Dayton, "The Use of Scripture in the Wesleyan Tradition," in *The Use of the Bible in Theology/Evangelical Options*, Robert K. Johnston, ed. (Atlanta: John Knox, 1985), p. 128.

[34] Wesley, *Works*, vol. 13, p. 9.

[35] *Ibid.*, vol. 6, pp. 64, 65.

[36] Wesley, *A Plain Account of Christian Perfection*, pp. 54, 60, 61; Dayton, "The Use of Scripture," in *The Use of the Bible*, p. 127. (Italics supplied.)

[37] See Benjamin Breckinridge Warfield, *Studies in Perfectionism* (Phillipsburg, N.J.: Presbyterian and Reformed, 1958), pp. x, 58; L. Berkhof, *Systematic Theology*, 4th rev. and enl. ed. (Grand Rapids: Eerdmans, 1949), pp. 538-540.

[38] Laurence W. Wood, "A Wesleyan Response," in *Christian Spirituality*, pp. 84, 85; Wesley, *A Plain Account of Christian Perfection, passim.*

[39] Wesley, *Works*, vol. 12, p. 207.

[40] *Ibid.*

[41] For a major study that buttresses my conclusions on the relationship of E. G. White to Wesley's ideas on salvation and perfection, see Woodrow W. Whidden II, "The Soteriology of Ellen G. White: The Persistent Path to Perfection, 1836-1902" (Ph.D. diss., Drew University, 1989).

# Chapter 8

# Ellen White on Perfection and Sinlessness

One of the most obvious facts in Adventism, both present and past, is that those who emphasize perfection as a sort of perfect sinlessness having absolute implications heavily rely on the writings of Ellen White and are weak in scriptural presentations of the topic. The reason for their dependence on Ellen White is that one cannot prove sinless perfectionism from the Bible.

## Methodological Confusion Between the "Lesser" and the "Greater" Lights

I would like to suggest that neither can sinless perfectionism be demonstrated in Ellen White. For one thing, she has plainly stated that her "testimonies are not to give new light, but to impress vividly upon the heart the truths of inspiration already revealed" in the Bible. "Additional truth is not brought out."[1]

Interestingly enough, Ellen White linked her no new light position to the topic of Christian perfection. On the same page as the above quotations, we read: "If you had made God's word your study, with a desire to reach the Bible standard and attain to Christian perfection, you would not have needed the *Testimonies*."[2]

The purpose of the *Testimonies* is not to provide new light on perfection and other topics, but to simplify "the great truths already given" in the Bible. According to her, God gave to the Adventist Church "a lesser light [her writings] to lead men and women to the greater light [the Bible]."[3] One of the most serious problems in Adventism is that it has too often used the lesser light to lead people away from the Bible rather than toward it.

Such has been the case with the never-ending compilations on perfection. I cannot remember one of them suggesting that the real scene of the-ological action was the Bible, and that, therefore, Adventists should study the topic in the Word that she did not add anything to. To follow Ellen White means to let her writings bring "them back to the word that they have neglected to follow."[4]

My first point, therefore, is one of theological methodology. Adventists ought to go to the Bible for their basic understanding of Christian perfection rather than to Ellen White.

My second point is that because she builds upon the Bible, we must interpret her writings on perfection within the framework of the biblical teachings on that topic. Such a procedure will lead us to see that in actu-ality Ellen White has not contradicted the biblical teaching on perfection as love and maturity in daily life within a faith relationship to God through Jesus.

Of course, there always exist quotations from her that can be violently ripped out of the context of her entire message to prove extremes she never taught. But that approach can also be used for Bible writers.

For example, *I could have a field day of fanaticism if I took 1 John 3:9 out of context*: "No one born of God commits sin; for God's nature abides in him, and *he cannot sin*." If I as a Christian "cannot sin," then everything I do has God's mark of approval. Many perfectionists in history took exactly that view, but their lives turned out to be something less than sanctified.

However, when we read 1 John 3:9 within the total context of 1 John, as we noted in chapter 7, we see that the disciple is talking about rebellious and ongoing sin rather than absolute sinlessness. *The irresponsible collector of quotations can do great injustice to the message of the Bible by seeking out extreme statements on a topic, but Ellen White's writings are liable to a thousand times the problem due to the bulk of her literary corpus.* Quotation collectors on perfec-tion have had and are having a field day.

*Our only safety is to read Ellen White within the context of the biblical frame-work of perfection, which she claims not to go beyond.* In addition, we need to be careful to interpret her writings on the topic within her total message and not to select out the most radical statements and present them as her balanced position.

In our examination of Ellen White's teachings on perfection in the rest of this chapter and the next, we will see that she does indeed agree with the Bible she uplifted throughout her ministry. That is good, because she gave us no authorization to find in her writings teachings that supersede the Bible as the Word of God.

## Ellen White's High View of Character Perfection

It will come as no surprise to the readers of this book that Ellen White had an extremely high view of character perfection. Some would say that her understanding of perfection is related to forensic justification by faith; that the Christian is perfect because the perfect Christ has covered his or her sins; that Christ is their vicarious perfection; that they are "clothed in" His "perfection."[5]

That view is true, but it is not her whole viewpoint. She also held to a very explicit concept of character perfection as a possibility and an ideal for every Christian. Thus while there is a perfection involving what God does *for* us, there is also a perfection involving what God does *in* us through the dynamic power of the Holy Spirit. Richard Lesher summed up Ellen White's position nicely when he observed that for her "perfection" "is unquestionably the goal of sanctification" and "the goal of Christian life."[6]

That Ellen White meant character perfection *in* Christ's followers and not merely vicarious perfection *for* His followers is clear from the following quotations. "The Lord requires perfection from His redeemed family. *He calls for perfection in character-building."* *"Perfection of character is attainable* by every one who strives for it." "We can overcome. Yes; fully, entirely. Jesus died to make a way of escape for us, that we might overcome every evil temper, every sin, every temptation, and sit down at last with Him."[7]

One of Ellen White's most forceful discussions of character perfection occurs in her treatment of the parable of the talents (Matt. 25:14-30) in *Christ's Object Lessons.* "We should," she penned, "cultivate every faculty to the highest degree of perfection. . . . *Moral perfection is required of all.* Never should we lower the standard of righteousness in order to accommodate inherited or cultivated tendencies to wrong-doing. . . . Those who would be workers together with God must strive for perfection of every organ of the body and quality of the mind." "Perfection of character . . . will reach out to perfection in action."[8]

Not only did Mrs. White hold to the necessity of character perfection as the apex of sanctification, she also noted that Satan "is constantly seeking to deceive the followers of Christ with his fatal sophistry that it is impossible for them to overcome. . . . He [Christ] declares . . . : 'My grace is sufficient for thee.'. . . Let none, then, regard their defects as incurable. God will give faith and grace to overcome them." "Satan is jubilant when he hears the professed followers of Christ making excuses for their deformity of character." Furthermore, she argued that "those who say that it is not possible to live a perfect life throw upon God the imputation of injustice and untruth."[9]

Ellen White leaves no doubt that she believed character perfection is both possible and expected. Thus it behooves us to examine what she means by the concept.

That task will take up most of this chapter and the next. Meanwhile, it is important to note that she held that God's forgiving grace runs side by side with His empowering grace. Thus Christ's vicarious justifying perfection still covers those who fall short.

In her thought, the issue of actualized character perfection will come to a head just before the second coming of Christ. Chapter 9 will treat that eschatological aspect of perfection. The rest of this chapter will explore her concepts of character development and sinlessness.

## Perfect Like Christ

A whole battery of Ellen White statements indicate that Christians are to develop Christlike characters. After citing Matthew 5:48 ("Be ye therefore perfect, even as your Father which is in heaven is perfect," KJV), she goes on to note that that command "is a promise. The plan of redemption contemplates our complete recovery from the power of Satan. . . . A holy temper, a Christlike life, is accessible to every repenting, believing child of God. *The ideal of Christian character is Christlikeness. As the Son of man was perfect in His life, so His followers are to be perfect in their life. . . . His character is to be ours.*"[10]

Again she penned: "Christ has given His Spirit as a divine power to overcome all hereditary and cultivated tendencies to evil, and to impress *His* own *character* upon His church. . . . *The very image of God is to be reproduced in humanity. The honor of God, the honor of Christ, is involved in the perfection of the character of His people.*"[11]

Those powerful quotations leave us in no doubt that God wants to reproduce His character perfectly in His children.[12] It is a mistake to seek to explain away the radical forcefulness of such statements. We will return to the implications of perfectly reproducing the character of Christ—a recurring Ellen White theme—in chapter 9.

Meanwhile, we should note that Herbert Douglass is correct when he suggests that we should avoid absolutist definitions of perfection based on Grecian philosophy rather than the Bible. "Perfection in the Biblical sense," Douglass pens, "is simply Christlikeness—combining a relationship with God such as Jesus had, with the qualities of character that Jesus manifested."[13] The qualities of Christ's character, as we shall see, are the central concern in understanding what it means to be like God and/or Christ.

One of the great themes of Ellen White's *The Desire of Ages* is that we can overcome just as Christ did—through the indwelling power of the Holy Spirit. Just as Jesus resisted the temptation to put His will at the center of His life (the very point at which Adam and Eve fell), so may we. He overcame that TEMPTATION of temptations. As a result, He could say at the end of His life that Satan had "no power" over Him (John 14:30).

"There was in Him," Ellen White wrote, "nothing that responded to Satan's sophistry. He did not consent to sin. Not even by a thought did He yield to temptation. So it may be with us."[14] As we noted in discussing the TEMPTATION of Christ in chapter 6, He refused to come down off His cross and exert His will in opposition to the Father's will.

God offers that same opportunity and power to those who accept Christ. Through the power of the Spirit, our will can stay surrendered to His will, and we can reject the TEMPTATION to return to the self-centered, self-serving life of sin. Transformation to a life of service and self-giving can become a permanent part of every born from above human life. Like Christ, each of us may pass over "the ground where Adam stumbled and fell," resist the TEMPTATION to live a life in rebellion to God, and actively live out the great law of love in daily life.[15]

Christ "was fitted for the conflict by the indwelling of the Holy Spirit. And He came to make us partakers of the divine nature. So long as we are united to Him by faith [i.e., 'in Him'], sin has no more dominion over us. God reaches for the hand of faith in us to direct it to lay fast hold upon the divinity of Christ, that we may attain to perfection of character."[16]

At this juncture it is crucial to note that Ellen White held that even though Christians are to reproduce the perfect character of Christ, they will never equal it. Thus, she wrote, "He is a perfect and holy example, given for us to imitate. *We cannot equal the pattern*; but we shall not be approved of God if we do not copy it and, according to the ability which God has given, resemble it." It is interesting that she made that statement in the context of loving others and rejecting selfishness, since, as we shall see, that was the central element in Christ's character.[17]

Along the same line, Mrs. White penned that "Christ is our pattern, the perfect and holy example that has been given us to follow. *We can never equal the pattern; but we may imitate and resemble it according to our ability.*" In another connection she flatly claimed that "no one is [ultimately] perfect but Jesus."[18]

After reading the last few pages, you should be suffering from a bit of intellectual tension. After all, Ellen White has suggested both that we are to perfectly reproduce Christ's character and that we will never perfectly equal His pattern.

It is interesting that those readers who frequently reiterate the perfectly reproducing the character of Christ statements are quite concerned that no one explain away the forcefulness of those seeming absolutes. But then they turn around and seek to downplay the less than equaling the pattern quotations. The reverse procedure is the practice of those who emphasize the less than equal statements.[19]

The best way to handle the apparent conflict is to let Ellen White provide her own explanation. The key to a balanced understanding seems to lie in her oft-repeated comment on Matthew 5:48: "As God is perfect in His sphere, so man may be perfect in his sphere." Woodrow Whidden perceptively points out that "the bottom line" of such statements "is that perfection is something different in God's sphere than it is in the human sphere."[20]

In yet another connection, she seemingly suggests that variations in perfection even exist between people. Thus she could write: "With our limited powers we are to be as holy in our sphere as God is holy in His sphere. To the extent of our ability [which apparently differs between individuals and within the same individual across time], we are to make manifest the truth and love and excellence of the divine character."[21]

On the other hand, the central core of all perfection, regardless of varying "ability," remains the same. A few lines farther down the page, therefore, she can claim that "wherever there is union with Christ there is love. Whatever other fruits we may bear, if love be missing, they profit nothing. Love to God and our neighbor is the very essence of our religion."[22] That love is the golden thread that runs across and throughout the various spheres of divine and human perfection. It is the key that unlocks the mystery of what it means to be perfect like Christ.

**Perfection: A Dynamic Process**

Closely related to the idea of the relativity implicit in Ellen White's concept of spheres of perfection is her view of perfection as a dynamic, ongoing process—one in which a converted Christian constantly grows in approximating the character of God but never reaches the goal.

In at least three of the above quotations Ellen White linked perfection with an individual's endowments. Consequently, degrees of relative perfection vary from one person to another, since not all have the same endowments. She can therefore write that "the specific place appointed us in

161

life is determined by our capabilities. Not all reach the same development or do with equal efficiency the same work. God does not expect the hyssop to attain the proportions of the cedar, or the olive the height of the stately palm. But each should aim just as high as the union of human with divine power makes it possible for him to reach."[23]

Note, however, that although there exist great variations in individual achievement and potential, there is a constant that runs across all levels of ability—total dedication to the purposes of God so that He might use each of us to our greatest potential. That total or perfect dedication to God's will is an important aspect of Christian perfection. Needless to say, total dedication is the polar extreme of that rebellion that stands as the hallmark of SIN.

Perhaps more important than variation between the earthly potential of individuals is the fact that people grow in perfection. Ellen White can point out, therefore, that even though Jesus was perfect as a child, He grew in grace, according to Luke 2:52. Thus, she concluded, "*Even the most perfect Christian may increase continually in the knowledge and love of God.*"[24] That internal growth, it seems to me, implies a developing perfection in outward action as people put to use their increasing love and knowledge.

R. N. Flew helps us see the outworking of that idea when he talks of the carpenter who puts his all into making tables and chairs. Although they are not "perfect," they are the best he can do at that stage of life. Since "he is offering all his powers and his daily work as a sacrifice to God," he is therefore "fulfilling the purpose of God."[25]

In another connection, Ellen White penned that "at every stage of development our life may be perfect; yet if God's purpose for us is fulfilled, there will be continual advancement."[26] It is of crucial importance to recognize that the perfect Christian is the developing Christian. That development begins at conversion, grows throughout one's earthly life, and will continue to progress, as we shall see in chapter 10, throughout eternity.

Thus while perfection has a solid core that consists of devotion to God's will and love to Him and other people, there is also a relative aspect as one's abilities and knowledge increase. But because of the inner core, one puts the new developments to sanctified uses.

Ellen White, therefore, agrees with Paul that a person can be perfect but not yet perfect (Phil. 3:15, 12, KJV). The same applies to her concept of sinlessness. As with Paul (Rom. 6) and John (1 John 3:9; 1:9-2:1), for Ellen White a person may be simultaneously sinless and not yet sinless.

## Sinless But Not Yet Sinless

She is quite explicit in her statements that a Christian may live a sinless life here on earth. For example, in 1906 she told her hearers at a California camp meeting that "every one who surrenders fully to God is given the privilege of living without sin, in obedience to the law of heaven."[27]

In a similar vein, in a 1902 article on "Satan's Rebellion," Ellen White claimed that "every one who by faith obeys God's commandments, will reach the condition of sinlessness in which Adam lived before his transgression."[28]

By way of contrast, she noted that only "when the saints of God are glorified . . . will it be safe to claim that we are saved and sinless." "We cannot say," Ellen White declared on another occasion, " 'I am sinless,' till this vile body is changed and fashioned like unto His glorious body." She went on to claim that those who will stand before the "throne of God without spot, or wrinkle, or any such thing" will be "complete in Christ" because they are "robed in His righteousness." That last statement indicates that the saints will need the covering righteousness of Christ right up to His second coming.[29]

How is it, we must ask, that Ellen White can say we can live without sin and be as sinless as Adam before the Fall on the one hand, while stating that we cannot claim sinlessness and will need the merits of Christ until the Second Coming on the other hand?

The answer lies, as it did in the case of the Bible writers, in her definition of sin and sinlessness. Sin, as we noted in chapter 2, is an act of rebellion against the person and authority of God. A conscious, willful attitude and act, sin is, Ellen White wrote, "a virtual denial of God, a rebellion against the laws of His government." Such sins are "willful" and "known." "Let none deceive themselves," she penned, "with the belief that they can become holy while *willfully* violating one of God's requirements. The commission of a *known sin* silences the witnessing voice of the Spirit and separates the soul from God." But "*to be led into sin unawares— not intending to sin . . .—is very different from the one who plans and deliberately enters into temptation and plans out a course of action.*"[30]

From the above quotation it is plain that Ellen White held that there are both conscious, known, intentional sins on the one hand, and sins of ignorance on the other, that are both unintentional and unconscious. It is important to note, however, that she regards both types as sins.

On other occasions, she refers to unintentional sins as "mistakes." She could therefore write that "when we are clothed with the righteousness of Christ, *we shall have no relish for sin*; for Christ will be working with us. *We may make mistakes, but we will hate the sin that caused the sufferings of the Son of God.*"[31]

With that background in place, we can begin to understand Ellen White's apparently conflicting statements that we can live sinless lives, yet we cannot claim sinlessness. Those who "are living without sin" and who "reach the condition of sinlessness in which Adam lived before his transgression" will not be participating in rebellion or willful sin any more than Adam did before the Fall. Because their attitude is right with God, they are without rebellion toward Him and His law of love.

On the other hand, they will still make mistakes. They will still commit unwillful and unconscious sins. Thus they are not sinless. It is with that tension in mind that Arnold Wallenkampf could suggest that one can have a perfect attitude of love to God even though he or she may fall short in achievement. John Fowler, in his doctoral study of Ellen White's concept of character development, came to a similar conclusion. Perfection, Fowler wrote, "calls for the absence of *cherished* sin."[32]

By now it should be clear that Ellen White's view of sinlessness is the same as that of the New Testament writers and of John Wesley, as examined in chapter 7. It should therefore not surprise us to discover that she blamed the same culprit for the shortfall between the lack of cherished sin and total sinlessness. It is the old issue of "mortal bodies" that Paul wrestled with in the book of Romans (see, for example, Rom. 6:12) and elsewhere.

"All," she stated, "may now obtain holy hearts, but it is not correct to claim in this life to have holy flesh. . . . If those who speak so freely of perfection in the flesh, could see things in the true light, they would recoil with horror from their presumptuous ideas. . . . While we can not claim perfection of the flesh, we may have Christian perfection of the soul. Through the sacrifice made in our behalf, sins may be perfectly forgiven. Our dependence is not in what man can do; it is in what God can do for man through Christ. . . . All may be made perfect in Christ Jesus. Thank God that we are not dealing with impossibilities. We may claim sanctification. . . . *While sin is forgiven in this life, its results are not now wholly removed.*" That will take place at the Second Coming.[33]

In conclusion, Ellen White, as does the Bible, holds to a tension between Christians being sinless but not yet being completely sinless. Such sinless Christians are the same as perfect Christians. They are those who share in a faith relationship with Jesus and who have totally surrendered their hearts, minds, and wills to doing God's will. Thus they are as free from rebellious sin as Adam before his fall. On the other hand, due to ignorance and other infirmities of the flesh, they still make mistakes and commit unwillful sins. But a fuller state of perfection and sinlessness awaits them at the second coming of Jesus, when He will "change our vile body, that it may be fashioned like unto his glorious body" (Phil. 3:21, KJV; cf. 1 Cor. 15:44, 50-54). We will examine the effect of that change on perfection and sinlessness in chapter 10.

**The Character of Character Perfection**

Before leaving Ellen White's view of perfection, it is important that we come to grips with her understanding of the nature of character perfection. We encounter two approaches to that topic. The first focuses on the "bits and pieces" (that is, a life of flawless acts) that make up perfection, while the second emphasizes a principle-centered view of character perfection. Even though the bits-and-pieces idea seems to be most evident in popular interpretations of Ellen White, her writings actually lead us toward the opposite interpretation.

She is concerned with a person's loyalties, that one's heart and mind be in perfect accord with the heart and mind of God. Right actions—the bits and pieces—will flow naturally out of a right attitude and allegiance.

Her view of principle-centered character perfection has at least two aspects. One she nicely expresses when she comments that "the essence of all righteousness is loyalty to our Redeemer. This will lead us to do right because it is right—because right doing is pleasing to God."[34]

She highlights the second aspect of character perfection in writing that it was Christ's mission to make "men partakers of the divine nature, to bring them into harmony with the *principles* of the law of heaven."[35] Of course, as we saw from the Bible, both the "divine nature" and the "principles of the law" focus on *agapē* love (1 John 4:8; Matt. 22:36-40).

Ellen White links the bits and pieces of Christian living to basic principles in a consistent pattern that is quite in harmony with the biblical presentation. For example, in *Christ's Object Lessons* she flatly states that "*God requires perfection of His children.*" She goes on to note that "His law is a transcript of His own character, and it is the standard of all character. This infinite standard is presented to all that there may be no mistake in regard to the kind of people whom God will have to compose His kingdom. The life of Christ on earth was a perfect expression of God's law, and when those who claim to be children of God become Christlike in character, they will be obedient to God's commandments. Then the Lord can trust them to be of the number who shall compose the family of heaven."[36]

Thus far we could interpret the law-oriented perfection of this passage in terms of either the bits-and-pieces model of outward actions or from the perspective of the paradigm of principles. Taken out of context, most would probably read the bits-and-pieces concept into it. But we should always let Ellen White speak through the fuller context.

In the next paragraph she points out that many "profess to be Christians, . . . yet they feel no need of a transformation of character." Such have never recognized either their need of faith in Christ or of true repentance. "They have not overcome their hereditary or cultivated tendencies [tendencies are best seen as the overall direction of one's heart and mind] to wrong doing. . . . Many who call themselves Christians are mere human moralists [those who merely keep the bits and pieces of the law without being transformed through a saving relationship with Christ]."[37]

On the next page Ellen White becomes more explicit in unpacking her idea of the kind of perfection "God requires . . . of His children." "The righteousness of Christ," she explains, "will not cover one *cherished* sin [thus implying that His righteousness does cover nonrebellious sins]. A man may be a lawbreaker in heart; yet if he commits no outward act of transgression [he manages to live up to the bits and pieces], he may be regarded by the world [and probably most people in the church] as possessing great integrity. *But God's law looks into the secrets of the heart. Every act is judged by the motives that prompt it.* Only that which is in accord with the *principles* of God's law will stand in the judgment." Her next words are that "God is love," thus bringing into focus the all-important principle.[38]

The above passage is typical of Ellen White's discussions of character perfection. She is concerned mainly with the great motivating principle of love that shapes and transforms a person's tendencies through God's grace. The bits and pieces of the law are important to her, but only in the context of the great principle of the law. Even at that, in the above passage she carefully specifies that it is the "cherished" bits and pieces of rebellious action that is the problem and not all the bits and pieces as such. Thus her view of character perfection in that passage is a principle-centered perspective.

That same understanding emerges again and again in her writings. Thus in commenting on the rich young ruler's encounter with Christ in his quest for perfection, she points out that while he had the bits and pieces of the law taken care of, he had missed Christ's ideal. "Christ read the ruler's heart.

Only one thing he lacked, but that was a *vital principle*. He needed the love of God in the soul. This lack, unless supplied, would prove fatal to him; his whole nature would become corrupted. . . . *That he might receive the love of God [the missing principle], his supreme love of self must be surrendered.*"[39]

She continued on to emphasize that "*Christ made the only terms which could place the ruler where he would perfect a Christian character.*" Later in the passage she stressed that the point at issue is "obedience to His law, not merely a legal obedience, but an obedience which enters into the life, and is exemplified in the character."[40]

Thus she followed her oft-repeated pattern of relating the bits and pieces of righteous living to the great central principle of character development in her discussion of character perfection. She leaves no doubt as to her focus. The essence of character perfection involves the perfect heart and mind and undivided allegiance to God. Such a view thoroughly agrees with her (and the Bible's) view of perfection and sinlessness as being attitudinal rather than absolute perfection of action. We will examine the gap between the perfect attitude and perfect actions in chapter 10.

In the meantime, it is important to emphasize that character perfection does not primarily consist of what one avoids. People will never become perfect by avoiding this sin and that transgression, even if they are able to escape all of them. On the other hand, character perfection is intimately linked with SIN—the attitude that places my self at the center of my life and focuses my *agapē* on that self rather than on God and others. C. Mervyn Maxwell makes a helpful point when he notes that "it is essential to emphasize the positive aspects of character perfection."[41]

Ellen White repeatedly drives home that same point. "Gospel religion," she penned, "is Christ in the life—a living, active *principle*. It is the grace of Christ revealed in character and wrought out in good works. The principles of the gospel cannot be disconnected from any department of practical life. . . . *Love is the basis of godliness*. Whatever the profession, no man has pure love to God unless he has unselfish love for his brother. . . . *When self is merged in Christ, love springs forth spontaneously. The completeness of Christian character is attained when the impulse to help and bless others springs constantly from within*—when the sunshine of heaven fills the heart and is revealed in the countenance."[42]

That principle-based "completeness of Christian character" is in essence the definition of character perfection. Ellen White can therefore write that "no man who has the true ideal of what constitutes a perfect character will fail to manifest the sympathy and tenderness of Christ. The influence of grace is to soften the heart, to refine and purify the feelings, giving a heaven-born delicacy and sense of propriety."[43]

Before leaving the topic of perfection in Ellen White, we should note two points. First, she never separates character perfection from Christ's empowering and transforming grace. Jean Zurcher has concluded that "an honest examination of Ellen White's writings will reveal that not once does she refer to character perfection without indicating that Jesus Christ is the only means of attaining it."[44]

A second thing to keep in mind is that it is easy for Ellen White readers to misapply her writings on perfection because of personal factors or mindsets. Ann Burke makes an excellent point when she indicates "it is unfortunate that, because of our temperaments, overconscientious believers often single out strong statements probably intended for careless Christians. They whip themselves with these statements, while careless church members find false security in those no doubt meant to comfort the oversensitive."[45] It is plain, of course, where the Pharisees would fall in such a scheme.

In this chapter, we have seen that Ellen White's definitions of sinlessness and perfection, when we read her statements in the context of both specific passages and in that of the general tenor of her writings, thoroughly reflect the biblical perspective. One of the most unfortunate tendencies of many Adventists is to quote Ellen White out of context in a way that pushes her beyond the biblical framework that she claims she never transcended. It is difficult to see how we can view that practice as being "faithful to Ellen White's straight testimony."

The issue of stilted definitions of perfection is especially problematic in the area of end-time perfection. It is to that topic that we now turn.

---

[1] White, *Testimonies for the Church*, vol. 5, p. 665.

[2] *Ibid.*

[3] *Ibid.*; Ellen G. White, *Colporteur Ministry* (Mountain View, Calif.: Pacific Press, 1953), p. 125.

[4] White, *Testimonies for the Church*, vol. 5, p. 663

[5] White, *The Desire of Ages*, p. 357. See Helmut Ott, *Perfect in Christ: The Mediation of Christ in the Writings of Ellen G. White* (Washington, D. C.: Review and Herald, 1987).

[6] William Richard Lesher, "Ellen G. White's Concept of Sanctification" (Ph.D. diss., New York University, 1970), pp. 242, 263.

[7] White, *Seventh-day Adventist Bible Commentary*, vol. 5, p. 1085; White, *Selected Messages*, book 1, p. 212; White, *Testimonies for the Church*, vol. 1, p. 144. (Italics supplied.)

[8] White, *Christ's Object Lessons*, pp. 330, 332. (Italics supplied.)

[9] White, *The Great Controversy*, p. 489; White, *The Desire of Ages*, p. 311; White, *Review and Herald*, Feb. 7, 1957, p. 30.

[10] White, *The Desire of Ages*, p. 311. (Italics supplied.)

[11] *Ibid.*, p. 671. (Italics supplied.)

[12] See White, *Christ's Object Lessons*, p. 69.

[13] Herbert E. Douglass, "Men of Faith—The Showcase of God's Grace," in *Perfection: The Impossible Possibility*, p. 14.

[14] White, *The Desire of Ages*, p. 123.

[15] White, *Selected Messages*, book 1, p. 226; White, *Testimonies for the Church*, vol. 8, p. 208.

[16] White, *The Desire of Ages*, p. 123.

[17] White, *Testimonies for the Church*, vol. 2, p. 549. (Italics supplied.)

[18] White, *Review and Herald*, Feb. 5, 1895, p. 81; White, MS 24, 1892, in *1888 Materials*, p. 1089. (Italics Supplied.)

[19] For an argument from Ellen White urging her readers to read with balance and common sense, see George R. Knight, *Myths in Adventism* (Washington, D.C.: Review and Herald, 1985), pp. 17-25; George R. Knight, *Reading Ellen White* (Hagerstown, Md.: Review and Herald, 1997).

[20] White, *Testimonies for the Church*, vol. 4, p. 591; vol. 8, p. 64; White, *Patriarchs and Prophets*, p. 574; Ellen G. White, *Medical Ministry* (Mountain View, Calif.: Pacific Press, 1932), pp. 112, 113; Whidden, "The Soteriology of Ellen G. White," p. 350. Cf. Ellen G. White, *The Spirit of Prophecy* (Battle Creek, Mich.: SDA Pub. Assn., 1877), vol. 2, p. 225.

[21] White, *Selected Messages*, book 1, p. 337.

[22] *Ibid.*

[23] White, *Education*, p. 267.

[24] White, *Testimonies for the Church*, vol. 1, p. 340. (Italics supplied.)

[25] Flew, *The Idea of Perfection*, p. 405.

[26] White, *Christ's Object Lessons*, p. 65.

[27] White, *Review and Herald*, Sept. 27, 1906, p. 8.

[28] White, *Signs of the Times*, July 23, 1902, p. 3. Cf. White, *Seventh-day Adventist Bible Commentary*, vol. 6, p. 1118.

[29] White, *Signs of the Times*, May 16, 1895, p. 4; March 23, 1888, p. 178.

[30] White, *Mount of Blessing*, p. 51; White, *The Great Controversy*, p. 472; White, *Our High Calling*, p. 177. (Italics supplied.)

[31] White, *Selected Messages*, book 1, p. 360. (Italics supplied.)

[32] Wallenkampf, *Justified*, p. 134; John M. Fowler, "The Concept of Character Development in the Writings of Ellen G. White" (Ed.D. diss., Andrews University, 1977), p. 148. (Italics supplied.)

[33] White, *General Conference Bulletin*, 1901, pp. 419, 420. (Italics supplied.)

[34] White, *Christ's Object Lessons*, pp. 97, 98.

[35] White, *Mount of Blessing*, p. 50. (Italics supplied.)

[36] White, *Christ's Object Lessons*, p. 315. (Italics supplied.)

[37] *Ibid.*

[38] *Ibid.*, p. 316. (Italics supplied.)

[39] White, *The Desire of Ages*, p. 519. (Italics supplied.)

[40] *Ibid.*, pp. 520, 523. (Italics supplied.)

[41] Maxwell, "Ready for His Appearing," in *Perfection: The Impossible Possibility*, p. 196.

[42] White, *Christ's Object Lessons*, p. 384. (Italics supplied.)

[43] White, *Mount of Blessing*, p. 135.

[44] Zurcher, *Christian Perfection*, p. 53.

[45] Ann Cunningham Burke, "The Adventist Elephant," *Adventist Review*, Aug. 27, 1987, p. 9.

Chapter 9

# Perfection
# and the Final Generation

It is no accident that Seventh-day Adventists have consistently believed that some sort of perfection is important. Even a cursory reading of Revelation 14—the chapter central to Adventist self-understanding—leaves one with thoughts of a perfect people at the end of earthly history.

### The Bible on Final Generation Perfection

Revelation 14 opens with the 144,000, who are sealed with their Father's name in their foreheads (Rev. 14:1; 7:4). The chapter announces that these end time people "have not defiled themselves" with false religion, that they "follow the Lamb wherever he goes," that they are honest, and that they are "spotless" (14:4, 5). G. C. Berkouwer says of the 144,000 that they are "radically committed" to Christ.[1]

It is the word translated as "spotless," however, that leads one to think of perfection for this end-time people. The King James Version translates the word as "without fault before the throne of God," and the New International Version renders is as "blameless."

Robert Mounce points out that "when used of NT believers, the Greek word uniformly means *ethically blameless.*" And George Eldon Ladd suggests that these people have "faultless dedication" to God.[2] No matter which way you look at it, the 144,000 end-time people possess some sort of perfection that Scripture appears to emphasize because it is an out-of-the-ordinary historical experience.

Adventists early saw themselves in this passage. They also glimpsed themselves as representing the three angels of the following verses (Rev. 14:6-12). Their message to the world was that "the hour of his judgment has come," that Babylon has fallen, and that keeping the commandments of God is a sign of those who are loyal to Him as opposed to those who give their allegiance to the beast power and receive its mark.

The next thing after the preaching of those three messages is the second coming of Christ and the harvest of the earth (verses 14-20). It is not difficult to understand why those who saw themselves in Revelation 14 wanted to be ready for the harvest by becoming "spotless" through obedience to "the commandments of God." The idea of end-time harvest perfection has been built into the fabric of Adventism from the very beginning of its history.

It seems to me to be useless to try to explain away the "spotless" perfection of God's end-time people. The real issue concerns why God apparently expects more from the final generation of earthlings than from any other.

The answer to that question does not lie in some kind of dispensationalism in which God treats them differently from those who have gone before, but in the effect of the end time crisis portrayed in Revelation 12:17 and 13:11-17. That crisis polarizes all humanity into two camps—one in total allegiance to the God of the universe and the other in complete loyalty to the dragon (Rev. 12:9) as represented by the beast powers of Revelation 13.

Revelation 12:17 previews the unprecedented crisis when it tells us that the dragon will make war with those who demonstrate their loyalty to God by obedience to His commandments. That war comes to a head in Revelation 13:16, 17, in which those who refuse loyalty to the beast in effect find themselves put under a death penalty (they cannot "buy or sell"). Revelation 14:13 records the fate of some of them as those who "die in the Lord henceforth"—that is, between the start of the preaching of the third angel's message and the great harvest of the earth.

It is in that stilted context that people become polarized in an unprecedented manner toward choosing either the principles of God's kingdom or those of Satan's dominion. According to Revelation 12:17-14:20, there will be no space for end-time neutrality. Those who attempt to do so merely receive the beast's mark in their hand rather than in their forehead (see Rev. 13:16). The mark in the forehead indicates intellectual acceptance of the beast's principles, while that in the hand represents passive submission to the dragon's principle of self-centered rebellion that lies at the root of all sins.

As a result, no middle ground will exist. In the clear light of the final conflict, those not accepting the mark of the beast must consciously opt for total allegiance to God's principles. Scripture therefore describes them as "spotless," as uncontaminated by false theology, as keepers of God's commandments, and as those who have faith in Jesus (see Rev. 14:4, 5, 12).

Martin Luther helps us see the effect of crisis on polarization when he notes that "God has many lovers" "in times of peace." In good times it is easy to think that we really love God, but times of crisis distinguish internalized love and allegiance from the merely external.[3]

During the crisis of Revelation 13 and 14 the issues in the great conflict between Satan and God become crystal clear for the first time in history. That very clarity and the principle-based decisions it forces on people living at that time has the effect of purifying the allegiance of men and women either toward God or against Him. Thus end-time people will have a unique experience in world history. That experience, as my former colleague Kenneth Strand has suggested, is not unique in kind but in magnitude. Humanity has always faced problems, but not of the intensity and clarity of the crisis predicted in the Apocalypse.

Those Christians living through that unprecedented period of earth's history will be done with rebellion (SIN) against God. Their allegiance and dedication to Him will be "spotless," "without fault," and perfect. God will be able to describe them as those who have "the patience of the saints" in awaiting the harvest, as those who "keep the commandments of God," and as those who have the same kind of faith that Jesus had in the Father (Rev. 14:12, KJV). As a result, "when he appears" in the clouds of heaven to harvest the earth, they "shall be like him" (1 John 3:2).

Not only did the early Adventists focus on perfection because of their understanding of the book of Revelation, but also because, as Ladd puts it, "sanctification has an eschatological goal. It is God's purpose that the church should be finally presented to him in splendor, 'without spot or wrinkle or any such thing, that she might be holy and without blemish' (Eph. 5:27; see Col. 1:22; 1 Thess. 3:13; 5:23)."[4]

Donald Guthrie points out that "the final dissolution of all things is held out as a motive for the present pursuit of a life of holiness" by the apostle Peter.[5] "Since all these things are thus to be dissolved," the apostle queried, "what sort of persons ought you to be in lives of holiness and godliness, waiting for and hastening the coming of the day of God?" (2 Peter 3:11, 12; cf. 1 Peter 1:13-16).

Part of the impetus for improving Christian conduct down through church history has been a "fear" (or respect) of judgment to come. After all, didn't Paul write that "we shall all stand before the judgment seat of God" (Rom. 14:10)? Again, he wrote to the Corinthians: "We must all appear before the judgment seat of Christ, so that each one may receive good or evil, according to what he has done in the body" (2 Cor. 5:10).

With the above texts in mind, we should not think it strange that a church believing itself to have been especially raised up to preach "the commandments of God" and "the hour of his judgment has come" should have serious thoughts about perfection as its members readied themselves for "the harvest of the earth" (Rev. 14:15). To the contrary, it would have been odd for such a people not to think about spotlessness or perfection.

Adventists, of course, have not fallen short in such endeavors, even if some of their concepts of perfection have not adequately reflected the biblical teaching on the topic. In the rest of this chapter we will examine Ellen White's understanding of end-time perfection. That perspective, as I noted earlier, must be viewed within the framework of the biblical concepts of perfection, sinlessness, sin, and redemption. Beyond that, it must be faithful to the total thrust of her teachings on those topics and to the immediate literary context of her several statements on end-time perfection.

### Ellen White on End-time Polarization and the Cleansing of the Sanctuary

One of the great contributions of Ellen White's writings is the fact that she picks up and expands the final controversy theme that runs from Revelation 12:17-14:20. In agreement with Revelation 12:17, she pictures an intensification of Satan's work as the accuser "as we approach nearer to the close of this world's history." Seeing his time running out, the devil "will work with greater earnestness to deceive and destroy. He is angry when he sees a people on the earth who, even in their weakness and sinfulness, have respect for the law of Jehovah. He is determined that they shall not obey God." That results in his heightened activity as explicated in Revelation 12:17.[6]

Also central to Ellen White's theology is the separation of the world into two camps and the ripening of the harvests of righteousness and sin set forth in Revelation 13 and 14. Perhaps her most explicit statement on this topic appears in *The Desire of Ages*. "The warfare against God's law, which was begun in heaven, will be continued until the end of time." It will test every person, as obedience versus disobedience is *the* question that the entire world must decide. "*All will be called to choose between the law of God and the laws of men. Here the dividing line will be drawn. There will be but two classes. Every character will be fully developed; and all will show whether they have chosen the side of loyalty or that of rebellion.*

173

*"Then the end will come."*[7]

Ellen White repeatedly links character development with Christ's second coming. That connection is so prominent that we can think of it as a theme in her writings.

She plainly states that the Lord did not return soon after the 1844 Millerite disappointment because "the people were not yet ready to meet their Lord. There was still a work of preparation to be accomplished for them." The disappointed believers would receive new light, new duties, and a new message. That new light and message would center on the Most Holy apartment of the heavenly sanctuary, where Christ would vindicate the faith of the saints during the pre-advent judgment that would extend from the disappointment to just before the Second Coming.[8]

Interestingly, or perhaps I should say, characteristically, she ties this waiting period to character purification in the believers. "While the investigative judgment is going forward in heaven," she penned, "while the sins of penitent believers are being removed from the sanctuary, there is to be a special work of purification, of putting away of sin, among God's people upon earth. . . . When this work shall have been accomplished, the followers of Christ will be ready for His appearing." During the time of Christ's second apartment mediation, they are "to perfect holiness in the fear of God."[9]

Ellen White leaves no doubt that believers living during the final period of earth's history dwell in serious times, even though they may still have joy and assurance because they are in Christ Jesus. Before the Second Coming, "there will be among the people of the Lord such a revival of primitive godliness as has not been witnessed since apostolic times." They are to "vindicate His character before the world," achieving "spotless perfection" as they advance toward the "full and final display" of His grace.[10]

The natural question, of course, is what does Ellen White mean by "primitive godliness," "His character," and "spotless perfection"? We will look at that question in the next few sections of this chapter as we examine what it means to perfectly reproduce the character of Christ, stand through the time of trouble without a Mediator, and possess the translation faith of an Elijah or an Enoch. We will then draw some conclusions from our findings.

### Perfectly Reproducing the Character of Christ

Undoubtedly the passage most often cited from Ellen White on the manifestation of the character of Christ in His people is the following:

"Christ is waiting with longing desire for the manifestation of Himself in His church. *When the character of Christ shall be perfectly reproduced* in His people, then He will come to claim them as His own."[11]

That passage is especially fascinating since it follows the sequence of the harvest picture of Revelation 14. The very next paragraph goes on to note that if all who believed in Christ would glorify His name, the earth would rapidly be sown with the gospel seed. "Quickly the last great harvest would be ripened, and Christ would come to gather the precious grain."[12] Given the parallelism with Revelation 14, it is not improbable, therefore, that it may shed some light on the nature of what it means to be "spotless" and have "the faith of Jesus" (Rev. 14:5, 12).

Now the key to the above Ellen White passage obviously lies in what it means to "perfectly" reproduce the character of Christ. That passage, unfortunately, has brought forth a lot of "strange fire" within the Adventist community.

The usual procedure for interpreting it is to yank it out of its context and to link it to "extremish" quotations from such books as *Counsels on Diets and Foods* (also taken out of their historical and literary contexts). The result is a "theology" that even Ellen White and God wouldn't recognize.

In my younger years I followed that line, becoming so stringent in my desire to perfectly reproduce the character of Christ that some feared I would "die of health reform."[13]

Some years ago Martin Weber published his journey along that same track in *My Tortured Conscience*. After becoming stricter than the strict in an Adventist self-supporting institution, he knew he was on the right track when even they recognized that he was a fanatic.

"*Great!*" he thought, "*everybody calls these people fanatics, and now they're calling me a fanatic. That makes me the fanatic of fanatics! Praise the Lord, I'll be a fool for Christ sake! These folks here just aren't spiritual enough to relate to what God is doing in my life.*"

The apex of Marty's struggle came when he decided he could really be like Christ if he prayed all night, concluding that "sleeplessness is the secret of perfection." His course of action had some interesting results, even if they weren't all sanctified.[14]

The tragic thing about all of this is that Marty was doing all these things for Christ and in the name of Christ. He later came to see his life as the worst kind of legalism. "It was *Christ-centered legalism—legalism by faith.*"[15]

Marty, myself, and many other Seventh-day Adventists could have saved ourselves (and others) a lot of pain had we read the balanced context of so many of the Ellen White statements that we so glibly compiled into Pharisaic monstrosities. By ignoring those contexts, we did violence both to her intent and to the God that we believe inspired her.

"Christ," Ellen White wrote in introducing the passage on "perfectly" reproducing the character of Christ, "is seeking to *reproduce* Himself *in the hearts* of men. . . . *There can be no growth or fruitfulness in the life that is centered on self.* If you have accepted Christ as a personal Saviour, you are to forget yourself, and try to *help others. . . .* As you receive the Spirit of Christ—the Spirit of *unselfish love* and labor for others—you will grow and bring forth fruit. . . . Your faith will increase, . . . *your love be made perfect. More and more you will reflect the likeness of Christ* in all that is pure, noble, and lovely."[16]

Perfectly reproducing the character of Christ means moving away from Pharisaic perfectionistic schemes that focus inward on my own self-improvement and toward losing my "self" in service for others.

Furthermore, perfectly reproducing the character of Christ means the caring relationship. It is not, as we see from the parable of the sheep and the goats in Matthew 25:31-46, what we eat (or don't eat) or even how we keep the Sabbath. Those *lifestyle issues are important, but only within the framework of a truly caring Christian life.* That is essentially what Jesus tried to tell us in Matthew 5:48, when He said, in the context of loving one's enemies, "Be ye therefore perfect, even as your Father which is in heaven is perfect" (KJV). The enlightening parallel passage in Luke 6:36, as we noted earlier, equates perfection with being merciful.

Thus the perfect Christian is the caring Christian. It is that characteristic that God desires for His "spotless" end-time people who have "the faith of Jesus" and have "perfectly reproduced" the character of Christ. Out of a transformed heart will flow transformed actions. The perfect Christian is in harmony with the great principle of the law—love to both God and one's fellow human beings (Matt. 22:36-40). "In so far as love is in man," Emil Brunner noted, "he really resembles God and shows himself to be the child of God."[17]

*Too much Adventist talk of character perfection deals with lifestyle rather than character itself.* That is a tragic mistake. How we eat and other lifestyle issues should be viewed as a means to an end rather than the end itself. Character is what the Lord of the harvest is after. He probably doesn't "lose any sleep" if you are eating intemperately, but He is upset when your intemperate eating makes you cranky and unjust to your children. The purpose of better health, and so on, is to prepare you to express more perfectly Christ's character to those around you.

*The unfortunate thing about confusing lifestyle with character is that it tends toward legalism—a legalism just as harsh, cold, joyless, and exacting as was that of the Pharisees of old. Thus perfectly reproducing the so-called Christlike character can lead to the antithesis of all that Jesus stood for.*

Ellen White did not suffer from that conceptual confusion. Her trumpet gave a loud, clear, and consistent blast. "The last message of mercy to be given to the world," she announced, "is a revelation of His character of love."[18] Thus she was in harmony with Jesus, who claimed that the world would know that we are His disciples if we "have love for one another" (John 13:35).

Some people would have Ellen White and Jesus put some form of perfect law keeping or lifestyle into their statements, but it seems to me that it is time to get things into perspective by letting God do the speaking rather than to see how close we can come to those Pharisees who held that Messiah (Christ) would come if Torah (the law) was kept perfectly for one day.[19]

Again and again, Ellen White drove home the much needed message that character perfection centers on the motivating principle of God's love in every aspect of Christian living. "When self is merged in Christ," she wrote, "love springs forth spontaneously. *The completeness of Christian character is attained when the impulse to help and bless others springs constantly from within—when the sunshine of heaven fills the heart and is revealed in the countenance.*"[20]

Such statements make short shrift of "pickle faced" perfection. Those possessing the character of Christ have nothing to fear for the future. "God is love," wrote the apostle, "and he who abides in love abides in God, and God abides in him. In this is love perfected with us, that we may have confidence for the day of judgment, because as he is so are we in this world" (1 John 4:16, 17).

### Standing Through the Time of Trouble Without a Mediator

Another group of passages that Adventists have traditionally tied to end-time perfection is those dealing with standing through the time of trouble (Dan. 12:1) without a Mediator—the implication being that in order to do that one must be sinlessly perfect in the fullest sense of the word. The very thought of such a prospect has led many Adventists to spiritual agony—much of it less than healthy.

Seventh-day Adventists have held that the time of trouble of Daniel 12:1 takes place between the close of probation (the point in time when every person's eternal destiny is finally settled—Rev. 22:11, 12) and the second coming of Jesus. Thus the standing up of Michael (Christ) in Daniel 12:1 is viewed as an allusion to Christ's ceasing His ministry in the second apartment of the heavenly sanctuary at the completion of the pre-advent judgment.

The language surrounding the final events in the writings of Ellen White contains numerous references to the perfection of the "spotless" ones of Revelation 14. For example, in discussing the latter rain of the Holy Spirit (Joel 2:23, 28-30) that will fall on God's people just prior to the time of trouble, she writes: "The ripening of the grain [as a result of the outpouring of the latter rain] represents the completion of the work of God's grace in the soul. By the power of the Holy Spirit the *moral image* of God is to be *perfected* in the character. We are to be wholly transformed into *the likeness of Christ.*

"The latter rain, ripening earth's harvest, represents the spiritual grace that prepares the church for the coming of the Son of man." The purpose of the latter rain is to fit God's end-time people for translation to heaven without seeing death and to strengthen them to pass through the time of trouble.[21]

Another end-time event immediately prior to the time of trouble is the completion of the sealing of the 144,000 (see Rev. 7:1-4; 14:1-5). Not only does John the revelator link the sealing with "spotlessness," but so does Ellen White. "The seal of God," she writes, "will never be placed upon the forehead of an *impure* man or woman. It will never be placed upon the forehead of the ambitious, *world-loving* man or woman. It will never be placed upon the forehead of men or women of false tongues or *deceitful hearts. All who receive the seal must be without spot before God.*" Again, "the seal of the living God will be placed upon those only who bear *a likeness to Christ in character.*"[22]

With the completion of the sealing, probation closes and God's people enter into the time of trouble. It is in connection with that event that Ellen White has employed some of her most forceful language regarding end-time perfection.

"Those who are living upon the earth when the intercession of Christ shall cease in the sanctuary above are to stand in the sight of a holy God *without a mediator. Their robes must be spotless, their characters must be purified from sin by the blood of sprinkling.* Through the grace of God and their own diligent effort they must be conquerors in the battle with evil." They must have already put away sin through a cleansing of the soul sanctuary during the pre-advent judgment.[23]

On that same topic, she also wrote that "now, while our great High Priest is making the atonement for us, we should seek to become *perfect in Christ. Not even by a thought could our Saviour be brought to yield to the power of temptation.* Satan finds in human hearts some point where he can gain a foothold; some sinful desire is *cherished,* by means of which his temptations assert their power. But Christ declared of Himself: 'The prince of this world cometh, and hath nothing in Me.' John 14:30. *Satan could find nothing in the Son of God that would enable him to gain the victory.* He had kept His Father's commandments, and there was no sin in Him that Satan could use to his advantage. *This is the condition in which those must be found who shall stand in the time of trouble."*[24]

The above statements and several others like them have had a profound impact upon Seventh-day Adventists. While some of that effect has been balanced and healthy, too much of it has lacked both balance and a clear understanding of what Ellen White actually wrote.

Thus A. L. Hudson (a man who for years read the statements regarding the condition of the saved in the time of trouble as meaning total sinlessness) points out that "this doctrine [living without a Mediator in the sanctuary above] has had bad effects in several ways in Adventism. Coupled with other ideas[,] it has led to the proposition that the final generation or 144,000 will have become so righteous, so clean, so holy they will no longer *need* a Saviour. This has led [in daily life] to untouchable self-righteousness (in anticipation) or to utter discouragement."[25]

Many, including the present writer, have experienced both the self-righteousness of "becoming perfect" and the utter frustration and discouragement mentioned by Hudson when we are finally willing to admit that in reality we are less "perfect" than we had imagined ourselves to be. We had taken the route of the Pharisees and had come to spiritual bankruptcy.

I would like to suggest that the real problem is not the Ellen White quotations listed above, but the way we interpret them. *One of the most difficult exercises for Adventists to perform is to read statements about human perfection unemotionally.* We generally make two mistakes with the above statements. First, we project meanings into the passages. Second, we often fail to heed their contexts.

The predictable results of such a procedure are more emotionalism about the topic of end-time perfection that tends to polarize people between a fanaticism that sets out to prove that one can become righteous enough to live without Christ, on the one hand, or that denies that there is any hope or reality in personal (as opposed to vicarious) perfection this side of the Second Advent, on the other hand. I have "lived through" both of those interpretations.

Now I see that a careful examination of such passages will lead to a moderate and balanced position of Christian character perfection. But such a reading must involve (1) *carefully reading the words actually written* (rather than supplying words from our fears, backgrounds, and/or imaginations), (2) carefully seeking to understand *what Ellen White meant* by those words (rather than supplying our own definitions or those of extremists or even moderates on the topic), (3) studying the *full context* of the statements as originally penned (rather than the snippets cited in either official or unofficial compilations), and (4) placing the statements within the *entire Bible and Ellen White framework of sin and salvation.*

If we consistently followed those four steps, we would see less self-righteous frustration and denial and more Christian balance. There is only one way to read a statement: that is to consider what the author *actually* wrote rather than what someone thinks (or fears) he or she did.

While I cannot in this book examine each of Ellen White's time of trouble without a Mediator statements in the detail of the four points set forth above, I will take the time to illustrate my meaning.

First, please note that she did not say that people would live without a Savior during the time of trouble. Rather, she consistently penned that they would live "without a high priest in the sanctuary," "without an intercessor," and "without a mediator" in the sense that Christ's intercession will have ceased in the sanctuary above.[26]

Christ does not forsake His people during the time of trouble. To the contrary, He flatly said, "I am with you always, to the close of the age" (Matt. 28:20). On the other hand, Ellen White does say that at least *one function* of Christ ceases when He leaves the heavenly sanctuary—He no longer will serve as the "Mediator." We will return to the implications of that below.

One reason Christ no longer needs to continue the work of mediation is that the pre-advent judgment has concluded, probation has closed, and God's saints have been sealed for eternity. In other words, by the beginning of the time of trouble every individual's case will have been forever decided. Both Matthew (25:31-46) and Revelation (chapter 14 and 22:11) indicate that but two classes will live upon the earth when Jesus comes again.

The close of probation signifies that all end-time human beings, in the pressure cooker atmosphere of the times, will have made a choice for either Jesus or Satan as their master. One group will have received the seal of God; the other the mark of the beast. Christ will leave the heavenly sanctuary because He has completed His work there. The loyalties of all have made themselves evident through the *principles* they have expressed in their lives. They have chosen either God's law of love or Satan's law of selfishness.

A second point to note about these statements is that they do not teach that the saints will have achieved a state of ultimate sinless perfection. Ellen White implies that when she points out that the purpose of the time of trouble is for the saints "to be placed in the furnace of fire" because "their earthliness must be consumed, *that the image of Christ may be perfectly reflected.*"[27] The end-time saints still have growing to do during the time of trouble.

A third and most important aspect of our current exercise is to examine the words Ellen White uses. Often in connection with time of trouble passages she expresses that the saints need to reflect or be like Christ's character. We demonstrated above, in the section on "Perfectly Reproducing the Character of Christ," that with that phraseology she refers to an attitude and life of loving action rather than to absolutely sinless behavior. A similar meaning undoubtedly lies behind the perfection of Christ's "moral image."[28]

Again, in the powerful passage in *The Great Controversy* (p. 623) that says that end-time believers need to be like Christ during the time of trouble, she indicates that "*cherished*" sins are the real problem rather than sins of omission or unconscious sins (mistakes). Focusing on the temptation of Christ, she wrote that "Satan could find nothing in the Son of God that would enable him to gain the victory." He had kept God's law.[29]

As we noted in chapter 6, the focal point in Christ's lifelong TEMPTATION was whether to put His self and His will or God and God's will at the center of His life. He overcame by choosing God and God's will. Christ's end-time followers can and must make that same choice. That "is the condition in which those must be found who shall stand in the time of trouble." They are "perfect in Christ. Not even by a thought" are they led into rebellious sin, because the Holy Spirit has wholly transformed their thoughts. The great polarization of end-time events has *forced* them into choosing either to live by the principles of God's LAW of love or by Satan's principles, and they have opted for the way of the LAW as exemplified by their Master. Thus they reflect Christ's character in their thoughts and lives. They are perfect in the sense that they no longer "cherish" SIN or sins.[30]

The time of trouble saints have no rebellious thoughts or actions. They therefore have no more need of the Mediator.

The pre-advent court session is finished, but that does not mean that the saints are either totally sinless or absolutely perfect. They are perfect but not yet perfect, sinless but not yet sinless.

While they have character perfection in terms of having internalized the great principle of law in their lives, they are yet in process toward total perfection. And they are sinless in the sense that they do not cherish sin and rebellion, but their ultimate sinlessness awaits the final trump of God.

*As Ellen White put it, "We cannot say, 'I am sinless,' till this vile body is changed and fashioned like unto His glorious body."* "While we cannot claim perfection of the flesh" until the Second Coming, "we may have Christian perfection of the soul."[31]

The root problem with achieving sinlessness on this earth, as we saw in chapters 7 and 8, is that even when our wills and attitudes are fully in harmony with God, the weaknesses of our bodies and minds still allow us to commit unconscious sins (or make mistakes) and to neglect to do the good through sins of omission. True sinlessness and perfection would be free from such problems.

Thus the end-time saints still need Jesus during the time of trouble. C. Mervyn Maxwell correctly points out that "Christ's caution, 'Without me ye can do nothing,' remains absolutely true throughout our earthly lives and even through eternity."[32]

Even though Christ has completed His mediatorial role in the heavenly sanctuary, His work as Savior still impacts the lives of those to be translated in at least two crucial ways. First, since they are still "in Him," their unintentional sins and sins of omission are still covered by His perfect life as imputed to every believer in their continuing justification.

Thus Ellen White writes that "only those who are clothed in the garments of *his righteousness* will be able to endure the glory of his presence when he shall appear with 'power and great glory.'"[33] Humans will never be like Christ in this earthly life in the sense that they will be able to stand in their own righteousness. They will never be sinless as He is sinless.

On the other hand, the saints will be like Him in loving character and intent of will. But even then they will not stand on their own, but will be empowered by His grace to live as Christians, just as they were before the beginning of the time of trouble.

What has changed is that they no longer need a Mediator, because they will have finished with conscious, willful, belligerent sin. They will have made their decision permanently to live the Christlike life. The God who does all He can to save His children has sealed their decision for eternity.

The time of trouble saints are sinless in attitude and conscious action. Their sinlessness will be complete at the Second Coming, when God will transform their mortal and limited bodies (having inbuilt weaknesses due to sin and a natural tendency to evil since the time of Adam) into "spiritual bodies" (having neither sinful tendencies nor the limitations caused by sin). The righteous will be "changed" "at the last trumpet." Christ at His return "will change our lowly body to be like his glorious body" (Rom. 6:12; 1 Cor. 15:44, 51-53; Phil. 3:20, 21).

Because of the changes that take place at the Second Coming, the saints will then cease to commit even unconscious sins. At that time both their wills and their bodies will be in line with God's principle of love. In that sense they will be sinless, even though they are not fully perfect. Growth in perfection after the Second Coming will be the topic of chapter 10.

## Possessing the Translation Faith of Enoch and Elijah

Perfectly reflecting the image of Christ through loving others as ourselves, the rejection of cherished and rebellious sin, and the continuous crucifixion of the self seem to stand at the center of Ellen White's definition of character perfection. Those elements will be central to those who will live through the time of trouble and be translated to heaven at the Second Coming.[34]

Such were the characteristics of the only two Bible characters to be translated without seeing death. Both men had apparently "walked" closer and closer with God in their lives of progressive sanctification. They finally came to the place where He could take them to heaven without their having to see death (see Gen. 5:21-24; Heb. 11:5; 2 Kings 2:11). Although the Bible does not have much to say on the topic, in late Judaism a considerable body of literature grew up around the translation of Elijah and Enoch and the possible state of sinlessness implied by that translation.[35]

Ellen White also had something to say on the topic. "Enoch and Elijah," she wrote, "are the correct representatives of what the race might be through faith in Jesus Christ if they chose to be. . . . These noble, holy men stood untainted, . . . perfected righteous characters, and were accounted worthy for translation to Heaven."[36]

183

Many cite that quotation without its all-important context. Taken as quoted, it could be interpreted to imply some sort of absolute perfection. But the paragraph in which it is embedded is a contrast between them and Moses. Specifically, Satan triumphed over Moses in tempting him to self-glorification, while Enoch and Elijah were overcomers. We can have that same victory as we choose to live the crucified life. Thus it is that "Enoch and Elijah are the correct representatives of what the race might be through faith in Jesus."[37]

Having overcome the TEMPTATION of temptations, Ellen White notes that Enoch and Elijah "stood untainted amid the moral pollution surrounding them." Thus not only did they not cherish sin, but their walk was one of consistent faith rather than one of rebellion.

In another connection, she wrote that "as was Enoch's, so must be their holiness of character who shall be redeemed from among men at the Lord's second coming."[38]

Once again, that statement usually gets quoted in isolation from its context and combined with other statements that leave the impression of some sort of ultimate perfection. But in the context Ellen White is quite explicit concerning the elements of Enoch's holiness. For example, the "love of God . . . became the subject of his meditations day and night. With all the fervor of his soul he sought to reveal that love to the people among whom he dwelt." Prayer became to him "as the breath of the soul," and "for three hundred years Enoch had been seeking purity of heart."[39]

In yet another place, Ellen White claimed that Enoch's "godly character . . . represents the state of holiness which *must* be attained by those who shall be 'redeemed from the earth' (Revelation 14:3) at the time of Christ's second advent." He had kept God's law of love and had turned his back on rebellion. "Like Enoch, God's [last-day] people will seek for purity of heart and conformity to His will, until they shall reflect the likeness of Christ."[40]

From what we can infer from these and other statements, the perfection of Enoch and Elijah lay in living the crucified life of faith, rejecting rebellion toward God and the rebellious sins of a wicked age, and reflecting the character of Christ. The fact that their lives did not arrive at some sort of absolute sinlessness can be inferred from Ellen White's statement that "Christ was the only sinless one who ever dwelt on earth" (cf. Rom. 3:23).[41]

In a passage quite disconnected from Enoch and Elijah, Ellen White wrote that *"when His image is perfectly reflected in them, they* [His people] *are perfect and holy, and prepared for translation."*[42]

Perfectly reproducing the character of Christ, as we have repeatedly noted in our study, stands at the very center of character perfection. We can never too strongly emphasize that she does not define that perfection in a legalistic manner that focuses on diet, Sabbath observance, or any other behavior or series of behaviors. Rather, she explicitly defines it as a spirit of "unselfish love and labor for others." As with the Bible, her definition of perfection and reflecting the likeness of Christ centers on perfect love.[43] It is an expression of the principles of the LAW rather than a mere acting out of the bits and pieces of the law.

Both the bits-and-pieces approach and the principle-based emphasis lead to changed lives, but one results in the kind we find among the Pharisees, while the other produces a life congruent with that of Christ.

## Two Kinds of Perfection and God's Final Demonstration to the Universe

*Two Kinds of Perfection*

We have come full circle from our discussion of the Pharisees in chapter 1. There we discovered that some of the Pharisees had arrived at the illusion of obtaining perfection by breaking SIN up into small "chunks" and then overcoming one "chunk" of sin at a time. Thus they came to see both sin and righteousness, in practice if not in theory, as a series of actions rather than as a condition of the heart and mind. In chapter 3 we also noted how even God's LAW had been fractured in daily life into a set of laws to expedite the attainment of Pharisaic righteousness. That whole way of looking at sin, law, and righteousness was undergirded by an inadequate view of the universality, subtlety, and power of sin in the lives of a people who wanted to be good but could not, due to their inborn "bent" to evil.

Also we saw in chapter 1 that the Pharisaic approach to righteousness has had a large following in Seventh-day Adventism. That has been true not only of the works-oriented righteousness of pre-1888 Adventism, but in the twentieth century through the writings of M. L. Andreasen and others.

Andreasen definitely saw sin as a series of discrete actions. He could therefore write that the person who got the victory over the tobacco habit had achieved a victory toward righteousness. "*On that point* [tobacco]," Andreasen wrote, "*he is sanctified*. As he has been victorious over *one* besetment, so he is to become victorious over *every sin*. When the work is completed, when he has gained the victory" over the whole set of discrete sins, "*he is ready for translation.* He has been tried in all *points.*" Thus "he stands *without fault* before the throne of God. Christ places His seal upon him. He is safe, and he is sound. God has finished His work in him. The demonstration of what God can do with humanity is complete."[44]

Andreasen's line of reasoning has led to a school of contemporary Adventist theology that both underestimates the power of sin and overestimates the ability of humans to overcome it. The upshot too often has been a striving after perfect sinlessness so that Christ can come again.

In contrast to Andreasen's atomized theology of sin, law, temptation, and righteousness, the present book has argued that SIN is first and foremost an attitude and a state of rebellion against God. That attitude has at least two results: a broken relationship with God and a series of actions that flow out of rebellion. Thus SIN leads to acts of sin, or as more commonly phrased, SIN leads to sins.

## SIN ⟶ sins

Some refer to any definition of sin that is not an action or series of actions as the New Theology. They should more accurately call it the *New Theology of the Sermon on the Mount.* One of Jesus' main points in His great sermon was to undercut the itemized definition of sin and direct His hearers to its inward aspects (see Matt. 5-7; 15:1-20).

Christ's definition of sin, of necessity, also contradicted Pharisaic understandings of righteousness. Whereas the Pharisees saw righteousness, sanctification, and perfection in terms of a series of actions, Christ saw those items from the perspective of a total transformation of heart and mind. If the heart and mind were transformed in love, then righteous acts in the daily life would be the natural fruit. Thus RIGHTEOUSNESS (a matter of the heart) leads to righteous acts in everyday living.

## RIGHTEOUSNESS ⟶ righteous actions

By way of contrast, righteous actions do not lead to RIGHTEOUS-NESS. RIGHTEOUSNESS can only come through the way of the cross, through faith in Christ, daily crucifixion, and a total recasting of heart and mind.

The transformationist view of RIGHTEOUSNESS also necessitates a wholistic view of the LAW as set forth in Scripture. The LAW is first and foremost the principle of love that stands at the center of God's character.

The transformed Christian has the LAW of love engraved on his or her heart. To obey the LAW is natural for those in Christ because its great principle has been internalized. Out of the principle of the LAW flow specific laws.

## LAW ⟶ laws

Whereas the Pharisees were obsessed with the letter of the specific laws, Christ focused on the spirit of the LAW. Because He was most concerned to do the loving thing (as demanded by the LAW of love), He often ran into conflict with the legalistic prescriptions of the Pharisees, who assumed that righteousness and perfection came from being faithful to the rules built up around the LAW. They eventually crucified Christ because His LAW conflicted with their laws.

Ideally, of course, LAW and laws are in harmony. But Pharisees are so busy defining and multiplying and keeping laws that they often transgress the LAW of love in their zeal. Thus we find the rude health reformer and the unloving Sabbathkeeper.

The import of the matter is this: the Pharisees of Christ's day focused on the law but failed to internalize the LAW. The teaching of the New Testament is that the law is good if, and only if, one keeps it in the spirit of love (the LAW).

Christ rejected the atomization of SIN, RIGHTEOUSNESS, and LAW. His followers were to avoid the way of the Pharisees.

Because of Christ's refusal to atomize, He had an entirely different view of temptation and perfection than that stipulated by the Pharisaic mentality. Temptation for the Pharisee was based on a particularized view of sin and law. Thus a modern disciple of the Pharisees might define temptation as being lured to steal a car or eat some forbidden item. While those enticements are temptations, they are not TEMPTATION. TEMPTATION is the enticement to put self at the center of one's life, to come down off the cross, to give up living the crucified life. Out of TEMPTATION flow temptations.

## TEMPTATION ⟶ temptations

When people overcome TEMPTATION through Christ and the power of the Holy Spirit, they will have no problem with temptations. I desire my neighbor's wife only because I have already fallen for the

TEMPTATION to put my self, rather than God's will and my love for both my neighbor and his wife, at the center of my life. Thus I have broken the LAW and committed SIN. That results in temptations, sins, and the transgressing of laws.

These two views of sin, righteousness, law, and temptation correlate with two distinct concepts of perfection. If I see sin as a series of negative actions, then righteousness becomes a series of positive actions in which I keep laws and avoid a host of temptations. When I finally stop doing all the wrong things and start doing all the right things, I am perfect in the sense that Andreasen defined perfection. Then Christ can come again.[45]

PERFECTION, on the other hand, consists in establishing a faith relationship with God in place of the natural SIN (rebellious) relationship, rejecting TEMPTATION through living the life of the cross, and internalizing the LAW of love in daily living. Righteous acts will flow from a heart set right with God. Such a person may not be absolutely sinlessly perfect as the Pharisee defines perfection, but he or she will be morally PERFECT.

It is of interest to note that these two opposing views of sin, righteousness, and perfection have tended to generate two spirits to accompany them. The paradox of the Pharisaic route to perfection is that it has often made its participants self-centered, joyless, harsh, judgmental, and vindictive. Thus Ellen White could speak of the "spirit of the Pharisees."[46]

By way of contrast, "the spirit of Christ" should lead us to be other centered; to be full of joy; to care for people more than rules; to accept harlots, publicans, and even Pharisees; and to be kind to other people, even when they differ from us.

In short, the spirit of Christ demands total transformation of heart, mind, and life, while the spirit of the Pharisees merely adds religious motivations and acts to the natural traits of human character.

### God's Final Demonstration

That brings us to the final demonstration to the universe of what God can do with human nature and how it relates to the coming of Christ. The Pharisees were clear on the topic: when the Torah (law) was kept perfectly for one day, the Messiah (Christ) would come.

Some Adventists today, in the tradition of M. L. Andreasen and his itemized version of sin and sanctification, apparently have the same view as the Pharisees. One gets the impression from some advocates of perfection that the final demonstration will center on those who have a perfect

diet and flawless lifestyle, but Ellen White put an end to all such speculation when she penned that "the last message of mercy to be given to the
world . . . is a revelation of His [God's] character of love." The context
goes on to line up that thought with the biblical definition of perfection as
caring for one another. That "final generation" statement is in harmony
with the context of her thought that "when the character of Christ shall
be perfectly reproduced in His people, . . . He will come to claim them as
His own."[47]

Wait, I hear some saying, what do we do about Andreasen's teaching
that God's closing of the work in the heavenly sanctuary is "dependent"
upon a totally perfect end time generation? After all, wasn't Andreasen
right when he penned that "through the last generation of saints God
stands finally vindicated. Through them He defeats Satan and wins His
case."[48]

Fortunately, Andreasen nullifies his own argument. In the same chapter as the above statements, he writes that to disprove Satan's accusation
that God's law could not be kept, "it is necessary for God to produce at
least *one* man who has kept the law. In the absence of such a man, God
loses and Satan wins."[49]

I would submit that that man was Christ. The victory was won when,
after living an absolutely perfect human life and going to the cross bearing
the sin of all humanity, Jesus cried out, "It is finished" (John 19:30).
*"Christ's death,"* Ellen White penned, *"proved God's administration and government to be without a flaw."* Contrary to Andreasen's *Sanctuary Service*, it is
through Christ that God defeated Satan.[50]

Beyond that, the very idea that God is dependent upon the Adventist
Church or any other group of people is the same misconception that mis-
led the Pharisees. They had forgotten that God's covenant is always con-
ditional. Its fulfillment depends upon human response (see Deut. 28:1, 15).
In their self-centeredness the Pharisees made God dependent upon them
and their law keeping. That very concept stands as the ultimate Pharisaic
arrogance. God wanted to use the Jews just as He would like to use His
end-time people, but if either refused to be totally transformed into His
loving likeness, He is free and able to cut His work short in righteousness.[51]
After all, God is God! Our place is not to tell Him what He can and cannot do, but to accept the *finished work of Christ* and allow Him to totally
transform our hearts and lives so that we might be ready when He returns.
That transformation of His end-time people and their expression of the
*principles* of His law in daily life is God's goal for His "spotless" ones. Their

demonstration of righteousness is not the DEMONSTRATION but a confirming validation of God's justice.

But, some may object, God cannot allow less than absolutely sinless people into heaven.

Knock out the "absolutely," and they are right. God will not pollute heaven with sinners—those in rebellion against Him. But, as is evidenced by the eventual resurrection of those having lived in all ages, He can without risk take to heaven those who still make mistakes and have sins of ignorance and sins of omission, problems that are rooted in the "bent" and limitations of sinful flesh.

After all, God's end-time people will have their hearts right toward God, they will hate both SIN and sins, and they will love both RIGHTEOUSNESS and righteousness. They will have demonstrated to the universe that love to others and faith in God can replace self-love and self-sufficiency. When people with such perfect attitudes and wills get their bodies transformed into "spiritual bodies" without the weaknesses caused by sin, and when such people are removed from a sinful environment, we can be assured that they, after all they have suffered, will not want to reinvent sin in heaven. It has been amply demonstrated that their one desire is to say yes to God with their entire heart and life.

Those with transformed, Christlike hearts and minds are safe to save for eternity. Add pure bodies in a flawless environment to pure hearts, and you have a fully redeemed people, a sinless people.[52]

Those redeemed people, however, will not be completely perfect yet. Their developing perfection is the topic of our final chapter.

---

[1] Berkouwer, *Faith and Sanctification*, p. 140.

[2] Mounce, *Book of Revelation*, p. 271; Ladd, *Revelation of John*, p. 192. (Italics supplied.)

[3] Luther, quoted in Althaus, *Theology of Martin Luther*, p. 146.

[4] Ladd, *Theology of the New Testament*, p. 520.

[5] Guthrie, *New Testament Theology*, p. 674.

[6] White, *Christ's Object Lessons*, p. 168.

[7] White, *The Desire of Ages*, p. 763. (Italics supplied.)

[8] White, *The Great Controversy*, pp. 424, 425.

[9] *Ibid.*, pp. 425, 488.

[10] *Ibid.*, p. 464; White, *Testimonies for the Church*, vol. 5, p. 746; White, *Testimonies to Ministers*, p. 18.

[11] White, *Christ's Object Lessons*, p. 69. Cf. White, *The Desire of Ages*, p. 671. (Italics supplied.)

[12] White, *Christ's Object Lessons*, p. 69

[13] I treat this episode more fully in Knight, *Angry Saints*, pp. 147, 148.

[14] Martin Weber, *My Tortured Conscience* (Washington, D.C.: Review and Herald, 1991), pp. 67, 70, 72.

[15] *Ibid.*, p. 72. (Italics supplied.)

[16] White, *Christ's Object Lessons*, pp. 67, 68. (Italics supplied.)

[17] Brunner, *Romans*, p. 155.

[18] White, *Christ's Object Lessons*, p. 415; cf. pp. 416-419.

[19] *Babylonian Talmud*, Sanhedrin 97b; Shabbath 118b; *Jerusalem Talmud*, Taanith 64a.

[20] White, *Christ's Object Lessons*, p. 384. (Italics supplied.) See also, White, *Testimonies for the Church*, vol. 6, p. 606; Ellen G. White, *God's Amazing Grace* (Washington, D.C.: Review and Herald, 1973), p. 235; White, *The Desire of Ages*, pp. 497, 498, 504, 637, 638; White, *Seventh-day Adventist Bible Commentary*, vol. 6, p. 1098; White, *Mount of Blessing*, pp. 25, 38; and many others.

[21] White, *Testimonies to Ministers*, p. 506; White, *Spiritual Gifts*, vol. 2, p. 226; White, *Testimonies for the Church*, vol. 1, p. 353. (Italics supplied.)

[22] White, *Testimonies for the Church*, vol. 5, p. 216; White, *Review and Herald*, 21 May 1895, p. 321. (Italics supplied.) Cf. Ellen G. White, *Early Writings* (Washington, D.C.: Review and Herald, 1945), p. 71; White, *Seventh-day Adventist Bible Commentary*, vol. 6, pp. 1117, 1118.

[23] White, *The Great Controversy*, p. 425. (Italics supplied.)

[24] *Ibid.*, p. 623. See also pp. 614, 649; White, *Early Writings*, p. 48. (Italics supplied.)

[25] A. L. Hudson, "Some Realities and Myths in Seventh-day Adventism," unpublished MS, 1989.

[26] White, *Early Writings*, p. 71; White, *The Great Controversy*, pp. 614, 649, 425.

[27] White, *The Great Controversy*, p. 621. Cf. White, *Our High Calling*, p. 321. (Italics supplied.)

[28] White, *Testimonies to Ministers*, p. 506; White, *Review and Herald*, 21 May 1895, p. 321; White, *The Great Controversy*, p. 621.

[29] White, *The Great Controversy*, p. 623; cf. p. 620; White, *Our High Calling*, p. 321. (Italics supplied.)

[30] White, *The Great Controversy*, p. 623.

[31] White, *Signs of the Times*, March 23, 1888, p. 178; White, *Selected Messages*, book 2, p. 32.

[32] Maxwell, "Ready for His Appearing," in *Perfection: The Impossible Possibility*, p. 190.

[33] White, *Review and Herald*, July 9, 1908, p. 8. (Italics supplied.)

[34] See White, *Testimonies for the Church*, vol. 1, p. 340 and section above on "Perfectly Reproducing the Character of Christ."

[35] *The New International Dictionary of New Testament Theology*, s.v. "Sin"; "Resurrection."

[36] White, *Review and Herald*, 3 March 1874, p. 91.

[37] *Ibid.*

[38] White, *Gospel Workers*, p. 54.

[39] *Ibid.*, pp. 51-53.

[40] White, *Patriarchs and Prophets*, pp. 88, 89. (Italics supplied.)

[41] White, *The Desire of Ages*, p. 72.

[42] White, *Testimonies for the Church*, vol. 1, p. 340. Cf. White, *Christ's Object Lessons*, p. 69. (Italics supplied.)

[43] White, *Christ's Object Lessons*, pp. 67, 68.

[44] Andreasen, *Sanctuary Service*, p. 302. (Italics supplied.)

[45] *Ibid.* Cf. Robert J. Wieland, *The 1888 Message: An Introduction* (Washington, D.C.: Review and Herald, 1980), pp. 105, 106; Donald Karr Short, "*Then Shall the Sanctuary Be Cleansed*" (Paris, Ohio: Glad Tidings, 1990).

[46] See Knight, *Angry Saints*, pp. 80-99.

[47] White, *Christ's Object Lessons*, pp. 415-419, 67-69.

[48] Andreasen, *Sanctuary Service*, pp. 321, 319.

[49] *Ibid.*, p. 316.

[50] E. G. White, MS 128, 1897, in *Seventh-day Adventists Answer Questions on Doctrine*, Annotated Edition, ed. George R. Knight (Berrien Springs, Mich.: Andrews University Press, 2003), p. 539; Knight, *The Cross of Christ*, pp. 141-142. (Italics supplied.)

[51] White, *Selected Messages*, book 1, pp. 67, 68, 118. See also White, *Christ's Object Lessons*, p. 303; George R. Knight, *If I Were the Devil: Seeing Through the Devil's Smokescreen: Contemporary Challenges Facing Adventism* (Hagerstown, Md.: Review and Herald, 2007), pp. 61-63.

[52] Cf. Douglass, "Men of Faith," in *Perfection: The Impossible Possibility*, pp. 28, 30.

Chapter 10

# Growth Toward Perfection Throughout Eternity

The unregenerate person would be completely out of place in heaven—
"quite out of his element," penned a Puritan divine, "as a swine in the
parlour, or a fish out of water."[1]

A general agreement seems to exist among those who have thought on
the topic that the purpose of the earthly life of Christians is to prepare them
for living in the perfection of heaven. At the time of their new birth "babes
in Christ" receive a new heart and mind. As a result, they are no longer at
odds—intellectually at least—with the principles of God's kingdom. A
Spirit-empowered growth in progressive sanctification as individuals develop a "fitness" for heaven then follows that birth.

While most would agree that perfection and sinlessness are God's obvious goals for the saints, there is a surprising unanimity (even among
those most concerned with perfection) that no one reaches full and final
perfection or sinlessness in this present life. Thus R. N. Flew correctly
concludes that "the full Christian ideal must span both worlds, the present life and the life to come. It is only completely realizable in the life
beyond the grave."[2]

If that is true, we find ourselves forced to ask, What is it that is sup-
posed to take place during the earthly life of a Christian, what is left for
heaven, and what makes the difference between success in growth toward
perfection in this life as compared with success in the next? Those three
topics will provide the subject matter for the rest of this chapter.

## The Nature of Earthly Perfection

The perfection obtained in sanctification is *character perfection* or moral
perfection rather than complete perfection. It has to do with the internalization of God's great principle of love and a reorientation of the life from

193

the rebellious SIN relationship to God to the faith relationship. John Wesley touched on this point when he wrote that "we may die without the knowledge of many truths," yet still be saved in God's kingdom, "but if we die without love, what will knowledge avail?"[3]

Ellen White put it somewhat differently when she pointed out that "the refining influence of the grace of God changes the natural disposition of man. . . . The propensities that control the natural heart must be subdued by the grace of Christ before fallen man is fitted to enter heaven and enjoy the society of the pure, holy angels."[4]

Stated more positively, she wrote that "the spirit of Christ's self-sacrificing love is the spirit that pervades heaven and is the very essence of its bliss. This is the spirit that Christ's followers will possess." "The completeness of Christian character is attained when the impulse to help and bless others springs constantly from within." Those who have permitted God's Spirit to work fully in their lives will be so in harmony with His will, "that when obeying Him" they "shall be but carrying out" their "own impulses."[5] Such people have reached the biblical standard of character perfection and are safe to save for eternity. They are indeed perfect like their Father in heaven (see Matt. 5:43-48).

Internalizing the character of Christ on this earth is important because, J. C. Ryle writes, we will not be able to enjoy heaven if we are out of harmony with its principles. "Death works no change. The grave makes no alteration. Each will rise again with the same character in which he breathed his last."[6] What possible enjoyment could those out of harmony with the principle of God's kingdom find there?

They would be more miserable than I was the first time I had dinner with a minister. At the time I was living on a merchant marine ship harbored in San Francisco Bay. My discomfort existed because all I did and lived for clashed with my perceptions of what a minister stood for.

I have since concluded that to be taken to heaven to spend eternity with the omniscient God if I were out of harmony with His character of outgoing love would be an eternal hell. In His mercy, God has declared that "without holiness no man shall see the Lord" (Heb. 12:14, paraphrase).

Because it is true that the traits of character we "cherish in life will not be changed by death or by the resurrection," it is also certain, Ellen White claims, that if the heavenly character is not acquired on earth, "it can never be acquired at all."[7]

*It is important to note that these statements imply character perfection for those who are resurrected as well as for those translated. The difference between the two groups, as we observed in chapter 9, is not one of kind, but of degree. All who go to heaven must be in love with the principle of love and must have internalized that principle into their daily living.* If they are not in love with love they will not be in harmony with God, who is love in His inmost being (1 John 4:8).

A "perfect" attitude toward God and His principles is a prerequisite for happiness in the hereafter. That perfect attitude expresses itself in both our desire to do the right (loving) thing in life and in sincere repentance when we realize that our rebellious acts put Christ on the cross. Born from above Christians may commit acts of sin, but when they come to their senses they will hate their sin in all its forms. They will also loathe the weaknesses that tilted them toward performing sinful acts.

## The Role of Resurrection and Translation
## in the Continuing Development of Perfection

One troubling aspect of Christian existence is the universal gap between attitudes and practice, between character and action.

The core of the problem appears to be that God's work for and in those being saved is not completed in the earthly life. Thus Paul can write that "I am sure that he who began a good work in you will bring it to completion at the day of Jesus Christ" (Phil. 1:6). That "day," of course, is the second coming of Christ.[8]

In a similar vein, we read in the book of Hebrews that those who have died in faith throughout the ages will "not be made perfect" "apart from" those living (Heb. 11:39, 40). In other words, God has a perfecting act that will take place at the Second Coming, when He resurrects the dead and translates the living (1 Cor. 15:42-56). Paul points to God's unfinished work when he claims that those who have been saved still await "the redemption of" their "bodies" (Rom. 8:23, 24). Jesus indicated the source of the gap between attitudes and practice when He said that "the spirit . . . is willing, but the flesh is weak" (Matt. 26:41).

God's full redemption includes that of the body. A problem with our "natural bodies" (see 1 Cor. 15:44, KJV)—the bodies we were born with—is that they have a weakness toward evil. Beyond that, being flawed, they house a less-than-adequate brain. Thus our thought processes are both limited and distorted. Those limitations, in turn, restrict our ability to respond and act in daily life. Coupled with those difficulties, human beings live in a world and community dominated by anti-Christian principles, principles quite attractive to the weaknesses of the "natural body."

Ellen White recognized the problem when she wrote that "we cannot say, 'I am sinless,' till this vile body is changed and fashioned like unto His glorious body. But if we constantly seek to follow Jesus, the blessed hope is ours of standing before the throne of God without spot . . . ; complete in Christ, robed in his righteousness and perfection." Along that same line, she also penned that in this life "we may have Christian perfection of the soul," even though "we can not claim perfection of the flesh."[9] Character perfection is a possibility during the present life, but a more complete perfection awaits the return of Christ.

Because of that, Alister McGrath notes that we do not "share the fullness of the resurrection life *here and now.*" And Leo Cox points out that "perfect love" is not "resurrection perfection. There is much ahead for those whose love is made perfect."[10]

That "much ahead" provides an important link in the New Testament teaching of perfection. In the paragraph after Paul's revealing discussion of the tension between being perfect but not yet perfect (Phil. 3:12, 15), he goes on to speak of the effect of Christ's second advent on perfection. "We await," he penned, "a Savior, the Lord Jesus Christ, who will change our lowly body to be like his glorious body" (verses 20, 21).

The glorification of the body described in Philippians 3 Paul elaborates on more fully in 1 Corinthians 15. There we read that the redeemed will be changed when Christ comes again. Part of that transformation will be the fact that they will have "spiritual" bodies (verse 44). C. K. Barrett points out that a spiritual body is one "animated by the Spirit of God," while F. W. Grosheide suggests that it is a body "governed by the Spirit of the Lord."[11]

Paul describes the resurrected body, by way of contrast to the natural body, as glorious, powerful, spiritual, incorruptible, and immortal (1 Cor. 15:43, 44, 53). It will be a body free from the weaknesses caused by sin.

Within the renewed body, of course, will be a brain that functions as God intended it should when He first created it, a brain without the limitations of the "natural body." With glorification, therefore, will come also a fullness of knowledge. In 1 Corinthians 13:12 Paul contrasts the less than perfect knowledge of our present life with the perfect that is to come: "For now we see in a mirror dimly, but then face to face. Now I know in part, then I shall understand fully."

After the resurrection, both our spirit and our bodies will be willing and able in the fullest sense of the word. Instead of being, according to John Wesley, "clogs" to our spiritual life, our resurrected bodies "shall be obedient and able instruments of the soul. . . . When we have obtained the resurrection unto life, our bodies will be spiritualized, purified, and refined from their earthly grossness; then they will be fit instruments for the soul in all its divine and heavenly employment."[12]

Like Ellen White, Leo Cox notes that Wesley "clearly distinguished between the present perfection of soul attainable in this life and the future perfection of human nature attainable in the next life. The first frees the believer from sinfulness of heart; the second will free him from all the evil consequences of sin."[13]

One of the great truths of Scripture is that when Christ comes again "we shall be like him" (1 John 3:2, NIV). He shall "present the church to himself in splendor, without spot or wrinkle or any such thing, that she might be holy and without blemish" (Eph. 5:27).

Another important change related to perfection that will take place at the return of Jesus is the destruction of the evil, temptation-fraught environment in which human beings have been trapped since the Fall. God's people now look forward to existence in an eternity in which the tempter has been forever eradicated (Rev. 20:10) and "righteousness dwells" (2 Peter 3:13).

Thus while the end of the present age will find people with character perfection, the second coming of Jesus will add perfect bodies and a perfect environment. Such individuals, after all they and the universe have experienced, will have no desire to reinvent sin. Rebellion will have run its course. The crucial aspect in the crushing of that rebellion in the lives of individuals will have been the transformation of their minds and hearts from SIN to RIGHTEOUSNESS. It is that radical change expressed in daily life that is the essence of character perfection.

Such people will not have become sinless in the fullest sense of the word at the time of their death or at the time of the Second Coming, but because their hearts and minds were right they will be safe to save. Once such "perfect" people receive "spiritual bodies" and are placed in a perfect environment, the last thing they would ever want to do would be to return to the misery of sin. From that point on they can claim to be sinless in the most complete sense of the word. But they still will not yet be ultimately perfect.

## Dynamic Growth in Perfection Throughout Eternity

*The good news is that human beings will never be absolutely perfect.* Absolute perfection is an attribute of God that human beings can approximate but never reach, even throughout the ceaseless ages of eternity. One of the exciting things about heaven is that it will not be dull and boring. The saved will continually encounter new opportunities to grow in knowledge, love, and service.

Perfection, as we have noted several times in this study, is best thought of as a line rather than a point. In fact, it is an endless line. "Even the most perfect Christian may increase continually in the knowledge and love of God." "It should be our life work," penned Ellen White, "to be constantly reaching forward to the perfection of Christian character, ever striving for conformity to the will of God. The efforts begun here will continue through eternity." "In heaven we are continually to improve" in character development.[14]

Mildred Wynkoop shared the same understanding when she declared that "perfection is not a static 'having' but a dynamic 'going.' Love is not 'perfect' in the sense of having reached its zenith, but in its quality as a dynamic relationship subject to infinite increase."[15]

Because perfection is an eternal dynamic, the Pharisaic road to perfection soon proves to be bankrupt. For one thing, the Pharisaic predilection to define sin as an act or series of acts is incapable of encompassing the dynamic, all-inclusive reality of an attitude toward God, other beings, and His universe that touches the motivations and inmost feelings as well as external acts. Pharisaic perfection, by viewing sin as only an act or series of acts, aims too low to capture the magnitude of the changes that Christ seeks for His people. The one advantage in the Pharisaic "act" definition is that it makes it easier for a person to become what he or she defines as perfect, but such perfection falls far short of that set forth by Christ in the new theology of the Sermon on the Mount.

A second, and equally disastrous, problem with the Pharisaic definition of sin and perfection is its negativity—a negativity that longingly looks forward to the time when the goal has been reached so that one can finally relax. One of the great lessons of the New Testament is that we must conceive of righteousness, sanctification, and perfection as what people actively do rather than what they refrain from doing—that is, perfection is positive rather than negative. "Perfect" Christians are not so much looking out for what they (or their neighbors) can stop doing as they are in finding new ways to reach out in love to God and other beings.

The problem with negative Pharisaic perfection is that its goals are not high enough. There comes a time when a person will have finally stopped doing all the negative things that should be avoided, but there is no end to the acts of love that one can shower on the universe. That is why the Bible frames its definition of perfection in the positive terms of outgoing love. Such love has the potential of infinite growth and development. For that reason, Ellen White could write that "in the future state, untrammeled by the limitations of sinful humanity, it is in service that our greatest joy and our highest education will be found."[16]

Vincent Taylor makes a most meaningful comment when he writes: "Nor, in love, is a perfection ever reached beyond which a richer manifestation is not possible. God is love; and love has the infinitude of His Being. From this it follows that *the ideal of Perfect Love is always attained and always attainable; it belongs both to this life and to that which is to come; it is here and yonder, at this moment and always.*"[17]

The great tragedy of Pharisaism down through the ages is that it has aimed too low, and, having aimed too low, it has consistently manifested a critical attitude toward those who cannot accept its formulations of sin and perfection.

One of the most astounding confrontations of Pharisaic righteousness took place when Jesus in His great sermon told His hearers that unless their "righteousness exceeds that of the scribes and Pharisees," they would "never enter the kingdom of heaven" (Matt. 5:20).

And one of the most wonderful promises of all the Bible is that Christ "is able . . . to save them to the uttermost that come unto God by him" (Heb. 7:25, KJV).

### SOLI DEO GLORIA

---

[1] Joseph Alleine, quoted in Ball, *English Connection*, pp. 69, 70.

[2] Priebe, *Face-to-Face With the Real Gospel*, p. 67; Davis, *How to Be a Victorious Christian*, p. 130; Warfield, *Studies in Perfectionism, passim*; Edward Heppenstall, "Is Perfection Possible?" *Signs of the Times*, December 1963, pp. 10, 11, 30; Zurcher, *Christian Perfection*, pp. 39-43; Lesher, "Ellen G. White's Concept of Sanctification," p. 257; Maxwell, "Ready for His Appearing," in *Perfection: The Impossible Possibility*, p. 171; Flew, *The Idea of Perfection*, p. 400.

[3] Wesley, *Works*, vol. 5, pp. 5, 6.

[4] White, *Acts of the Apostles*, p. 273.

[5] White, *Steps to Christ*, p. 77; White, *Christ's Object Lessons*, p. 384; White, *The Desire of Ages*, p. 668.

[6] Ryle, *Holiness*, p. 42.

[7] Ellen G. White, *The Adventist Home* (Nashville: Southern Pub. Assn., 1952), p. 16; White, *Testimonies for the Church*, vol. 2, p. 267. Cf. White, *Christ's Object Lessons*, pp. 270, 280.

[8] Jac. J. Müller, *The Epistle of Paul to the Philippians*, The New International Commentary on the New Testament (Grand Rapids: Eerdmans, 1955), p. 42; F. W. Beare, *The Epistle to the Philippians*, Harper's New Testament Commentaries (San Francisco: Harper & Row, 1959), p. 53.

[9] White, *Signs of the Times*, March 23, 1888, p. 178; White, *General Conference Bulletin*, 1901, pp. 419, 420.

[10] Alister E. McGrath, *The Mystery of the Cross* (Grand Rapids: Zondervan, 1988), p. 33; Cox, *Wesley's Concept of Perfection*, p. 192.

[11] C. K. Barrett, *The First Epistle to the Corinthians*, Harper's New Testament Commentaries (Peabody, Mass.: Hendrickson, 1987), p. 372; F. W. Grosheide, *Commentary on the First Epistle to the Corinthians*, The New International Commentary on the New Testament (Grand Rapids: Eerdmans, 1953), p. 385.

[12] Wesley, *Works*, vol. 7, pp. 482, 483.

[13] Cox, *Wesley's Concept of Perfection*, p. 102.

[14] White, *Testimonies for the Church*, vol. 1, p. 340; White, *Review and Herald*, 20 Sept. 1881, p. 193; White, *Christ's Object Lessons*, p. 332.

[15] Wynkoop, *Theology of Love*, p. 66.

[16] White, *Education*, p. 309.

[17] Taylor, *Forgiveness and Reconciliation*, p. 179. (Italics supplied.)

# Index of Biblical References

# Index of Names and Topics